LOVE NEVER DIES

PRAISE FOR *LOVE NEVER DIES*

"In *Love Never Dies*, Cole does a beautiful job of describing the many ways romance, the desire for connection, shows up in horror films. Each chapter ends with a summary of how each movie mentioned lines up with terms used to define the romance genre. It is said that horror is an emotion, and I thoroughly enjoyed Cole's take on how desire flavors the disturbing aspects of movies I have watched and now need to rewatch."

—LINDA D. ADDISON, award-winning author, Horror Writers Association Lifetime Achievement Award recipient, and Science Fiction and Fantasy Poetry Association Grand Master

"Emma Cole has assembled a macabre catalogue of films for your next date night. *Love Never Dies* is a bloody love letter to those horrors that have drenched the silver screen over the decades. The Happily Ever After here for dear readers is a comprehensive list of grisly films that pluck on our heartstrings . . . only to rip the whole organ out and hold it up to the movie projector's light."

—CLAY MCLEOD CHAPMAN, author of *Devil Inside*

"Emma Cole takes us on a delightful journey through cinema's obsession with making our hearts pound. A love letter to the horror of love that makes a case for romance being that much better when it has a bit of a bite."

—DONYAE COLES, Bram Stoker Award–nominated author of *Midnight Rooms*

"The most fascinating lunch date an avid horror fan could want. Pull up a stool beside Emma Cole. Raise a glass to the genre films we love. Then drink deep as Cole expounds on why love can be such a horror. Nostalgic, insightful, and thought-provoking."

—JAMIE FLANAGAN, screenwriter of *The Haunting of Bly Manor*

"Emma Cole puts the bloody, beating heart back in horror with *Love Never Dies*, an ode to the romance at the core of some of the scariest movies of our time. Cole's passion and knowledge will delight horror and romance fans alike."

—EMILY C. HUGHES, Bram Stoker Award–winning author of *Horror for Weenies: Everything You Need to Know About the Films You're Too Scared to Watch*

"*Love Never Dies* is a masterfully curated marriage of two seemingly opposed genres. As an editor of romance and an avid fanatic of horror, Emma Cole is the perfect person to explore the crossroads."

—JENNY KIEFER, Bram Stoker Award–nominated author of *This Wretched Valley* and *Crafting for Sinners*

"The tension between wanting and fearing, wanting *despite* fearing, is the engine of every great horror story and every great love story. Emma Cole maps that territory with wit, warmth, and an infectious passion for the films that dared to let their monsters fall in love."

—CYNTHIA PELAYO, editor of *Something Followed Us Home* and Bram Stoker Award–winning author of *It Came from Neverland*

"A page-turning, century-spanning delight. *Love Never Dies* explores horror's many cinematic loves and losses, eyeing canon classics and forgotten gems with equal affection. Horror and romance are the carnal genres, and Cole shows them gripping each other by heart and claw."

—HAILEY PIPER, Bram Stoker Award–winning author of *Queen of Teeth* and *A Game in Yellow*

"I love the way Emma looks at horror through the lens of love. It's fresh, intelligent, and makes us think twice about the stories we're drawn to."

—YIGIT TURHAN, author of *Their Monstrous Hearts*

LOVE NEVER DIES

ROMANCE IN HORROR MOVIES

EMMA COLE

BEACON PRESS, BOSTON

BEACON PRESS
24 Farnsworth Street
Boston, Massachusetts
www.beacon.org

Beacon Press books
are published under the auspices of
the Unitarian Universalist Association of Congregations.

Printed in Colombia

29 28 27 26   8 7 6 5 4 3 2 1

This book is printed on acid-free paper that meets the uncoated paper
ANSI/NISO specifications for permanence as revised in 1992.

Text design and composition by Kim Arney

Library of Congress Cataloging-in-Publication Data
Names: Cole, Emma 1979– author
Title: Love never dies : romance in horror movies / Emma Cole.
Description: Boston : Beacon Press, 2026. | Includes bibliographical references. | Summary: "From vampires and monsters to slashers and psychological thrillers, Love Never Dies explores the enthralling nature of horror romance films that are full of heart. It's just that sometimes, those hearts are on the outside"—Provided by publisher.
Identifiers: LCCN 2026024413 (print) | LCCN 2026024414 (ebook) | ISBN 9780807024959 trade paperback | ISBN 9780807025123 ebook
Subjects: LCSH: Horror films—History and criticism | Love in motion pictures | Thrillers (Motion pictures)—History and criticism | LCGFT: Film criticism
Classification: LCC PN1995.9.H6 C635 2026 (print) | LCC PN1995.9.H6 (ebook) | DDC 791.43/6164—dc23/eng/20260514
LC record available at https://lccn.loc.gov/2026024413
LC ebook record available at https://lccn.loc.gov/2026024414

The authorized representative in the EU for product safety and compliance is Easy Access System Europe 16879218, Mustamäe tee 50, 10621 Tallinn, Estonia: https://beacon.org/eu-contact.

CONTENTS

SPOILER ALERT

If you're familiar with the romance genre, you'll be aware of the term "HEA," or Happily Ever After. It would be impossible to discuss the romance in these horror movies without considering the full narrative, which of course includes the ending, plot twists, and other aspects of the story. I'm one of those people who doesn't find spoilers to be a problem, because I'm more interested in *how* the story is told than *what* is being told. So, if you're spoiler averse, be forewarned! I hope you can skip over those films that are new to you and still enjoy the rest of the book. I've included a list of all the movies I discuss throughout *Love Never Dies*, so do yourself a favor and watch these fantastic films, then come back and read more about them.

INTRODUCTION

HORROR AND ROMANCE

Opposites Attract

One of the best things about being a book editor is spending time talking to folks about what they love to read, watch, and listen to. After all, since I'm trying to acquire projects that will resonate with readers, it makes sense to know what people enjoy, right? While most of my workdays revolve around romance in all its forms, sometimes I get to dip my toes into different genres. Which is great, because my first love is horror. Since I was a kid, sneaking to the top of the stairs to catch a glimpse of the lizard people in *V* or accidentally watching the most terrifying Disney film of all time (*The Watcher in the Woods*) and having a recurring nightmare about it for six weeks, I've been fascinated by all things scary.

I know there are those who think romance and horror are far too different to be combined. I've seen people complain about love and relationships inserted into the horror they enjoy, and I've also seen romance fans put off by stories they think are too scary or extreme. In romance (fiction, at least), there absolutely must be an HEA, or a Happily Ever After, for the main characters; in horror, if protagonists end up happy, many folks would argue it's not horror after all. But for me, horror and romance are the perfect combination. Both genres require high stakes and very high emotion, and I think one is simply the flip side of the other.

FIRST THINGS FIRST: THE HEA

Before we can get into all the gory, gruesome horror in this book, we need to have a conversation about the romance. Though romance and horror may seem to be at odds at first glance, I think they can absolutely work together in interesting, nuanced, emotionally fraught stories. To properly appreciate horror romance, we just have to adjust our definitions of each genre slightly. And the biggest challenge for horror romance is something called the HEA.

Romance stories need to have, by definition, an HEA, or a Happily Ever After. The expectation, especially in romance fiction, is that the primary romantic relationship ends up resolved, with the couple happy and together at the end of the story. You can put characters through any number of trials, from the smallest misunderstanding to the largest life-and-death stakes. But if your couple (or throuple, or whatever the romantic situation might be) doesn't end up together at the end, you'd better watch out because there will be romance readers calling for your head (or at least vowing to never read your stories again). Sometimes, happy endings involve a wedding and a baby. Sometimes, things are a little more casual, with the story reaching its end as the characters set off to begin a relationship—this is known in romance circles as HFN, or Happy For Now. Whether the romance is also a drama or a comedy or a space opera (not too many of those around, sadly), the main thing is that the story needs to have an emotional, satisfying resolution in order to be a true romance. Not to be confused with Tony Scott's crime thriller *True Romance*, which is technically also a romance since the main characters end up happy.

So, what is it about a romance that makes it a romance? As a genre, romance is more of an emotional qualifier than a specific set of plot points (except for that HEA) or particular setting. You can't have a historical costume drama that takes place in the present day—it needs a setting that is, well, historical. Likewise, it's difficult to call your film a western if it doesn't take place in a new frontier of some kind, though it doesn't necessarily have to be the American West. In a genre like romance, there are many subgenres that all fit under the wider umbrella of capital-*R* Romance. The underlying emotional journeys of the characters are similar no matter the setting or the time: they're always moving toward an HEA. Films like *A Room with a View*, *Down with Love*, and *Crazy Rich Asians* couldn't be more different in their execution, settings, and time periods, yet they remain proper romances with happily-ever-after endings.

ADDING ROMANCE TO HORROR

Often, romance in horror films serves as a code or a key for exploring more taboo subjects that are frowned upon by mainstream audiences. Early horror films like *Island of Lost Souls* tempt our hero away from traditional, chaste monogamy with wild, uninhibited, animal women (viewed by many critics as code for Black women, a common stereotype of the time). As the studio system falls in the late 1960s, horror films begin exploring more progressive sexual politics, with romance tropes and characters used as shorthand for queerness; the signs are subtle enough to be missed by mainstream audiences, but if you know what you're looking for, you can find them. Monster romances ask audiences to grapple with the idea of xenophobia: We're all just looking for companionship, no matter if we're white, Black, or gilled. Romance is sometimes the transgressive catalyst that pushes the film further into the horror genre; a movie like *Hellraiser* uses a torrid affair between Julia and her husband's brother Frank as a way to give the audience a more layered villain. Frank's search for hedonistic pleasures doesn't end in death, and Julia is eager to seemingly continue her relationship, adding grotesque nuance to a horror film that blew me away when I first saw it.

Romance in horror is often a stand-in for something *else*. It's about characters looking for acceptance and stability in the face of terrifying, sometimes deadly circumstances. Or maybe instead of being repulsed by the darkness surrounding them, characters are attracted *to* the darkness, wanting to join the monster or let the monster inside of them out. Take someone like Sarah, Susan Sarandon's character in *The Hunger*. Sarah gravitates toward Catherine Deneuve's Miriam not only because she is attractive and welcoming, though that is certainly the case; Sarah is also drawn to the darkness in Miriam, much as she tries to resist it initially. That darkness is a stand-in for power, for sexuality and the freedom that comes from being uninhibited. The romance here is a way for the audience to empathize, to interact with the story on a deeper level than they would with a typical vampire story (though I could argue that most, if not all, vampire films contain at least a hint of romance).

One of the other reasons horror and romance are so complementary, especially on film, is that they're, well, wet. The two genres thrive in depictions of the body: lips bitten in anticipation, breaths catching in lust or in fear, hearts pierced with arrows, whether from Cupid or Jason Voorhees. The flesh, whether it's being adored or mutilated, plays an incredibly important role in both horror and romance. To fully understand both genres, I think you need to embrace the visceral, though not necessarily by spraying viscera all over the place (there's still room for slow burns and atmosphere over outright violence). The most successful films in the genre understand that the emotions evoked need to be reflected onscreen through the characters' physical reactions. Audiences want to be aroused or disgusted (or maybe both?) while they're watching these movies. Truly memorable romantic horror films are full of bodily fluids, either onscreen or implied, delivering equal parts dread and excitement.

Many successful horror romance movies luxuriate in the physical over the intellectual. The emotions of fear and lust are not clinical and detached—they're reactionary, reflexive. A film like *Don't Look Now* doesn't work the same way if you watch it hoping to explain the mystery. But if you let him, director Nicolas Roeg will transport you into a heartbreaking, sexy, and incredibly tender story about grief, marriage, and a killer dwarf. The romantic tension in *Don't Look Now* is heightened by the uncertainty and fear the characters face, and vice versa. Will Donald Sutherland's John and Julie Christie's Laura stay together after the tragedy they've experienced? Will the premonitions and supernatural happenings keep the two from an HEA? Likewise, David Cronenberg's *The Fly* is a masterclass in wedding the joys and the horrors of the flesh. Jeff Goldblum's brilliant scientist Seth and Geena Davis's talented journalist Ronnie give into physical pleasure when they embark on their relationship, only to be undone by the stomach-churning decay of Seth's gruesome transformation into a human/fly monster. The initial romantic journey of the characters is heightened and complemented by the horror here, and the emotional connection of the couple only deepens the awful sinking feeling as the audience realizes there's no saving Seth.

While there are, of course, overlaps between other genres, horror romance feels like a balance that can be tricky to achieve. It's easy to add a romantic flavor to almost any kind of story, and you can inject horror into many genres, too—from western to sci-fi to historical drama. Both are emotion-forward kinds of storytelling: Horror and romance focus on the audience's experience of the emotional reactions in the story, in contrast to other genres that may center the external conflict or setting. And since the emotional endpoint for horror is often the polar opposite to that of romance, a satisfying horror romance must look at genre in a slightly different way. At the end of *Bram Stoker's Dracula*, Vlad gets a happy ending of sorts, finally resting after searching for the love of his life across oceans. But Mina doesn't ride off into the sunset with him, much as part of her is drawn to his dangerous, monstrous character.

In a horror film, instead of reaching an emotionally satisfying HEA conclusion, characters often start out in a place of relative comfort and safety and become unmoored, thrust into violence and terror. Even in a very straightforward slasher film, the Final Girl is arguably transformed by the end of the movie, forever traumatized by the death she's witnessed. Horror is not comfortable; it's the opposite of comfortable, which certainly puts it at odds with romance.

All right, so horror moves from comfort to tension, and romance moves from tension to comfort. How do you put these two together in a rewarding way? It's not necessarily about equality. Think about it: If a movie was totally committed to both horror *and* romance for its full running time, audiences would probably struggle because there wouldn't be any room to alleviate the tension that ramps up throughout the film. You'd go from *will they or won't they kiss* to *will they or won't they survive* with no break. Chances are, you'd end up with a jumbled mess of disparate tones and scenes. Instead, successful romance elements in horror films are often used more sparingly. Maybe the film begins with a sweet romance that is torn apart in spectacular fashion, like in David Cronenberg's *The Fly*. Or perhaps two people find themselves and each other in the midst of a traumatic and horrifying situation, à la *Zombieland*.

Too much of a happy ending completely undermines the horror, so the audience needs to be satisfied with a different kind of happy ending. The characters must be fundamentally changed by their experience, whether that means they're traumatized, literally transformed into monstrous creatures, or perhaps even dead. The most effective films blend the two genres into a slightly different form, or instead, begin as one genre and change into something else.

As you go through the book, you'll notice that if I do a deeper dive into a particular film or filmmaker, I'll mention the common romance tropes you'll find in the movie and explain how they fit the story. I'll also point out the Dark Moment, the part of the film when the characters veer from their emotional journeys toward the HEA. In romance fiction, this moment is usually the last hurdle the couple needs to overcome before they find their way back to each other and their happy ending. In horror romance, this is usually the time when things start to go very wrong. But as you'll see, that doesn't always mean there won't be an HEA—it might look a little different from a typical fairy-tale ending, but sometimes love prevails even when lives don't.

Before we really get into it, a note about the content in this book: You will surely disagree with some of my observations. I don't pretend to be an expert in all things romance or horror—I usually describe myself as an enthusiast. My life has shaped the way I look at a film, and I'm sure that my experience will be different from yours or another reader's. My opinions are my own, and hopefully you find them entertaining even if you think they're wrong.

If you're looking for a book that is going to go deep into proper film criticism, this one may not be for you. What I try to do is communicate my love for these films, and for the tropes and themes that come up again and again in many of them. This is not a definitive reading of a particular film or genre; I think in film, like in books and other art, there are many ways to interpret meaning.

The delineation between film eras isn't always clear, so I've tried to group movies together by theme or trope, recognizing that there are some areas of overlap between chapters. I've read a lot of books about film over the course of my life, and I've compiled a list (at the end of this book) of titles that you might be interested in should you want to explore horror or film in general in more detail. But *Love Never Dies* is mostly just a collection of movies I love and how their stories embody both romance and horror in various ways.

There are far too many romantic horror films for me to come even close to watching and writing about. I've tried to stick to movies that are generally accessible in one way or another, and movies that I've seen at least once or twice that, for me, fit the theme of romantic horror. Again, you may disagree with my choices! If I missed a film or a director you really loved, sorry, but I don't have an infinite number of pages to wax poetic about every production. Certain themes resonate more deeply for me than others, so there are most certainly movies in each category that I've not seen (probably some things I've never even heard of). Please write a book about those films so I can read it!

I'm still on the lookout for a perfect horror romance novel (*Twin Peaks* romance, anyone?), so for now films will have to do. I'm glad there are so many wonderful ones to choose from, and that just as horror and romance have evolved separately, horror romance movies have found new ways to combine the two genres into something both scary and heartwarming.

CHAPTER ONE

MEET CUTE

Where Does Horror Romance Start?

If you haven't spent a lot of time watching older films, you'd be forgiven for assuming that they're all fussy, straitlaced, somber pictures or screwball comedies. I know when I used to work in a video store, some customers' eyes would glaze over if we tried to recommend a black-and-white film or anything released earlier than the 1980s. But a lot of films from the 1920s and early 1930s are pretty racy. They tackled everything from premarital sex and homosexuality to murder, and much more bluntly and frankly than some modern movies. The film industry was full of people excited to experiment with this new medium, especially once sound was introduced, and they wanted to see what they could get away with (not that *Babylon* [2022] was completely accurate, but there were definitely some hedonists in Hollywood). Since the industry was so new, there weren't many guardrails in place, and as long as a studio put up the money to produce and distribute it, filmmakers could create some wild stories onscreen.

Early films from the 1930s were truly shocking in their portrayals of sex and violence. In public spaces, particularly in areas outside of urban cities, divorce was only discussed in whispers.

But Norma Shearer's defiant portrayal of a woman who is an adulterer and a divorcee was frank and captivating in the 1930 film *The Divorcee*. Although the story eventually ends with the reconciliation between husband and wife, it's not before both parties have sought companionship with others (also married, in some cases), and everyone is far from monogamous. Barbara Stanwyck's character in 1933's *Baby Face* is even more bold: The unapologetically ambitious Lily Powers begins the film as a prostitute, and she seduces man after man as she climbs the corporate ladder. And *Mayor of Hell* (1933) situates a sordid gangster story alongside the tale of a boys' reform school where horrible things befall the troubled young men. As much as audiences flocked to many of these movies, there were people who didn't appreciate the boundary-pushing studios making these pictures. Groups began organizing to push back against these brazen filmmakers (*Baby Face* is partly responsible for the organization of the Catholic Legion of Decency). The production code, created in 1930 (also known as the Hays Code) to ensure studios were more mindful and modest in their plots and imagery, was enforced more strictly.[1] Since the code was more focused on sex and nudity than on violence, some filmmakers found a loophole: horror films.

There were a few scary "nightmare pictures" that came and went in the silent era, like *M* (1931) and *Nosferatu* (1922). But in North America, horror really took off when studios began making their monster movies. While most people think of Universal Studios as the main purveyor of these horror films (their versions of *Frankenstein*, *Dracula*, *The Mummy*, and *The Wolf Man* obviously stand out as icons in the genre), many studios jumped on the horror bandwagon. From Paramount (with films like *Island of Lost Souls*) to RKO (with classics like *I Walked with a Zombie* and *King Kong*), these studios made films that dealt with monsters, mental illness (though not necessarily using the kind of language we'd use now), and murder. The production code was more concerned with crime thrillers and "realistic" kinds of violence. Allowing filmmakers to create fictional, supernatural reasons for the scares onscreen was a great way to skirt the rules and to cater to the audience's prurient interests. As long as studios focused on frights instead of sexual innuendoes, most censors were content to let the films find their viewers. The same is still often true today, with violence much more accepted in media than sexual content, in North America at least. Even romance novels have their detractors—social media algorithms like TikTok's have changed the way we even talk about sex in books; "spicy" code words allow book influencers to reference things happening in the stories they're loving without being deplatformed or shadow banned.

The Black Cat, released by Universal a month before the production code crackdown in the summer of 1934, features references to cults, necrophilia, animal cruelty, drugs, devil worship, and a character being skinned alive (shown in shadow)—it's *wild* that this got past the censors! The film is probably helped by being the first of eight films to feature both Bela Lugosi and Boris Karloff, each of whom had been made stars in *Dracula* and *Frankenstein*, respectively. Not to be confused with the sillier 1941 *The Black Cat* (both star Bela Lugosi), the 1934 film is a visceral, haunting rumination on vengeance and betrayal, and though it's not explicitly gory, it's a brutal experience nonetheless. The off-camera skinning scene is truly grotesque, and it's almost worse that it's left to the audience's imagination instead of portrayed with the practical makeup effects that would have been available at the time. And yet romantic elements are here as well. Though Karloff and Lugosi are the main characters, the secondary couple (who are essentially stand-ins for the audience) are newly married and deeply in love. They lend extra emotional tension to the plot as they innocently try to figure out what shared history the two protagonists are trying to hide while staying safe from a demonic cult.

The monster movies of the 1930s often used romance cues in their tales: A monster would fixate on an ideal human mate, and a burly hero needed to step in to save his beloved. But both *Island of Lost Souls* and *King Kong* can also be viewed as speaking to the societal anxiety that many white Europeans and Americans felt about race mixing, with the panther woman Lota in *Souls* and the monstrous gorilla in *Kong* standing in for Black people. Other characters in these movies reinforced the *savage* stereotypes many white audiences consumed in both film and literature at the time. Racial integration in the US was still a number of years away, but the anti-miscegenation (or anti–interracial relationship) rhetoric in the 1930s that was spreading in Nazi Germany fanned the flames of fear and distrust among white people in many parts of the world. (For more on portrayals of Black people in cinema, do yourself a favor and read Robin R. Means Coleman's *Horror Noire*; it is excellent.)[2] Even though Black actors were given roles in a number of mainstream films, there was certainly not any chance of an interracial romance onscreen. Apes or panther women falling in love with humans were perfectly acceptable, though, at least at the movies.

Island of Lost Souls (1932), based on the classic novel *The Island of Dr. Moreau* by H. G. Wells and directed by Erle C. Kenton, features both a monster romance of a sort—between the protagonist, Parker, and Lota, a panther woman created by Dr. Moreau—as well as a more traditional romance between Parker and his fiancée, Ruth, who ultimately rescues him from the island. In addition to questions of whether or not a woman created by a scientist with panther DNA can truly consent to a romantic relationship with a human (not to mention whether it's okay for a man to pursue this creature even after he knows she's not consenting), *Souls* also features Moreau's other creations. Are the ape men who attack Ruth sexually motivated or not? It's not quite explicit, but there is definitely an undertone of sexual menace. Once they are liberated from their creed to never harm a human, these monsters dispatch Dr. Moreau in vengeful, violent fashion for his horrific and torturous treatment of them in the House of Pain.

The story in *Island of Lost Souls* has been seen as a metaphor for the male hero who needs to have one last free sexual encounter before falling in line and becoming a devoted spouse.[3] Lota, the wild woman/cat hybrid created by the doctor, represents lust, animal sexuality, and forbidden temptation when compared to the more chaste and straitlaced Ruth. As in many films of the era, the hero was allowed to get away with all kinds of mistreatment of his significant other, provided he returned to her at the end of the film, where she'd forget all his indiscretions. The audience wanted to live vicariously through the hero as he engaged in these forbidden passions, but also wanted to be reminded that in essence he represented a wholesome, "traditional" relationship, leaving his adventurous past behind and settling down.

King Kong (1933, codirected by Merian C. Cooper and Ernest B. Schoedsack) takes the monster romance trope even further, with the giant ape fixating on Ann Darrow (Fay Wray). Ann doesn't reciprocate the monster's feelings, so it's a one-way romance. Once again, we can see how Kong can be a stand-in for lust and wanton sexuality, trying to overcome a female companion who is brought back to her chaste, virginal persona by her true love. The natives of Skull Island who are in thrall to the giant monster are uncharitably depicted as merciless savages, sacrificing the women of the tribe to satiate their deity, and all these stereotypes are, of course, racist in their origins. Upon seeing the pale, blond Ann, the tribe is willing to give up all their women to possess this rare beauty, and Kong is ready to tear down the world in order to claim her. In many monster romance movies throughout the studio era (from 1930 until an antitrust case caused studios to divest from theater chains in 1949), women characters are rarely outright interested in their monster counterparts (and it's almost always women as objects of lust and male-presenting monsters; the monstrous females will show up a bit later). However, there is sometimes some nuance at play, some I-can-fix-them undertones where the women are at least a little sympathetic to the creatures lusting after them. They don't necessarily want to commit to a relationship, but they're flattered by the thought that even nonhumans are attracted to them.

Not every horror film of the 1930s is a creature feature, however. Tod Browning's *Dracula* (1932) is one of Universal's first forays into the monster movie genre, and it features characters of the more human (or mostly human) variety. Vampires are inherently sexual (we'll get into that in another chapter), and although this early film is less romance forward than John Badham's 1979 version starring Frank Langella, or my favorite, Francis Ford Coppola's *Bram Stoker's Dracula* from 1992, the dark and brooding Bela Lugosi wasn't *un*romantic. In fact, Universal decided to play up the romance in ads before the film was released, calling it "The story of the strangest passion the world has ever known!" Adapting Bram Stoker's epistolary novel into a more straightforward, linear horror tale focused on the love triangle between Jonathan Harker, his fiancée Mina, and the Transylvanian Prince Dracula. Actually, it's a bit of a love square, since Mina's friend Lucy is also seduced by the vampire. We'll see this play out in a bigger, more explicit way in the 1992 version of the film. While the details are a little vague in the Universal picture, the overarching themes remain the same. The hold Dracula has on the vulnerable Mina means this romance isn't exactly on a level playing field, and that's typical of many early horror films. The women were objects of the monster's attraction, and usually they only reciprocated because of a curse or magical means; they didn't have any agency. While on the surface it seemed that the women in the early monster romance films were going along with the seduction, the relationship was usually one of dubious consent.

This same sense of a woman as prize to be won or an object to be used shows up again and again. *The Mummy* (1932), directed by Karl Freund, centers the ancient mummy Imhotep (the fabulous Boris Karloff), who is resurrected as Ardath Bey and searches for his long-lost love Anck-es-en-Amon, and discovers what he thinks is a reincarnated version of her in Helen (Zita Johann). His single-minded pursuit of Helen is where the real horror is revealed, as any woman who's felt like she can't get away from an ardent suitor can attest to. There's also the whole killing and mummifying thing, which definitely doesn't help. Karloff as the mummy is fantastically menacing, his silent stalking lending wonderful suspense to a movie that on its face seems rather tame. The film ends not by Helen rebuking Imhotep or by her present-day love saving her, but by her invocation of the spirit of the goddess Isis as she reclaims her ancestry and destroys the mummy. The update of *The Mummy* in 1999 uses a very similar plot but plays up those romance and adventure cues, with Rachel Weisz's Evie as a strong foil to Brendan Fraser's Rick. There's a lot less horror in that version, but many (many!) more beautiful people. So many beautiful people.

Variations on these same themes appear in horror films of the 1930s and '40s, and some, of course, don't feature romantic elements at all. Others, like *Freaks* (1932), subvert romance tropes in particularly interesting ways. The central love triangle in that film is another love square: Circus performers Hans and Frieda are engaged, but the beautiful Cleopatra and her lover Hercules want to swindle Hans out of his large inheritance. Cleopatra steals Hans away from Frieda, until she accidentally reveals she's really in love with Hercules. The "freaks," Hans's friends, ultimately thwart Cleopatra and Hercules's plan and transform Cleopatra into one of them, a human/duck hybrid to be gawked at in the circus. Romance plots and elements feature heavily in the film, and many secondary characters are given layered and nuanced love stories in addition to the central story.

Director Tod Browning creates a universe where the outwardly beautiful people are hiding the ugliest insides, and gives us an empathetic view of the much-harassed circus performers in the film, each with some quality that makes them undesirable in the eyes of the visitors to the circus and the able-bodied folks working there. *Freaks* rejects the common trope of damsel in distress or virginal heroine; here Cleopatra is devious, cruel, and conniving. Frieda, in contrast, suffers through Hans's rejection and, depending on the version of the film you see, doesn't get to experience an HEA. In one version, there is an epilogue of sorts, where Frieda visits Hans at his new estate and declares she still loves him. But the original release of the film simply ends with horrifying images of the mutilated Cleopatra.

Films have always relied on specific hooks to get audiences in the door, and playing up horror was certainly one way to do it in the early days of the studio era. Though many of these films feel a bit tame by current standards, there's no question that a lot of them have some great unsettling and eerie moments. When the studios felt that horror on its own didn't entice audiences, it was clear that adding in some romance elements was a surefire way to convince viewers to shell out for the cinema experience, regardless of any HEAs. Not only did romance allow for a more emotional story; casting a beautiful actor in the leading lady role was also a draw for moviegoers. The original scream queens like Fay Wray, Gloria Stewart, and Helen Chandler all helped convince the hero to step up and defeat the evil lurking in the shadows. This idea hasn't ever really gone away; from Janet Leigh in *Psycho* to Jamie Lee Curtis (her daughter) in *Halloween* to Mia Goth in *X*, *Pearl*, and *MaXXXine*, there is no shortage of attractive women luring moviegoers to frightening films.

EARLY HORROR STANDOUTS

Island of Lost Souls (1932; dir. Erle C. Kenton)

TOP TROPES: Love Triangle: Engaged couple Edward and Ruth are separated when Edward is shipwrecked on a mysterious island. His benefactor, the sinister Dr. Moreau, keeps Edward safe and comfortable at his estate and introduces him to the beautiful and strange Lota. She turns out to be a creation of the unhinged doctor, a woman/panther hybrid who nevertheless infatuates the naive Edward. When Ruth shows up to bring Edward back to civilization and a monogamous marriage, he must give up the pleasure he may have found with Lota.

MONSTER ROMANCE: Though Lota is mostly humanoid in form, the reveal that she is in fact a creation of Moreau's derived from a panther pushes the movie into monster romance, albeit a very tame version. The only real monstrous aspect of Lota is her animal-like fingernails.

DARK MOMENT: While Ruth, Edward's fiancée, doesn't show up at all in the first half of the film, once she arrives, the film's tone shifts to more danger and less mystery. The horrible torture Dr. Moreau is perpetrating on the residents of the island takes center stage, and the couple doesn't experience much in the way of doubt or external barriers to their relationship. The fact that Edward is unfaithful is never really addressed, and Edward is able to escape with Ruth without having to explain his actions. And Lota is conveniently dispatched, so Ruth is none the wiser.

HEA? Yes. Edward and Ruth escape together, ready to put their perilous time on the island behind them and presumably start their life together.

Dracula (1932; dir. Tod Browning)

TOP TROPES: Monster Romance: Although Dracula looks mostly human in this version, he *is*, of course, a monster. Dracula uses his mind-controlling powers to feed on both Lucy Weston and Mina Seward, and though both make small attempts to stop him, they are powerless to resist him. The romance here is one of *dubious consent*, a trope that features heavily in many dark romances that are having a moment in the romance literature space. Couples with a power imbalance (typically a man in a position of dominance) have become more popular in recent years, particularly in the indie publishing space, and sometimes feature explorations of kink in addition to more traditional boss/assistant or billionaire/working-class combinations.

DARK MOMENT: Mina must confess to Jonathan that she can no longer marry him. Though she doesn't say it out loud, Dracula's violation of her makes her believe she needs to cut ties with her fiancé. Infected with vampire blood, she attacks Jonathan and tries to kill him.

HEA? Yes. Jonathan and Van Helsing defeat the monster, which returns Mina to her normal, human self so she can leave with Jonathan to start their life together.

CHAPTER TWO

FORBIDDEN LOVE

Monster Romance

In many of the most popular early horror movies, romance was fairly one-sided if there was a monster involved. Sure, King Kong might have been enthralled by Ann Darrow, but she wasn't reciprocating any of his feelings. However, romance does bloom between humans and monsters in a whole host of early horror films. Sometimes the monster isn't aware they are *other* when they meet their significant other; sometimes, that otherness is what draws their partner in. There's a spectrum of monstrosity here, from mostly human in *Phantom of the Opera* (1943) to humans who transform into monsters (as in *The Wolf Man*), all the way to full-on strange creature, like the dinosaur in *Tammy and the T-Rex* (not exactly a horror film, but it's definitely got both horror and romance elements).

Many early monster romance films featured monsters who were closer to human than not, rather than creatures of other species: *Dr. Jekyll and Mr. Hyde*, *The Wolf Man*, and *Phantom of the Opera* all portray monstrous humanoid characters and feature romances of a sort. Audiences flocked to see these films (the 1943 version of *Phantom of the Opera* is the only Universal monster film to receive an Oscar nomination), and the studios loved the popularity of these scary (or scary-adjacent) stories. Many studio heads thought it made sense to continue producing more derivative sequels and remakes while they were profitable (we can see the same trends today in both film and publishing, with remakes and retellings still very much on trend). The horror films of the 1940s seem to take one of two positions: The main character ends up a monster, in which case they must be destroyed (largely due, as I mentioned, to the requirements of the production code), or the main character is able to defeat the monster and allowed to celebrate with an HEA.

The 1943 adaptation of Gaston Leroux's *Phantom of the Opera* is quite different from the 1925 version, which features an iconic performance with incredible makeup from Lon Chaney. Director Arthur Lubin's remake is much less focused on horror, but I think it's worth mentioning here anyway, as it is the kind of film that was trying to straddle the horror/romance line. There aren't a lot of outright scares here, though there is violence. The film spends a significant portion of its running time showcasing full operatic performances, but on the plus side that means director Arthur Lubin gets to reuse the opulent sets of the Paris opera (in beautiful Technicolor) from the 1925 version to tell the tale of Erique and Christine. The story may be familiar to anyone who's seen the popular Andrew Lloyd Webber musical or movie version of the stage play. (Huge thanks, by the way, to my grade-seven elementary school teacher who took a group of awkward, moody tweens on a four-hour bus ride to see the incredible production in Toronto, an experience that definitely helped shape me into the dramatic goth teen I became.)

Erique (Claude Rains) is a frustrated violinist who is losing the use of his fingers and is unable to play as well as he used to. When he's dismissed from the opera, he's furious—especially after his composition is stolen. Erique strangles the publisher of the stolen work who manages to throw acid on Erique's face, horribly scarring him. While the opera company believes Erique has disappeared after the incident, of course he's just escaped to the sewers under the opera house, hiding his face with a prop mask he steals. From the shadows, Erique continues to champion singer Christine DuBois (Susanna Foster) and secretly plots to get her a leading role in a new opera for which she is the understudy, drugging the lead to give her a chance at the spotlight as well as causing the spectacular chandelier crash that features heavily in subsequent adaptations.

Rains, the actor behind such characters as the Invisible Man, Prince John (opposite Errol Flynn) in *The Adventures of Robin Hood*, and, my favorite, Captain Louis Renault in *Casablanca*, does a wonderful job portraying the tortured artist Erique, though he doesn't get as much to do in the second half of the film. The romantic aspects between Christine and Erique are played down here. The original script for this version had Erique revealed as Christine's father, and I think you can tell that something's been omitted, because there are lines that foreshadow the reveal that never comes. That's not to say there's no romance here, though. Christine is in a love triangle with police inspector Raoul Dubert (Edgar Barrier) and opera baritone Anatole Garron (Nelson Eddy), and the film uses the men's pursuit of Christine to comedic effect as they both try to capture the phantom to prove their love. The film ends, surprisingly, with Christine choosing neither man. Instead, she decides to focus on her singing career, so in a way she chooses Erique and his devotion to her. And Anatole and Raoul end the film going to dinner together (the beginning of another beautiful friendship, perhaps).

Another one of Universal's monsters, one of only a few not based on a novel, is *The Wolf Man* (1941), played by Lon Chaney Jr., the son of the original Phantom of the Opera. Claude Rains stars in George Waggner's picture as well, as John, the father of Chaney's Larry Talbot, a man returning to his home in Wales after the death of his brother. The romance in this film is, as in *Phantom of the Opera*, rather one-sided. When Larry meets Gwen, a local villager, he is smitten with her, although she doesn't seem to reciprocate his affections. In fact, she tells him she is already engaged, but Larry pursues her anyway, refusing to take no for an answer. And he hasn't even been turned into a monster yet. The power dynamics are amplified by the class system in place: Larry is the son of the lord of the area, and he isn't used to taking no for an answer. Does Gwen reluctantly agree to meet with him because she feels she has no choice? It's not made explicitly clear, but it's implied that a person of lower social class would be expected to abide by the aristocrat's whims and wishes. There's some similarity here to the storylines of many billionaire or royalty romance novels: A persistent, confident, wealthy man sets his sights on a woman and through force of will (and often, especially in older novels, through more insidious means of coercion) ends up with a wife.

After meeting with a fortune teller, Gwen and Larry are attacked by a large wolf, and Larry fights it off with his silver wolf-headed cane, but not before he is bitten. With that, the curse of the werewolf is in him, and much of the rest of the film plays out like a mystery, with Larry trying to prove his innocence after the fortune teller Bela and Gwen's friend Jenny are found murdered. As Larry tries to clear his name and find out what's happening to him, the hint of romance grows as well. The villagers start to whisper that Gwen and Larry are engaged in an affair. Even though Gwen's fiancé believes she is innocent, both she and Larry are vilified. The rumor mill is too strong to overcome, especially since Larry *was* trying to convince Gwen to spend time with him. The pair aren't officially in a relationship, but there is an element of romance that lingers, suggesting that perhaps they might be together if Gwen wasn't already engaged. She certainly seems to feel some sympathy for Larry as he navigates the terrible situation he's dealing with.

As in *Cat People* (1942), a character's transformation to savage beast can be interpreted as them becoming overwhelmed by lust and impulsive behavior. In many films featuring transformation and body horror, sexual connotations may be more or less overt—depending on the era of the film, the director, etc.—but are almost always present. Larry can't control his desire to kill those who stand in the way of his pursuit of Gwen, just as Irena in *Cat People* can't control her jealousy (for more on *Cat People*, see chapter 3). The difference between the two characters is that Irena is fully committed to repressing her murderous feelings as long as she can, whereas Larry can't or won't make the same effort. Perhaps this difference stems from the perception of gender roles at the time: Women were not allowed to give into lustful feelings because they would be shunned for being too brazen. Men, on the other hand, could let their animal sides out, provided they were properly contrite once they came to their senses.

While *Cat People* and *The Wolf Man* are very different in execution, their endings are quite similar. Larry's father, John, doesn't believe him when he confesses he's the wolf man who has been terrorizing the village, so John fails to restrain Larry when the full moon rises once again. When Larry chases down Gwen, he is defeated before he can harm her, bludgeoned by his own silver cane.

Both Larry and Irena, thrust into situations out of their control, are unable to escape their fates. Would things be different if they were able to tamp down their murderous, lustful impulses?

The 1940s also brought a different kind of transformation in *Dr. Jekyll and Mr. Hyde*. Robert Louis Stevenson's 1886 novella has been adapted more than one hundred times and was one of the most adapted stories of the silent film era.[1] The 1931 film starring Fredric March won him an Oscar, but I prefer the not-as-well-loved 1941 film starring Spencer Tracy as the doctor, Lana Turner as his love Beatrix, and Ingrid Bergman as Ivy, the woman pursued by the sinister Mr. Hyde. While the 1931 version relies on some fantastic special effects to allow Jekyll to change into Hyde, the 1941 version uses little in the way of makeup to signal the switch from the good doctor to the evil Hyde. Instead, Spencer Tracy uses his physicality and acting ability to portray the two characters as very different people, which feels much closer to the novel (it reminds me of Jeremy Irons's dual performances in *Dead Ringers*, though the movies are quite different).

I think director Victor Fleming makes some interesting choices, as do the cast members. Lana Turner and Ingrid Bergman were originally cast in opposite roles, but the two actors wanted to avoid being typecast. I know I'm probably in the minority, but I like the friction that comes from someone like Bergman, known at this point in her career largely for being demure and quiet (although sometimes a victim, as she is here) taking on a character as brash and as flawed as Ivy, the sex worker who draws Hyde's interest. Lana Turner has a bit of a thankless role as Beatrix, Jekyll's fiancée, and I don't think playing against type works as successfully for Turner here.

The romance in the 1941 version of *Dr. Jekyll and Mr. Hyde* feels more central to the story. Perhaps the focus on acting rather than special effects makes everything feel a little more intimate. While the makeup effects in the 1931 version were very well done, they pull the emotional punch of the story. The March version of the film shows Hyde as a truly monstrous, almost caveman-like figure, which fits his brutish and violent nature very well. But that seems like a very easy way to let Jekyll completely off the hook for his actions, and I don't think he should be. The decision to make Jekyll's alter ego almost identical in the 1941 film changes the focus from that of a character transformed into a completely different being to someone unleashing a horror that's always been within. Even before Jekyll transforms into Hyde for the first time, we see that Jekyll's fanaticism and drive to perfect his medicinal pursuits (he's trying to create a serum to separate good and evil within a person) are a problem. Jekyll's problem is so disturbing that his fiancée Beatrix's father encourages her to take a break from the doctor. One of the biggest flaws in the film, for me, is that we don't really get to see the fallout from this decision in a satisfying way. What was the relationship like before Beatrix left (early in the film) on a trip with her father? Was Jekyll already showing signs that he would be uncontrollable and drawn to the dark side, or does his time away from his intended catalyze his eventual capitulation to Hyde's hideous nature? Lana Turner isn't given enough to work with, and the early love story is mostly set aside to focus on Hyde's more lurid and horrifying relationship with Ingrid Bergman's Ivy.

That relationship is definitely not romantic. Hyde becomes obsessed with Ivy, and he goes even further in his pursuit than any of the other men we've discussed so far. He doesn't just try to get her to fall in love with him. He abducts her, then sexually and physically assaults her while she is trapped. Even when Jekyll returns to his old self, the doctor does not set Ivy free; he provides her room and board, and since she can't see any other choice she stays, though she lives in fear of Hyde coming back to assault her again (which he does). The idea that Jekyll and Hyde are truly separate, that the monster is not part of the man, doesn't ring true. Would Jekyll have gone back to see Ivy one last (fatal) time after Beatrix returned home to him if he wasn't linked to Hyde? I don't think so. Hyde is an inextricable part of Jekyll, which is what makes this monster so compelling.

One development that really helped the rise of monster romance was the proliferation of 1950s creature features. North American audiences became enamored (and wary) of the Atomic Age. Giant monster films like *It Came from Beneath the Sea* and *Them!* were less interested in outright horror, but many (probably most) of them do feature romances between alpha heroes and plucky women. These early, effects-driven pictures were more about big monsters and bigger destruction, so there was less room for the nuanced and often more character-driven horror films that had been popularized by paranormal ghost stories (like *Cat People*, *The Uninvited*, or *The Ghost and Mrs. Muir*). Though many of these monster movies can seem rather silly to modern audiences, there's a lot to enjoy about them (and the giant ants in *Them!* legitimately unsettled me the first time I watched them attack).

The love interests in these '50s fright films (usually the women) are often interchangeable, almost afterthoughts to the plots. They either don't have much to say at all or are dismissed as being cold or analytical. Rather than having any agency, they are often used more like set dressings or as catalysts for the action. In these movies, the plot points are the same regardless of the kind of monster we're dealing with: Someone (usually a scientist) warns the army about a creature that may attack the city. The army laughs them off, thinking that they will be able to hold off the creature (or downright dismissing the scientist altogether). Often, a beautiful woman (maybe a fellow scientist, or a reporter, or a schoolteacher—she usually has a job of some sort) is the only one who believes the hero, either because she's always been in love with him or because she's seen this creature for herself. The monster attacks, sometimes damaging whole city blocks (like the huge octopus creature created by Ray Harryhausen in *It Came from Beneath the Sea*, one of my favorite films in this genre). The military finally listens to the hero, he helps them defeat the monster, and then he gets the girl. The very rigid gender roles and racial stereotypes feel incredibly overdone in many of these films, and there isn't a lot of room to deviate from the typical storyline, though there are a few gems here and there.

As we get to the end of the 1950s, the sci-fi horror trend begins to fracture into very different genres, though it takes a while to get to the full space operas that piqued viewers' imagination in the mid-1970s. But the creature features of the late '50s become less rooted in real science and more interested in the special effects that created the monsters. As special effects makeup becomes more polished and accessible, movie makers use these effects to create more believable creatures, ones who can be shown in more emotional relationships.

The years 1958 and '59 are when horror and B movies start to surface in a big way, in large part due to the confluence of all the factors I've mentioned already along with the popularity of drive-ins (particularly for the older teen demographic).[2] Directors and producers like William Castle and Roger Corman contributed to the popularity of these movies as well. Corman began directing films in 1955 and made some cheap westerns before he started making sci-fi and horror, with movies like *It Conquered the World* and *Attack of the Crab Monsters*. Many of his early films were made on shoestring budgets, but as he began to establish himself in the horror space, particularly in the 1960s with a string of gems starring Vincent Price, Corman became known not only for his own films, but also as a producer who helped break out a huge number of successful filmmakers, from Martin Scorsese to James Cameron, and launched several actors' careers as well. Though it's easy to laugh off movies like *She Gods of Shark Reef* and *Ski Troop Attack*, many of Corman's films are highly entertaining and inventive (I absolutely love the completely bonkers *X: The Man with X-Ray Eyes*). One of Corman's earlier works, *The Wasp Woman*, is a strange little film that isn't necessarily about romance and thus is not really in keeping with the theme of monster romance, but it is about women and societal expectations, in line with recent films like Coralie Fargeat's *The Substance*. It's worth a look.

So, where's the romantic horror? One film from the 1950s stands out to me as rising far above the rest of these earlier monster romances: *The Creature from the Black Lagoon*. The sexuality in *Creature* is a little more overt than it was in the films of the '30s and '40s. Maybe that's partly because the rules begin to relax a little as filmmakers become more comfortable skirting the edges of what's acceptable. But maybe it's just that an aquatic monster is a good excuse for an actress in a bathing suit (Julie Adams as Kay Lawrence). What begins as a film that can essentially be called *King Kong* underwater quickly transforms into a monster's terrifying pursuit of the beautiful woman he sees and is entranced by. The Gill-Man is a relentless and mysterious creature. The audience never gets a true sense of his motivations or feelings; the characters guess at his motivations, but they're really just projecting. The two men leading the expedition into the Amazon, Mark (Richard Denning) and David (Richard Carlson), are ostensibly both men of science. But Mark is in it for the glory, whereas David (and his girlfriend, Kay) are there to learn and research, and they're much less bloodthirsty as a result. Much of the film is spent arguing over whether the team should kill the creature and bring him back as a trophy or let him live unbothered by the humans encroaching on his territory.

I don't think director Jack Arnold intended *The Creature from the Black Lagoon* as a full-on monster romance (Kay certainly doesn't seem interested in the Gill-Man as anything more than a scientific anomaly), but there is a bit of romantic conflict that bubbles up to the surface on a few separate occasions. Mark surprises Kay and David as they share an intimate kiss, and the camera lingers on his irritated face just long enough for the audience to wonder if there's more to his annoyance than simply disapproval of making out on the job. Kay acknowledges to David the awkwardness between the three of them, and hints that Mark may have made his feelings known to her in the past, and either she brushed him off or it didn't work out. That extra tension adds more suspense to many of the underwater scenes, particularly when the two men are diving together. Will Mark try to harm David so he can get the girl? Will each leave the other to a terrible fate, attacked by the creature? Not knowing how the two men will react when they're away from the rest of the crew adds a fascinating little layer to this story.

The visuals of the creature stalking Kay underwater are similar to scenes in many horror films. *Friday the 13th*'s killer uses a similar POV as they watch unsuspecting teens. And *Vertigo*'s Scottie follows Madeleine around San Francisco using this perspective as well (more on my feelings about *Vertigo* as horror movie later). As someone who is unnerved (okay, outright afraid) of being out in deep water where I can't see the bottom, the underwater scenes when the Gill-Man is lurking just beyond the reach of the main characters are genuinely creepy, and they are even more impressive when you realize how technically challenging they must have been to film. (If you want to know more about the creature design, do yourself a favor and check out Mallory O'Meara's absolutely fantastic book *The Lady from the Black Lagoon*, a fascinating look at Milicent Patrick, the woman who designed the creature for this movie.)[3]

As much as the creature itself might look a little silly to audiences unfamiliar with older rubber suit costumes (in the words of my teenage son, Gill-Man "looks a little goofy"), I think the movie holds up as a super effective creature feature. I love the tension throughout, and there are some genuinely nail-biting sequences. The underwater scene where the Gill-Man is mimicking Kay, swimming just below her, is mesmerizing and beautifully shot. And the romance between Kay and David feels refreshingly modern for the most part, as David confides in Kay, asks her opinion, and generally treats her as an equal. They're not married, and both seem okay with that, which is a departure from films like *Cat People* (or many romance novels) where folks get married at the drop of a hat. There's a sadness to the creature, who's clearly alone and seems to just want some companionship but doesn't know how to communicate that. And the idea of humans invading the Gill-Man's space and wanting to destroy his habitat kind of makes you want to root for the monster, which perhaps is why the Gill-Man has endured as a horror icon, though the film has not been remade endlessly.

Guillermo del Toro takes the creature of the Gill-Man to even more emotional depths in *The Shape of Water* (which I'll discuss in more detail later), where the implied romantic feelings of the monster are much more overt (and are reciprocated). Once again, the romance angle here is a stand-in for other, wider feelings of anxiety. The idea of a woman perhaps being interested in or available to a creature of a different species echoed the anxiety among white people about interracial relationships. Many male moviegoers were troubled by a fear of the Other, epitomized by the scenario of a love interest being swept away by someone (or something) who doesn't fit the idealized version of the Western hero.

While many early monster romance stories feature monsters that are still mostly human, or at least look mostly human, I think I would be remiss if I didn't mention, at least briefly, one of the most memorable monster romance films I've seen: 1981's *Possession*, starring Sam Neill and Isabelle Adjani and directed by Andrzej Żuławski. I know some of you are reading this and saying, huh? It *is* a romance, though, in many ways, even though the bulk of the film is perhaps the most unromantic movie I've ever watched.

The story follows Mark (Neill), a Cold War spy of some kind who comes home to his wife Anna (Adjani) and their young son Bob (Michael Hogben). Though it is deliberately kept vague, it seems that Mark has been away for some time, and during his absence, Anna has carried on an affair. As the film begins, we infer that Anna has asked Mark for a divorce. What follows is an absolute tour de force performance of anger, grief, and confusion from Neill and Adjani (whose portrayal of Anna won her the Cannes best actor award). The film cuts quickly between perspectives and abruptly shifts scenes, leaving the audience with a disjointed view of how the couple are reacting to each other. We watch their increasingly unhinged behavior both toward each other and toward the other people in their lives, from their son, Bob, to Anna's lover, Heinrich, to family friend Margie. Mark vacillates between rage and sadness, one minute imploring Anna to stay so they can move past her infidelity, and the next throwing over tables and slapping her in the face (a brutal and exhausting scene). Anna, for her part, cannot bear to be stuck in the apartment with Mark and Bob, and physically recoils at her husband's touch. She is casually cruel to him, but at the same time she seems devastated by her circumstances and the hurt she's causing.

If the film was simply an encapsulation of this couple's divorce, it would be an incredibly moving, uncomfortable piece of work, but it wouldn't fit in this book. Luckily for us, about halfway through, the tone shifts, and the movie goes from being a searing drama to something much, much weirder and more horrifying. After Mark suffers a beating from Anna's lover, Heinrich, after confronting the man, Mark hires a private detective to follow Anna. She's not staying with her lover, so where is she? The detective eventually finds her in a moldy, decrepit apartment building, and under the pretense of being from the building management, he gains access to her apartment. What he finds there, lurking in the dark corner of one of the bedrooms, will make you sit up and murmur to yourself, *WTF*. The wet, bloody, wormlike creature that the audience sees in the shadows entrances the detective, just long enough for Anna to stab him with a broken wine bottle. Again, I cannot say enough about Adjani's performance here: She is at once calculating and reckless, full of murderous rage that she unleashes on the unsuspecting detective.

Now that Żuławski has introduced this horrific speculative element to the story, things get progressively stranger. It turns out that Heinrich is not the only one who has been sleeping with Anna; she has been regularly having sex with the creature in her apartment. She isn't satisfied in her marriage, and she is no longer fulfilled by Heinrich either. Even when she tries to make amends with Mark, coming home to see him again, she realizes she can't stay, as she is too drawn to the creature. Mark is at a loss, and as he tries to put the pieces of his life back together, he meets Bob's teacher Helen, who inexplicably looks almost identical to his estranged wife. In a romance novel (well, a slightly macabre gothic romance novel, anyway . . . or at least a soap opera), this is where we would realize that Helen and Anna are the same person, or identical twins, or otherwise two people scheming to frame Mark or punish him for his treatment of his wife. He'd see the error of his ways and beg for forgiveness. But that is not how *Possession* works. Instead, we find out the origins of the creature who has stolen Anna's affections away from her husband and her lover. It is a scene that is hands down one of the most visceral, unapologetic, jaw-dropping performances I've ever seen (one that has been referenced in everything from Massive Attack's music video for "Voodoo in My Blood" to Arkasha Stevenson's *The First Omen*). Anna is beset by some unknown force in a subway tunnel, throwing herself into the wall, rolling around on the floor, screaming endlessly until she is oozing blood and bile and other bodily fluids from her mouth, her neck, everywhere. She tells Mark this was a miscarriage that she suffered, but we're not offered any real explanation. We can surmise that the miscarriage resulted in the creature that Anna has been nurturing and growing in her apartment, the same creature she's now having sex with. But nothing is ever fully explained here. It's incredible, uncomfortable, and truly something that must be seen, as no amount of written explanation will do this justice.

Anna continues to take care of this creature, who is becoming more human in appearance each time we see it. Mark finds Anna in flagrante delicto with the monster toward the end of the film, the half-human, half-tentacled creature bringing her to orgasm as she yells "Almost." It's only at the end of the film that we truly understand what that means. Mark, pursued by unknown operatives, ascends a spiral staircase, injured but still trying to escape. As he stops to rest, Anna and her creature appear, and he's now Mark's doppelganger, almost identical except for his eyes. Is this the embodiment of Anna's frustration and rage, her attempt to remake Mark as she wishes he was? Is this creature her possession, or does he possess her? We aren't given any answers. As Mark and Anna are both killed by those chasing Mark, his double leaves to find Helen (Anna's lookalike), who has been watching Mark's son. Though Bob pleads with Helen not to open the door to the Mark creature, somehow sensing that it's not his real father, Helen says she wants to see him anyway, disregarding Bob's worry and fear, which leads him to drown himself in the bathtub (a callback to a bathtub scene earlier in the film). The movie ends on an ambiguous note, with Helen at the door while a strange, grasping Mark waits on the other side.

Though *Possession* doesn't end with an HEA (though there might be one coming between Helen and Mark's doppelgänger just off screen), it's a fascinating, grueling film—one of those sticky movies that never leaves you once you've experienced it. It's both a romance and a tragedy, a searing drama and a weird, speculative thriller, and if you haven't seen it, you should.

The accessibility and realism of special effects in the 1980s and 1990s made it easier for filmmakers to show monsters as fully realized characters rather than shadowy figures that needed to be obscured so the audience could suspend their disbelief. Some of the monster romances in that time period include *My Demon Lover*, *Swamp Thing*, and "Lover's Vow," one of the stories in *Tales from the Darkside: The Movie*. The balance in these movies skews more romance or comedy, with not much in the way of horror. But in 1992, a more sinister monster is brought to life in *Candyman*, directed by Bernard Rose.

Wait, is *Candyman* a monster romance? Well, yes and no. Certainly, the character of Candyman, played by the wonderful Tony Todd, is no longer human; he's a vengeful spirit who was murdered by slave owners for having an affair with his master's daughter. And he has a rib cage full of bees, so he's definitely monstrous. But is there a romance? I think there are hints, though the film doesn't follow the typical romance formula. Helen Lyle (Virginia Madsen) is a researcher and grad student who is researching urban legends. She comes across the story of Candyman, a spirit/monster who haunts the Cabrini-Green housing project in Chicago. The original story by Clive Barker ("The Forbidden" in his *Books of Blood* collection) takes place in a similar housing development in Liverpool, England, but the shift to Cabrini-Green introduces racial dynamics that aren't present in Barker's story. As a white woman intruding on the predominantly Black neighborhood (even though she's sure she's helping the residents, Helen oversteps a number of times), the residents are reluctant to speak with Helen as she tries to learn more about the legend. When she discovers that Candyman's former lover was a white woman who looks quite a lot like herself, Helen is even more drawn to the legend, trying to figure out if she really has some connection to him.

I think *Candyman* is an example of a monster romance where it's not the monster who's pursuing the heroine, but the other way around. Helen's drive to learn more about Candyman and, I think more importantly, her need to be the person who brings his legend to a larger (whiter, richer) audience is what propels the story forward. Even when the people around her are being killed by the hook-handed monster, Helen persists. She can't stop herself from wanting to get close to his danger, even though he tells her explicitly he wants her to surrender to him and become his victim. Helen might tell herself that she's doing all of this work to save the boy Candyman abducted, or to help the residents of Cabrini-Green remove the threat of the monster. But there's a part of her who seems drawn to Candyman, whether it's because she's somehow linked to his lover from a past life or because she just likes dangerous men (who are very different from her current partner). Ultimately, her obsession with Candyman leads to her death; though she saves the young boy from Candyman, she succumbs to his darkness and is burned alive, destined to be Candyman's victim once again. The denouement makes this story even more interesting: Helen is reborn as a monster similar to Candyman, taking on his role and his powers. The final scene of the film of Helen appearing to murder her husband when he says her name five times cements her descent into darkness.

Nia DaCosta's 2021 *Candyman* is a direct sequel to the 1992 version, and I find it to have some incredibly interesting things to say about the nature of a monster who seeks to be eternal, and how the shared memories and legends of a community will both protect and haunt the residents. I think it's well worth watching, though it doesn't have much in the way of romance.

I won't get into the racial dynamics of the story, and the way white women have been weaponized against Black men in the past, but if you'd like to know more about that perspective, you should read Dominique Brown-Sampayo's excellent Medium article on *Candyman*.[4]

The 1990s gave birth to a few great monster romances (the gothic revival notwithstanding), and though *Candyman* is a little bit of a stretch, 1994's *Wolf*, starring Jack Nicholson, Michelle Pfeiffer, and an absolutely stellar list of costars ranging from the always sinister James Spader to David Hyde Pierce and Christopher Plummer, is most definitely a monster romance. Directed by Mike Nichols, this is a film that would probably bill itself as "elevated horror" nowadays; it's just as much a male-midlife-crisis drama as it is a werewolf movie. Legendary makeup artist Rick Baker is responsible for the transformation, but there's no graphic *An American Werewolf in London* body horror; instead, Nichols keeps our main characters mostly recognizable as themselves with a few subtle changes. Maybe when you get Jack Nicholson to play a werewolf you want to make sure audiences can tell it's Jack Nicholson (stunt doubles aside).

The film opens with Nicholson as Will Randall, a senior editor at a boutique publishing house (before all those houses were scooped up as imprints of the now Big Five). He's driving back from Vermont on a snowy evening and hits an animal. When he approaches, he realizes it's a wolf and it's still alive. The wolf bites Will before it runs off into the woods, and now we've got our story. We're told Will is a nice guy, a bit of a pushover who loves the work he does but isn't power hungry or cutthroat in the way he does business. He's also about to find out whether the billionaire who's taking over the publishing house, Raymond Alden, will keep him on the job. His protege, Stuart Swinton (smarmily played by James Spader), has secretly been gunning for the editor-in-chief position and at a party hosted by Alden, Will is unceremoniously demoted and learns of Stuart's betrayal. Incensed, Will stumbles around the estate, hiding from the partygoers (including his wife) as he struggles with what he thinks is a panic attack. Luckily, he's found by Alden's beautiful and sullen daughter, Laura (played by Michelle Pfeiffer). Though Will assures Laura she doesn't need to be cautious around him, the audience (especially an audience familiar with romance tropes) knows the stage is set and that the spark between Will and Laura will eventually grow into a flame. It feels like Nichols is going for a bit of a Humphrey Bogart/Lauren Bacall vibe here (Pfeiffer is thirty-six to Nicholson's fifty-seven), but let's face it, not many on-screen couples have the same sizzle that Bogey and Bacall had.

Will begins to realize that the wolf bite has given him some strange side effects, from incredibly sharp hearing to a stronger sex drive, and he keeps waking up with no recollection of his nocturnal adventures, which include running through the forest and killing a deer, among other activities. Meanwhile, his animal instincts have also given him the ruthless qualities he had been lacking, leading him to concoct a plan to get his job back and destroy Stuart in the process. Not only did Stuart steal his career, he'd also been sleeping with Will's wife, Charlotte (Kate Nelligan in a bit of a thankless role). When Will discovers Stuart's second betrayal, they get into a fight and Will bites Stuart (we'll come back to that in a minute). But more importantly, since this is a monster romance, Charlotte's infidelity has allowed Will to pursue the woman he's most interested in: Laura.

Some obnoxiously outdated romance tropes are at play here as the audience watches the courtship develop. Laura is standoffish but still decides to spend the entire day with the rather rude (though he'd probably call himself a "straight shooter" or something like that) man whom she barely knows. She's intrigued by his confession that the wolf bite has made him feel transformed. When he collapses, she takes care of him, and even after he disappears without acknowledging her, she still decides to forgive him and meet him at his hotel.

Obviously, Laura is drawn to a hint of danger, which is not only telegraphed but spoken aloud pretty explicitly when she talks about her past and her rebel wild-child life before she came home to her father's house. She's especially drawn to Will because despite his threatening nature, she feels largely in control: Though he pursues her, he's willing to lock himself up so he doesn't hurt her and is trying to push her away. So, she feels confident that she can steer this relationship. Until the police show up and she realizes that Will isn't as safe as she thought he was.

Charlotte is murdered, her throat ripped out, and when Laura speaks with the police, they tell her Will has been cleared. There is canine DNA mixed in with the rest of the evidence, so of course Will couldn't be responsible. Will and Laura decide he needs to be kept in her barn so he can't hurt anyone else, since he's clearly dangerous. But she had forgotten about Stuart, whom she runs into at the police station. The makeup effects here on James Spader are very subtle at first, which is so effective; the audience slowly (or quickly, depending on how good you are at guessing twists) remembers that Will bit Stuart during their altercation, so he must be transforming into a werewolf as well. He seems different, but since Laura doesn't know him well, she doesn't seem to notice anything other than the fact that he's a little aggressive and making advances on her. This isn't a full-on love triangle, since Laura isn't interested in Stuart at all. However, Will and Stuart are vying for power and she's the crux of their struggle. Once Will defeats Stuart in a struggle at Laura's, he runs off into the forest. Will gets away, Stuart is destroyed, and Laura is left to pick up the pieces. Except there is an interesting coda that leaves things much more open to interpretation.

As the police try to sort out what happened on the estate, Laura walks out of her cottage, looking much more femme fatale than she has at any point previously; she's got makeup on, her hair is a little wilder, and she seems more confident, more predatory. As she walks away from the detectives, we realize that she not only has a heightened sense of smell but also hears exceptionally well. As the camera closes in on Laura's eyes as she walks toward the lens, we see her irises change color and realize that she too is transforming into a werewolf. Was she always a wolf in disguise? Was she bitten during the fight with Stuart? Did having sex with Will trigger the beast in her? The ending is left ambiguous. I think the most interesting interpretation is based on something a scholar says to Will when he's investigating his wolf symptoms: Some people already have the spirit of the wolf in them, and they don't need to be bitten. I like the idea that Laura was always inherently a wolf, she just didn't know it, and that her attraction to Will was partly a case of two similar beings finding each other. She unlocks this hidden part of herself when she gives in to her more animal instincts.

Though *Wolf* isn't the last mainstream monster romance to be released in the '90s and 2000s, there don't seem to be many that focus on a real romantic relationship the way many earlier films do. Either the romance is played more for laughs, as in *Warm Bodies*, or it's much more horrific and much less consensual, as in the 2010 remake of *The Wolfman*, starring Benicio del Toro and Emily Blunt. But in 2017, director Guillermo del Toro brought his (and story co-creator Daniel Kraus's) take on *The Creature from the Black Lagoon* to life in *The Shape of Water*, easily one of the more outright love stories in this book. Though it might not be as full of horror as some other films here, the antagonist pushes the movie from straight fantasy to dark fairy tale. Audience reaction was generally quite positive, which may be a little surprising given that this film is most definitely a romance. Elisa (played by Sally Hawkins in a wonderful performance) is fully committed to a relationship with an Amphibian Man, whose design pays terrific homage to the original Gill-Man made by Milicent Patrick (again, for more on the invention of the Creature, read Mallory O'Meara's book). The movie won best picture at the Oscars in 2018, a rare feat for a fantasy (or really any "genre") film.

Del Toro had such fond memories of the 1950s creature feature that he wanted to film a version of the story where the female lead reciprocated the feelings of the so-called "monster," where the real bad guys were the scientists and military men who wanted to exploit the aquatic discovery for their own purposes. This is a prevalent theme in del Toro's work, culminating in his 2025 adaptation of *Frankenstein*. Elisa, who is mute, gravitates toward the Amphibian Man. Perhaps she senses the loneliness in him and recognizes that isolation within herself—she only has two companions in life: her coworker Zelda (Octavia Spencer) and her neighbor Giles (Richard Jenkins). From the moment the Amphibian Man is brought to the secret Baltimore facility where Elisa works, she is drawn to the mysterious creature, and he seems interested in her too, maybe simply because she shows him kindness. It's a far cry from the treatment he receives from Colonel Richard Strickland, who captured the Amphibian Man and wants to take him apart to study him and see whether there's anything about him he can exploit. Michael Shannon's

Strickland is a truly horrible man: racist, sexist, cruel, and petty. He terrorizes everyone he can, from Michael Stuhlbarg's scientist Robert Hoffstetler (really a Russian spy undercover) who wants to keep the Amphibian Man alive, to the creature himself, to Elisa, whose quiet strength seems to both anger Strickland and turn him on.

The love story in the film is played completely straight; there's no sense that Elisa ever considers the Amphibian Man to be weird or funny. He can't speak her language, and she can't speak at all; in finding new ways to communicate with each other, the two grow closer together and become intimate. Del Toro does a wonderful job of playing up the fairy-tale aspects of the story, and Doug Jones is a marvel, imbuing so much humanity in the role while completely obscured by his costume and makeup. The color palette shifts from cold greens and blues to warmer tones, and when Elisa starts to feel the love of the creature, she glows, swapping out her typical monotone wardrobe for bright red shoes and a headband that drive home the shift in her perspective. These are beautifully crafted touches that show the audience how much care del Toro has taken in bringing the romance to life.

Elisa shows the Amphibian Man the joy of hard-boiled eggs and record players, and brings him some solace and comfort, a respite from his torturous sessions with Strickland, who is not only quick to beat and electrocute the creature, but is also increasingly interested in Elisa. For her part, Elisa slowly becomes less and less the model cleaning woman at the facility; her interest in the creature unlocks her desires in a broader way. Zelda, seeing Elisa slowly become a little more defiant and less complacent, inadvertently helps Elisa formulate her plan to smuggle the Amphibian Man out of the lab to freedom by showing her where she hides from the cameras to take breaks. The suspense increases as Elisa enlists help from her friends to save the Amphibian Man from his death at the hands of Strickland and the military, and once they pull off their mission, Elisa is free to pursue her relationship with the Amphibian Man in a much more open way. There are a whole host of moments here that would fit into a number of more contemporary and less weird romances: The two shyly maneuver around each other before finally giving in to their feelings and consummating their love in a completely outlandish and ultraromantic scene where Elisa fills her entire bathroom with water so they can swim and love together.

Del Toro doesn't see the "monsters" in his films as creatures to be frightened of or repulsed by (see *Hellboy* or the Faun in *Pan's Labyrinth*). Rather, the authoritarian humans in his stories are the ones who should be avoided, a theme that shows up time and again in del Toro's films. His particular brand of dark fantasy always has horrific elements but ultimately believes in hope and love, and that's definitely the case here. Elisa decides she must let the Amphibian Man go to keep him alive. In return, he brings her back from the dead, and the movie ends with the two of them embracing after he plunges into the ocean carrying her. Is *The Shape of Water* an outright horror film? Not really. Though there are horrific moments throughout (and Strickland's necrotic fingers are truly disgusting), the overall arc moves from a place of unease and distress to a place of comfort, where Elisa and the Amphibian Man end up in a happy relationship under the sea.

Monster romance is a wide spectrum, from atmospheric stories with mostly humanoid creatures to wild tales of alien-like characters, and everything in between. While some of these films lean to the romance side of things and others feature much more horrific moments, it's clear that audiences have been fascinated by these unusual love stories since the early days of horror films. Monster romance has definitely risen in prominence recently, with books like Ruby Dixon's *Ice Planet Barbarians* and Lindsay Straube's *Kiss of the Basilisk* satisfying the curiosity of readers intrigued by characters like the Gill-Man but who want more agency in their romance. Meanwhile, movies like 2024's *Lisa Frankenstein*, *Your Monster*, and del Toro's transcendent

Frankenstein are capturing the attention of modern film audiences. I suspect we may be exploring these unlikely pairings for quite a while.

NOTABLE MONSTER ROMANCE

The Wolf Man (1941; dir. George Waggner)

TOP TROPES: Doomed Protagonist: Larry Talbot's plan to woo the woman of his dreams, Gwen, is shattered when he's exposed to a werewolf who bites him. From that moment on, no matter how Larry or Gwen really feel, their potential romance doesn't have a chance.

STALKER ROMANCE: Though Gwen certainly warms to Larry over the course of the movie, he's a persistent pursuer and gives off creepy vibes even before he turns into a murderous werecreature.

DARK MOMENT: Larry realizes that he won't be able to stop himself from attacking Gwen once the full moon is out, so he tells her goodbye and asks his father to restrain him.

HEA? No. At least Larry doesn't kill Gwen in a fit of werewolf pique, but he does end up dead.

The Creature from the Black Lagoon (1954; dir. Jack Arnold)

TOP TROPES: Damsel in Distress: Kay is being watched and coveted by the Creature who follows her as she swims in the South American waters, and also by the scientist Mark, who is jealous of her relationship with David.

SYMPATHETIC MONSTER: though the Gill-Man is not fully in the right, he's not totally wrong either; his habitat has been invaded by the scientists' expedition and he's both protecting his home and searching for a companion, so his drive to capture Kay is mostly instinctual.

DARK MOMENT: Kay is kidnapped by the Gill-Man (a dark moment for her and David, but kind of a win for Gill-Man).

HEA? Not for the Gill-Man; he's killed by David and Mark as they rescue Kay.

The Shape of Water (2017; dir. Guillermo del Toro)

TOP TROPES: Beauty and the Beast: Elisa is drawn to the frightening and frightened Amphibian Man, sensing a kinship with him that blossoms into a full-on love story.

TOUCH HER AND DIE: Strickland's pursuit of Elisa comes to a grisly end when the Amphibian Man lashes out after Elisa is shot.

DARK MOMENT: When Elisa realizes that the bathwater she's given the Amphibian Man isn't enough to keep him safe and healthy, she knows she must let him go so he can survive in the ocean, thinking she won't be able to stay with him.

HEA? Yes! Elisa and the Amphibian Man plunge into the depths and the Amphibian Man uses his powers to give Elisa gills so the two of them can live happily ever after underwater.

CHAPTER THREE

Deep Dive

Romance and Repression in Cat People

The horror films of the 1930s (and even earlier, but those are beyond the scope of this book) captivated audiences who wanted to be scared at the cinema. Filmmakers and studios began to branch out a little from adapting classic tales like *Frankenstein* and *Dracula* to crafting their own stories featuring different, sometimes original stories. As the tropes and trappings of the genre solidified, writers, directors, and producers were a little freer with their storytelling methods. This happens in fiction as well—as a new subgenre or theme emerges, more authors start writing within the guardrails of that trope or that established storyline. There's more room to explore the nuances of the genre in ways that might have been trickier for audiences to get into when they were completely unfamiliar with a particular style, trope, or theme. Look at romantasy, for example: Taking the existing tropes or expectations from a specific genre like romance and imposing them on a story of a different genre, like fantasy, allows the writer to express ideas or emotions in a novel way. These shifts can pull enthusiastic readers of either genre toward reading different kinds of stories. Jacques Tourneur broke the horror genre open with his trifecta of films with producer Val Lewton for RKO: *Cat People*, *I Walked with a Zombie*, and *The Leopard Man*. While all three of these films offered something new and different in horror, for me *Cat People* is the most interesting.

Cat People (1942) features many similar tropes as films like *Island of Lost Souls* or George Waggner's *The Wolf Man*. There's the supernatural element of shapeshifting, the underlying murder mystery, and characters who aren't quite what they seem. But sexuality and romance are explored through a slightly different lens here, because the main character in the film is Irena Dubrovna, played by the lovely Simone Simon. Irena is a young woman from Serbia who is working as a fashion illustrator. She's also plagued by an almost overwhelming fascination with big cats.

The film opens with Irena sketching a panther at the zoo. She crumples up her paper and attempts to throw it in the trash can, but she misses. Oliver Reed (Kent Smith), a marine engineer, notices the paper, then notices Irena, and is almost instantly smitten. He strikes up a conversation with her, and though she's initially a little standoffish, she allows him to walk with her back to her apartment (which is incredible, by the way).

When Irena invites Oliver in for tea, it's the first hint that she might be more interested in him than she let on when they first met. This opening section of the film is very romance forward and could easily fit in with any number of romances of the same era. Even the score is lilting and upbeat, reinforcing the idea that these two strangers might be on their way to a beautiful relationship. There are small hints of tragedy in Irena's past; she explains she left Serbia to get away from a terrible situation. But Oliver is drawn to her despite, or maybe because of, this underlying darkness. This is another example of the I-can-fix-them trope, and in this case there's also a little bit of a white knight vibe; Oliver seems to fancy himself as Irena's savior, offering her a stable "American life." Never mind that Irena is clearly self-sufficient and probably doesn't need his help—again, check out that apartment.

The film shows Oliver and Irena's brief courtship, a bit of a whirlwind where both seem to be falling in love with the idea of being in love rather than actually getting to know each other. We see further hints that Irena is hiding a terrible secret (animals are frightened of her), and she explains the history of the village she comes from in Serbia, where the king had to destroy the Satan-worshipping magic users who had taken over the area. Some fled to the mountains, cursed to transform into murderous big cats whenever they fell in love with a man. But these things don't seem to matter to Oliver, who is infatuated with his European love interest, and he proposes marriage. Irena agrees, but once they're married, and Oliver is ready to consummate the marriage, Irena confesses that she is afraid she will turn into one of the cat people, so they can never be together in a sexual relationship. Not exactly what Oliver wanted to hear.

The curse in the movie can be interpreted as a stand-in for women's repressed sexuality, as is true in many movies of the time, when the production code in full force made it difficult for unmarried sexual relationships to be portrayed onscreen. A number of readings of the film go even further, suggesting that the cat-people curse is in fact a reference to queerness, as Irena is unable or uninterested in consummating her relationship with her husband (I've read two great yet different takes on this idea).[1] In Irena's case, giving in to these lustful feelings unleashes murderous rage and transformation into a panther (panthers again, just like in *Island of Lost Souls*!) when she is faced with feelings of sexual arousal (another reason for the interpretation of lesbianism here, since her male love interest is nowhere in sight when she transforms in the pool scene I will discuss further on). But audiences might recognize their own feelings of jealousy and out-of-control anger in Irena. And although those emotions can be terrifying, they're also a little enticing. Oliver says at one point he can't help but be drawn to Irena, to want to touch her when she's near him, even though he knows she thinks that means she'll kill him. In a scene at the zoo, when Irena notices the key has been left in the door of the panther cage, she is tempted to keep it, to hold on to the danger. As her psychiatrist says, everyone is a little fascinated with death.

For all the clear romantic tropes in *Cat People*, and the obvious courtship between Irena and Oliver, Tourneur and producer Val Lewton make a choice that, to me, separates this film from many others of its time, certainly many romance-adjacent films: They don't give Irena an HEA. Instead, the happy couple at the end of the movie (who will go on to be a happy couple in the sequel, *The Curse of the Cat People*) turns out to be Oliver and his coworker, Alice (Jane Randolph). Introduced fairly early on as a confidante to Oliver as he first begins to fall in love with Irena, this other woman is depicted as the opposite of Irena and her mysterious ways. Alice is forthright, spending time with Oliver as a friend first before becoming increasingly bold in her intimations that she is in fact in love with him. Why she doesn't explain this to him before he decides to get married to Irena, we are never told. But Alice is the catalyst for Irena's downfall. When Irena comes home to find Alice and Oliver deep in conversation, we see her jealousy and annoyance at Alice's pushing of boundaries—we can infer that it would be pretty out of the ordinary for a married man to invite an unmarried woman into his apartment without a chaperone (plus, he had moved into Irena's apartment; it's not even his!). Oliver has violated Irena's trust by confessing her paranoia and obsession with cats to Alice, ostensibly to ask for help in finding a psychiatrist. But as someone who has read many romance novels can tell you, sharing these kinds of intimate details with someone you're not in love with is a big sign that you're with the wrong person.

I've spent a whole bunch of time here talking about the romantic elements of *Cat People*, but what about the horror? This is a slow-burn, atmospheric story; there isn't much in the way of monstrous images, but that doesn't mean it's lacking in the horror department. Instead, Tourneur uses a number of devices to crank up the paranoia and suspense in some incredibly effective ways, including one of the first jump scares onscreen. Though we don't see Irena transform into a panther, à la *An American Werewolf in London*, we do see the effects of her transformations, and much like other psychological horror films of the time, like *The Spiral Staircase* or *The Ghost Ship*, *Cat People* lets the audience's imagination fill in the blanks. The sequence where Alice is stalked through the park is a wonderful example of Tourneur ramping up the tension. Alice leaves Oliver to walk alone through the park, telling him she's a big girl and can take care of herself. We, the audience, know that Irena has seen the two of them together, and we also know Irena is convinced that her jealousy will cause her to turn into a panther. As Alice walks through the park from lamppost to lamppost, we hear her footsteps, watching her feet move quickly as she begins to think she's not alone. We know Irena is following her, and we wait for Alice to realize the same thing. She moves from darkness to light and back again, the editing cutting between Alice's scared face, the shadows and the streetlights, and her feet moving faster and faster as she tries to keep ahead of whatever is following her. Tourneur and Lewton keep this up for an agonizing length of time, the audience desperate for Irena in panther form to leap toward Alice at any moment. When Alice finally turns to look when she hears what might be a growl, we're surprised by a bus coming into the frame from the opposite direction: the first jump scare (dubbed the Lewton bus) that catches viewers off guard through misdirection and loud sounds.[2]

The next scary sequence in the film is one of my favorites and, again, features Irena and Alice. Alice checks into a spa/fitness club after meeting Oliver (and after she convinces him to ditch Irena), and she is unaware that Irena has followed her to the club. We see Alice getting ready to go for a swim, oblivious to the fact that Irena is lurking nearby. At this point, we know Irena is jealous and angry, and we're just waiting for a panther to come out and attack the unsuspecting woman. The lighting here is once again impeccable, with the ripples from the light on the pool reflecting and obscuring what's going on, and the shadows in the hallway leading from the changing room to the swimming area are stark and mysterious. Alice hears a noise, and she's convinced Irena has come to attack her, but she can't see her anywhere. We tense up along with Alice as she is stuck treading water in the middle of the pool; are panthers afraid of water? Will Alice tire and drown while she waits for the threat to pass? Once more, Lewton and Tourneur linger on the terrified Alice, drawing out the suspense as long as they can. When Alice finally screams, bringing the desk clerk in to her rescue, it's revealed that there was nothing to be scared of, as Irena innocently moves into the light, human as always. It's only after Irena leaves that we see that Alice's cover-up has been shredded by cat claws. Eerie and effective, these two sequences really elevate *Cat People* from a simple romantic drama to something much more unsettling.

Ultimately, the romance here is of a tragic sort. Irena can't escape her curse, and her husband won't even believe her, let alone save her. Instead, he leaves her, pretending to himself and his new love that it's for the best that they lock her away in an institution so they can be together (but not marry). The folk horror elements of curses and gothic trappings are transformed here, reimagining those tropes in a sleek, urban environment, which gives it a contemporary feel. Tourneur's fantastic chiaroscuro images and play with light and shadow helped evolve the language of film and inspired film noir as a genre (one he would perfect in one of my fave noirs, *Out of the Past*). The language of Lewton and Tourneur's film continues to resonate both in film and in fiction. Romantic suspense, monster romance, and stalker romance fiction all have some roots in films like *Cat People*, and the style of the film has influenced horror movies from *The Haunting* to *It Follows*.

TOP TROPES: Other Woman: Irena has a rival for Oliver's affections in Alice and ultimately loses him to the other woman. Secret Identity/Dark Secret: Oliver is unaware of Irena's past and her transformative nature, oblivious to the warning signs that she isn't quite what she appears to be. Insta-Love: Irena and Oliver take absolutely no time at all to get acquainted and immediately begin to get very attached to one another.

DARK MOMENT: When Oliver confesses to Irena that he's no longer in love with her and instead is in love with Alice, we see Irena's world collapse.

HEA? Not for Irena. The film ends with her being attacked and killed by a panther at the zoo. Oliver and Alice, however, are free to marry each other, and in the sequel, they are shown to be happy parents to the main character, Amy.

CHAPTER FOUR

Queer Representation in Horror Romance Cinema

Just a note as I begin this chapter: I'm a cis, hetero woman, and as such I want to focus on horror romance that features queer relationships as portrayed onscreen, rather than talking about the personal lives of actors, writers, and directors of horror romance. If you're interested in reading about horror films from a queer perspective, I highly recommend *It Came from the Closet: Queer Reflections on Horror* edited by Joe Vallese and *Corpses, Fools, and Monsters: The History and Future of Transness in Film* by Caden Mark Gardner and Willow Catelyn Maclay.[1]

Monsters aren't the only common tropes in early horror films. Ghosts and spirits play a large role in films like *The Ghost and Mrs. Muir* (which is more paranormal romance than horror), *The Uninvited*, and its follow-up, *The Unseen*. Even director Alfred Hitchcock, the Master of Suspense (whose true horror movies I'll discuss later), adapts Daphne du Maurier's *Rebecca* in 1940, and though it's more of a mystery than a horror film, the ghost of the late Mrs. de Winter certainly casts a heavy shadow over the characters at Manderley. These paranormal stories relied more on bumps in the night and atmosphere, and, of course, romance plays a part in many of them. Women were often in distress, haunted by unseen forces or past traumas, and the brave male heroes would help solve the mysteries and fall in love at the same time.

Hidden underneath these more overt storylines, however, is nuance often overlooked by mainstream filmgoers: queerness. Once the production code began to be enforced more strictly, explicitly queer characters were largely considered indecent and forbidden. Many filmmakers found ways to insert queer storylines, though, if people knew where to look for them. Horror, in particular, a genre so interested in transgressive messaging and exploring the unknown, was a perfect place to find queer stories. As regulations loosened over the years, LGBTQ+ stories became a little more acceptable, and in the 1970s and beyond, more and more queer stories were shown at the cinema, though many of these were still told from an outsider's perspective, since the producers, directors, and stars were usually straight, often white, and often men (at the very least, they weren't openly queer).

Rebecca (1940), Alfred Hitchcock's first US film, is the one that cemented him as a "Director," an auteur before auteurs were a thing. Producer David O. Selznick brought Hitchcock over to the US after his success with suspense thrillers like *The Lodger*, *The 39 Steps*, and *The Lady Vanishes*. Selznick had purchased the rights to Daphne du Maurier's popular novel, a gothic mystery, and wanted an accomplished director to oversee the film. But Hitchcock and Selznick disagreed throughout the production. Hitchcock's initial treatment for the film was very different from the book. Selznick wanted to stick closely to the novel, focusing on the second Mrs. de Winter's search for the truth about what happened to her husband's first wife, Rebecca (there are many behind-the-scenes accounts of the production issues; one of my favorite Hitchcock biographies is Patrick McGilligan's *Hitchcock: A Life in Darkness and Light*[2]). The film opens with a whirlwind romance between a young woman (who is never named), played by a wide-eyed Joan Fontaine, and Maxim de Winter (Laurence Olivier), a wealthy and rather mysterious gentleman whom the young woman seemingly saves from contemplating suicide (a trope that is reversed in Hitchcock's *Vertigo*). Max continues to spend time with his new love interest and unexpectedly proposes marriage. The woman is warned off; she's told that Max is still distraught over the death of his first wife, Rebecca, and his estate, Manderley, will be very difficult for the woman to run. But, with a classic I-can-fix-him determination, the woman, now the second Mrs. de Winter, thinks she will be able to thaw Max's icy demeanor and make him fall in love with her.

This story that started out oh-so romantically soon turns sour, as Max broods around his estate and his housekeeper, the severe Mrs. Danvers (Judith Anderson), taunts the second Mrs. de Winter, trying to convince her that she will never be able to take the place of Rebecca. In the years since the movie was first released, there has been much written about the character of Mrs. Danvers and the idea that she is a closeted lesbian in love with Rebecca.[3] Hitchcock clearly portrayed Mrs. Danvers as a woman in love with, and obsessed with, her former employer. She is so broken up over Rebecca's death that she does everything she can to manipulate the second Mrs. de Winter, trying to sabotage her marriage to Maxim. While the audience can never know for sure whether Rebecca reciprocated Mrs. Danvers's feelings, as the mysteries of Rebecca's life are revealed, it certainly seems possible that Mrs. Danvers had cause to be so upset. There clearly wasn't any real romantic connection between Rebecca and Maxim, and at one point Mrs. Danvers says Rebecca never loved any of her male companions. Mrs. Danvers ends up trapped (whether willingly or accidentally) in Rebecca's rooms as they catch fire, succumbing to the flames. Subsequent versions of the film have played up this romantic entanglement between Rebecca and Mrs. Danvers, which adds further nuance to the story. Because of the production code (and the idea that criminals needed to be punished onscreen), the ending of the movie is changed from the novel. In the book, Maxim really does kill Rebecca, and his new wife helps him get away with it. It would have been great to see Hitchcock keep that ending. Instead, we see Maxim and the second Mrs. de Winter absolved of any wrongdoing, and they are able to get their HEA.

The Uninvited (1944), directed by Lewis Allen, features two HEAs, though it gets there in a different way (and it's a different kind of happy ending). While the main romantic relationship in *Rebecca* is established at the beginning of the film, the central relationship in the first half of *The Uninvited* is between siblings Roderick and Pamela Fitzgerald, played by Ray Milland and Ruth Hussey, respectively. The two are very close, and they impulsively decide to buy Windward House together while on holiday in Cornwall, a house that is unusually inexpensive. The owner of the house, Commander Beech (Donald Crisp), has had trouble with tenants leaving because of "disturbances" following the death of his daughter, Mary Meredith, who fell to her death from the cliffs outside the home. Though Mary's daughter Stella (Gail Russell), who lives with her grandfather Commander Beech, is adamantly opposed to the sale, upset that she will lose her connection to her mother (who died when Stella was three), Beech goes through with the sale anyway. Roderick, a composer, is looking forward to using the artist's studio in the house, but when the two siblings open the door, they experience the first sign that the house is haunted by a restless spirit of some kind: an oppressive, uncomfortable cold. Though his sister finds the spirit more intriguing and sad than terrifying, they decide they must uncover the secrets of the house.

They soon realize that the (very young) woman named Stella holds the key to the mysteries of Windward House. She also seems to hold the key to Roderick's heart, as he is infatuated with her. I'm not sure how audiences felt about the age gap between

Milland and Russell in 1944, but it definitely gave me pause the first time I saw the film; he was thirty-seven and she was twenty, so the relationship feels a bit off-balance, particularly when they first meet. Rick is almost like a father figure to her, and both he and Pam talk about how they feel a bit sorry for her being so sad about her mother and the house she left behind. There *has* been a bit of a resurgence of age gaps in romance novels, even with the #MeToo movement highlighting the skewed power dynamics that can arise in these types of relationships. However, though Roderick has romantic feelings for Stella, aside from their first kiss, which he initiates after an argument, there doesn't seem to be much in the way of coercion on his part. Stella seems drawn to Rick and pursues him—that might be because she wants access to Windward House, but there appears to be genuine affection on her part too. He seems to care for her and wants to save her from the spirit that's haunting the house, since it seems to have nefarious plans for the young woman.

The horror in *The Uninvited* is mostly of the eerie variety; there aren't any gory or overly explicit scenes here. But the movie nonetheless projects an unsettling vibe with creepy moments and wonderful ghostly effects, particularly the séance where Stella is possessed by the ghost. The siblings, with the help of the local Dr. Scott (Alan Napier), who is rather interested in Pamela, uncover the mystery and reveal that the ghost is a Spanish woman named Carmel, Stella's real mother. She was having an affair with Stella's father, and his wife Mary (of course) hated her. Carmel died not long after Mary confronted her at the cliffs near the house, and they argued passionately before Mary fell over the edge onto the rocks below.

There's another layer to *The Uninvited* that echoes the earlier *Rebecca*. Mary is revealed to have had a very close relationship with Mrs. Holloway (Cornelia Otis Skinner), a woman who runs a women's shelter where Stella is sent by Commander Beech after her brush with unearthly spirits during the séance. The relationship between Mary and Mrs. Holloway echoes that of Rebecca and Mrs. Danvers, and it seems pretty clear (to me, at least) that the women's connection went much deeper than friendship, and that the two were romantically involved. With the production code and the Catholic Legion of Decency holding so much sway over the Hollywood studios, studios had to be very guarded about what they were allowed to show in terms of queer relationships, but as in *Cat People* and *Rebecca*, studios and filmmakers found ways to skirt the rules and provide hints of forbidden relationships. For instance, when Mrs. Holloway is speaking about Mary and how they were so close, the camera frames her with the large portrait of Mary hanging above her mantle, and everyone else in the frame is set a little apart.

This movie has a great denouement after everyone realizes that the ghost is Stella's mother and can be laid to rest. Just as the audience thinks everything is back to normal as Carmel is laid to rest and will no longer bother anyone, Roderick realizes that Mary's vengeful spirit is still haunting Windward House (the ghost effects in the film are really excellent, using trick photography in a way that was new to audiences at the time), and he has to banish her as well. It's an early example of one of my favorite tropes, where we think everything is resolved but there's time for one last scare (à la *Carrie* or *Friday the 13th*). Though we don't get a traditional Happy Ever After (there's no final declaration of love from Rick and Stella or Pam and Dr. Scott, or anything definitive like a marriage proposal), both couples end up together at the end of the film, and with the spirits laid to rest, the movie finishes on a positive note.

The late 1950s and early 1960s in North America was when the studio system truly ended (for a deep dive into this, check out Mark Harris's *Pictures at a Revolution*[4]). Many factors contributed to the downfall of what was known as the Golden Age of Hollywood. The US government had introduced antitrust legislation in 1948 to break up the studios' vertical pipeline, and film studios were no longer able to own the cinemas where they were distributing the movies they produced. This meant that there was room for smaller independent studios to show their films; by the mid-1950s, almost half of the films being shown in cinemas were made by independent studios or filmmakers who shopped their final movies around to distributors. The proliferation of drive-in theaters, which relied on B movie pictures, meant there was more space for these cheaper, shorter films. The film production code and censors became more lenient, and the opportunity for gorier, sexier, queerer, and more extreme horror presented itself, and with that came more romance as well. The true exploitation films of the 1960s (the ones shown in grindhouses) don't necessarily feature a whole lot of love as they give audiences glimpses of wilder violence and sexual situations. But the overall relaxing of rigid mores, in light of the Civil Rights Movement and early feminist movements, meant that movies were freer to explore different romantic relationships. And though homosexual couplings were still largely prohibited (and in many places, illegal), there were filmmakers who used genre as a way to cue queer lifestyles without making things so obvious that the censors took note.

Hammer Film Productions first began making horror films in the late 1950s (*The Curse of Frankenstein* was released in 1957). Many of their films in the 1960s were more extreme versions of stories that North American audiences had been loving since Universal Pictures started making black-and-white fright films in the 1930s. When Hammer decided to start filming in vibrant Eastmancolor, the BBFC (British Board of Film Censors) struggled to determine exactly how far the studio would be able to push their gory imagery, since blood in full color is different than in black-and-white footage. The censors were sometimes a little lax in their determination of what could be shown, especially since the BBFC didn't always get to view the entire film in color; sometimes filmmakers would submit black-and-white prints to skirt the rules.

In addition to the violence in these horror films, the romance and horror tropes begin to overlap quite closely, beginning with *The Curse of Frankenstein*.

The story in *The Curse of Frankenstein* will be familiar to anyone who's watched the earlier film version of Mary Shelley's novel starring Boris Karloff as the creature. But the Hammer production, directed by Terence Fisher, deviates from both the novel and the Universal film in a number of ways. Doctor Victor Frankenstein is vividly brought to life by the wonderful Peter Cushing. He would go on to play Frankenstein multiple times in Hammer's sequels and was a staple of the studio's gothic horror pictures, along with his counterpart Christopher Lee, who plays the Creature here. The film also introduces viewers to Elizabeth (played by Hazel Court), Frankenstein's cousin and fiancée (which is weird, but not completely unheard of for the time period), and Paul (played by Robert Urquhart), who serves in the Igor role here. He starts out as Victor's tutor, then assistant, but he grows increasingly uncomfortable with Victor's experiments in his quest to reanimate flesh.

Though the film definitely fits into the gothic horror genre (this movie essentially started the British gothic horror revival), the romance between Victor and Elizabeth is less pronounced than it is in some other adaptations (particularly Kenneth Branagh's version, which I'll explore later). In fact, the film is bookended with scenes of Victor in jail after having murdered his maid Justine (Valerie Gaunt), with whom he'd been carrying on an affair, so he wasn't particularly enamored of Elizabeth. There is a bit of a love triangle set up when Elizabeth first arrives at the castle, much to the chagrin of Justine, but I think the central relationship of the film is the one between Paul and Victor. While I don't know that director Terence Fisher intended for there to be a queer subtext present in the film, a few moments stand out to me. There's a scene where Paul tells Victor they need to stop because Elizabeth might find out. Ostensibly, this conversation is about the experiments they're conducting and the depravity they're committing by digging up bodies and harvesting them for parts. But I'm not alone in thinking there may be a hint of queerness here (you can read Samantha McLaren's excellent article about queerness in Hammer films in *Fangoria* for more.[5]) Peter Cushing is a wonderfully expressive actor, and his body language with both women in the film is much more standoffish and cold than it is with Paul, who seems to be the only person with whom Victor can truly be himself and explore his dark, transgressive thoughts—at least until Paul decides he can't continue to take part in Victor's experiments. Although overt, explicit queer representation was virtually nonexistent during this time period, many critics would agree that the symbolism in some of the Hammer horror films certainly has a queer bent.

The Curse of Frankenstein was a massive success for Hammer, both in the UK and in the US, and that success paved the way for the studio to become an absolute juggernaut in horror for the 1960s and most of the 1970s. Following Frankenstein, Hammer released *Dracula* in 1958, again starring Cushing and Lee (this time as Van Helsing and Dracula, respectively), and by 1965 they were releasing six horror films a year. Though critics were mixed in their reviews of *The Curse of Frankenstein* and it received an X rating for its full-color violence, its popularity with audiences has endured.

As Hammer reinvigorated the horror film genre, other studios began to explore variations on themes that seemed to be resonating with audiences. Of course, there were still creature features shown at drive-ins and midnight movie screenings, but some more serious horror films were getting traction as well, though perhaps not as frequently as they were in the 1930s and '40s. Were they also romances? Maybe not necessarily (or maybe not completely), but we'll look at a few here and see if I can convince you that there are at least some romantic vibes going on in some of these movies.

Though *The Haunting* was not a huge success when it was released in 1963, its status in the horror genre has grown significantly over time, with directors like Martin Scorsese championing the film as one of his favorite scary movies.[6] Based on Shirley Jackson's deliciously creepy novel *The Haunting of Hill House*, Robert Wise's movie stars Julie Harris, Claire Bloom, Richard Johnson, and Russ Tamblyn (Dr. Jacoby in my number-one favorite TV show of all time, *Twin Peaks*). Johnson plays Dr. John Markway, who puts out an ad for people to help him study the house and its paranormal activity. Luke Sanderson (Tamblyn), heir to the owner of the house, comes along, and the only other two people who apply are Theodora (Bloom), a psychic, and the central character of the film, Eleanor Lance (Harris). Eleanor experienced poltergeist activity when she was a child, and she is quite fragile emotionally, living in isolation after her mother's death. Nevertheless, Eleanor is invited to participate, and the foursome arrive at Hill House, a sprawling manor that just feels off: Angles are wrong, doors open and close by themselves, and everything seems a bit ominous, though Luke remains skeptical. It doesn't take long for everyone to start to believe supernatural forces are at play, however.

Theo and Eleanor experience a number of tense, ghostly events, and director Robert Wise does an excellent job of leaving things to the viewer's imagination. There are loud bangs and bulging doors, but we don't really get to see what exactly is causing all this supernatural activity. The film is a little more ambiguous than the book, and Eleanor's telekinetic ability is downplayed so we're never quite sure whether she has attracted a ghost, amplified the ones already haunting Hill House, or whether she is simply causing all the spooky activity herself. She's a tragic figure, but a tragic figure who makes terrible decisions, and her inevitable death (either by her own hand or assisted by the spirit of Hill House) is almost entirely predictable.

What about the romance? A few different romantic angles are present in *The Haunting*. Though Jackson was rather ambiguous about the character of Theo in the novel, in the film she's more definitely coded as queer (and Robert Wise has said there was a scene featuring Theo's breakup with her girlfriend that was filmed but cut).[7] Even so, her queerness is conveyed by knowing glances and seductive mannerisms rather than by coming out to her housemates. Theo seems to be attracted to Eleanor, and the two strike up a somewhat fraught friendship at first, sharing some lovely moments and opening up to each other about their lives outside of Hill House. Theo tells Eleanor she's unmarried and has recently left her love interest. Theo also guesses Eleanor's nickname, calling her Nel before Eleanor ever mentions it. But as the investigators spend more time in the house, experiencing more and more paranormal activity, Eleanor turns against Theo when she accuses Eleanor of writing ghostly words on the wall. Eleanor calls Theo unnatural and rejects her completely, which is perhaps when she begins her final spiral toward her ultimate demise. Eleanor's own infatuation with Dr. Markway comes to nothing when his wife arrives at the house, and Eleanor is increasingly isolated when her hope of any kind of romantic pairing is dashed.

One of the things about *The Haunting* that I think has allowed it to stay relevant and engaging over all this time is the unapologetic depiction of Theo's queerness. She is allowed to be gay, attracted to Nel (albeit in very subtle ways to appease the censors) while keeping her "feminine" qualities. Many lesbians on film at the time (*The Children's Hour* had been released a couple of years earlier) were required to suffer or be punished for their lifestyle; lesbianism was considered a mental disorder, and this kind of deviant behavior couldn't be shown without consequences. Allowing Theo to just *be* and experience her feelings without making her predatory or otherwise aggressive is quite refreshing, and frankly is still not as easy to find in cinema as it should be.

Horror films with queer characters become a little more mainstream in the 1980s and '90s, though there was still a long way to go. Even if films featured queer characters, they were not written, produced, or directed by queer people and fell back on tired stereotypes to tell their stories. There was also a homophobic backlash during this same time period, led by Reaganite conservatism in the US and Thatcherism in the UK. Nevertheless, movies featuring queer characters were being made, and horror was once again a space for folks to make films that could skirt the rules and norms of mainstream cinema to explore different perspectives. One of those is a personal favorite of mine: Clive Barker's *Hellraiser*.

Based on Barker's own splatterpunk novella, *The Hellbound Heart*, and directed by the author in his first filmmaking credit, *Hellraiser* (1987) tells the story of Larry, Julia, Frank, and Kirsty Cotton, and the creatures that they've summoned, the Cenobites. Even if you've never seen the film, you've likely seen these characters in pop culture—leather-wearing, body-modifying, genderqueer beings who are led by a character referred to as the Hell Priest, but subsequently known as Pinhead (due, of course, to their head full of pins). These creatures have given themselves over to an existence where pain exists simultaneously with pleasure. They devote themselves to the pursuit of sensation, offering everything you could ever want to feel, as well as everything you'd never want to feel again. The Cenobites are summoned by explorers who solve a puzzle box called the Lament Configuration, and one such explorer is Frank Cotton, a debaucherous, drug-using hedonist who has been carrying on an affair with his brother Larry's wife, Julia. Unfortunately for Frank, his pursuit of carnal pleasure comes to a horrific end when the Cenobites, who no longer differentiate between good or bad sensation, rip him apart with supernatural hooks and chains.

When Larry moves into Frank's house, hoping to reconnect with Julia, he accidentally brings Frank back to life when he spills blood on the spot where Frank was killed. Frank isn't quite all there though, and he needs Julia's help to bring him fully back to life. Julia, a wonderful embodiment of the evil stepmother trope, is still in love with Frank (even in his wet, bloody, not-fully-formed state), and she agrees to help him get his body back by bringing him unsuspecting male victims to drain. When Larry's daughter (and Julia's stepdaughter) Kirsty comes across her monstrous uncle, she narrowly escapes him and manages to grab the puzzle box before she gets away. Her accidental opening of the box and summoning of the Cenobites is the catalyst for the rest of the film. In exchange for her freedom, she convinces Pinhead that she can trap her uncle and give him back to the Cenobites he's escaped from.

The central romance in this film is obviously between a woman and a man (albeit a man back from the dead who's missing his skin). But the queerness in *Hellraiser* is intrinsic to the story. The Cenobites have moved beyond gender and conventional sex; their entire purpose is to push boundaries and keep finding more ways to experience sensation. Their transformation of their bodies, peeling back the flesh to feel in different ways and explore other avenues of potential pleasure, goes far beyond conventional depictions of sex and violence. The story that the film is based on is much more sexually explicit; Barker ran into problems with the censors who demanded cuts to some of the sexual content in the movie. Even with those cuts, though, *Hellraiser* remains a baroque, bombastic, bloody feast for the eyes, with beautifully grotesque creature design and a delightfully over-the-top feel. The sequels devolve into a bit of a mess, especially as Barker tried to distance himself from the increasingly silly plots. But the 2022 remake, featuring Jamie Clayton in the role of Pinhead, breathed new life into the franchise, offering an interesting and innovative new version of the now classic character. There's less sex and romance in the remake, but the quest for new sensations and pleasures is very prominent in the film, so it's very much in keeping with the feel of the original.

For a slightly more traditional (but maybe even more nightmarish) take on a queer romance, I rewatched *Mulholland Drive* recently. Director David Lynch (as you'll see in chapter 8) was one of the most sincere filmmakers around, and he often featured romantic stories within his dreamlike, bizarre, fascinating movies. *Mulholland Drive* (2001) is a romantic film—right up until it isn't. The film opens with a strange and unsettling sequence as we see a woman fall back onto a bed. Then we immediately shift to what is seemingly a different story, following a woman escaping from an attempted murder who hides out in an apartment in Los Angeles. The story flits back and forth between this mysterious woman and Betty, an aspiring actress who has just moved to California and is hoping for her big break.

Betty is played by Naomi Watts (who got her own big break in *Mulholland Drive*), and she is perfectly cast as the plucky, wide-eyed heroine here. Eventually, Betty stumbles across the mysterious woman (played by Laura Harring) in her aunt's apartment, where she had been hiding, and it turns out that this woman is suffering from amnesia and doesn't know who she is or where she came from. Betty names her Rita and decides to help Rita figure out who she is and get her back to her old life. Lynch intersperses the mystery solving with the story of director Adam Kesher (Justin Theroux), who is trying to make a film and is beset by demands from the shady and secretive studio heads, who tell him he needs to find the girl they want him to cast in his film. The story feels opaque at first glance, with many signature Lynchian details; things jump around, there are small vignettes that seem unrelated to the main storyline, and we get flashes of all-out strangeness (the scene behind Winkie's Diner is so damn unsettling; even on my most recent rewatch I jumped). But although the movie has been criticized for being hard to follow and making no sense, I genuinely think that if the viewer opens themselves up to Lynch's storytelling style, things do fall into place. Mostly.

About two-thirds of the way through the film, when it looks like Betty and Rita are about to make some discoveries, their romance also blossoms, and the two give in to temptation and sleep together. Their burgeoning love story feels like it's been taken out of a more typical romance storyline; they meet during a mix-up, they try to solve problems together, they grow closer as the suspense builds. But after their first sexual encounter, Rita convinces Betty to come with her to Club Silencio, where she thinks they will find answers about Rita's identity. Instead, though, they find a box and a key. The camera zooms in to the darkness of the box, and all of a sudden, things are different. Betty is no longer Betty; she's Diane Selwyn, an out-of-work actor who seems severely depressed and is mourning the loss of her girlfriend, Camilla Rhodes (Rita). Diane is so angry that Camilla is leaving her to marry director Adam that she decides to hire a hitman to murder Camilla. When Diane gets word that the hit has taken place, she kills herself. The first time I saw this movie, I really had no idea what was going on (and young me was very unforgiving of films that didn't "make sense"), and I kind of hated *Mulholland Drive*. Slowly, though, as I was exposed to more Lynch, and more weirdness in both fiction and film, I was able to come around, and I now think it's a beautiful, lyrical story that isn't quite as hard to follow as I first thought.

I agree with the fairly common interpretation of the film: that the bulk of the movie is actually a dream taking place in Diane Selwyn's head. Diane is Betty's doppelganger (both characters played by Naomi Watts), and the dream is Diane's way of reconciling her hurt and anger over the way her life has turned out. Her love of Camilla has turned into a toxic, desperate hate, and she can no longer go on with her life, feeling she's got nothing left. As she leaves this world, her subconscious creates a better version of her relationship and her career for her to dwell within, but the truth is too strong for Diane to overcome, so even in her dream things take a turn for the worse, devolving into strange, nightmarish sequences.

There's no HEA in *Mulholland Drive*, but I think that there is a fully realized romance within the film, and the connections between the characters make the horrible results of the story feel even more heartbreaking. Lynch's films are never straightforward genre pieces, and there are many layers in this one, but I think it fits squarely in a horror space, full of genuinely frightening and uncomfortable sequences, and blood and murder and strange occurrences. Like I said, the scene at Winkie's with the man behind the dumpster is one that will stick with me forever. The fact that Lynch is always so sincere and committed to getting the characters right means that everything resonates at a high level, and the terrifying things people face, or are willing to give themselves over to, make for some truly disturbing images.

I've avoided talking too much about vampires in this chapter, even though they are quite often characters who are more open or liberal in their sexuality. I've seen the argument pop up time and again on social media that vampires are inherently queer characters, and I think there's quite a bit of truth to that. More than anything, a vamp's motivation is the pleasure of the flesh and the blood, especially in many more recent adaptations (as opposed to the genuine creepiness of something like *Nosferatu*), and given that they are so often portrayed as immortal creatures living outside of time, it makes sense that they're not too concerned about their prey's gender. Social constructs must seem less important when you have lived through so many changes. We'll save most of the vampire discussion for chapter 7, but I did want to explore one vampire movie here: Tony Scott's *The Hunger* (1983), based on the book by Whitley Strieber.

The crux of the story is the same in both film and novel: Miriam, a centuries-old vampire, has taken a series of companions over the years, and her current companion, John, is about to reach the end of his preternaturally extended life. Miriam comes across a scientist, Sarah, whose research into sleep and aging may be able to save John, but as Miriam and Sarah grow closer, she realizes that perhaps she would rather Sarah replace John than save him. The novel gets bogged down in the science of the story, which feels quite outdated, and while it's told from Miriam's perspective, much of the prose in the novel feels clunky and a bit overwrought; the depictions of women in the story are eye-rollingly two-dimensional. To be fair, the movie also adopted some of these problematic interpretations of the characters, but Scott's incredibly stylish direction and the performances from the three main actors save the film. Catherine Deneuve plays Miriam with a haughty sensuality that is so captivating. Similar to Delphine Seyrig in *Daughters of Darkness* (discussed later), Deneuve exudes a power that tricks the audience into forgetting what a monster she is. David Bowie is her lover and companion, and he imbues John with an ethereality and androgyny that sets the stage for Miriam's subsequent queer relationship with Sarah, played by Susan Sarandon as a woman who seems a bit timid and perhaps repressed before she gives in to Miriam's advances.

The character of Sarah in the novel is very much coerced into her relationship with Miriam, but Sarandon plays Sarah in a more open way. Though Sarah initially reaches out to Miriam in the hopes of helping John, she's drawn to Miriam as well, and though she tries to stay away once she finds out that Miriam is older and more monstrous than she originally seems, Sarah eventually returns, curious to explore further. Miriam's bisexuality is a departure from depictions of many previous vampires in cinema. It was certainly more common for a male vampire to set his sights on a virginal young woman, and though female vampires were often coded as lesbians going as far back as Elizabeth Báthory and Carmilla, it was rare to see a vampire onscreen who was more interested in desire, pleasure, and blood indiscriminately, without seeming to have a preference for a specific gender. Scott leans into the lesbian relationship between Miriam and Sarah rather than the coupling of John and Miriam—the sex scene between the two women is much more of a focal point than any aspect of the emotional relationship between John and Miriam, even though theirs is the longer partnership.

Scott shoots the film beautifully, using gorgeous background lighting and billowing curtains to frame shots. The opening sequence, set to Bauhaus's excellent "Bela Lugosi's Dead," establishes the grim yet elegant tone of the movie. We see Miriam and John as vampires seducing and preying on an unsuspecting couple. This violent, sensual hunt is cut with footage of Sarah and her monkey test subjects who are resorting to violence of their own. The parallel editing situates the vampires firmly in the monstrous, animalistic side of the sexy vampire spectrum. As stylish and stylized as the film is, it doesn't shy away from the extreme violence of these characters. We may feel a hint of sympathy for John, rapidly declining as he waits for a cure that never comes, but we don't forget how truly awful he and Miriam are, and how many people they've murdered. The echoes of Miriam's previous companions, moaning as their withered husks are locked away in coffins, further reinforces just how alien and removed from humanity Miriam really is. Even as she uses her seduction techniques on her newest prospect, her cavalier treatment of John, discarding him so quickly after centuries together, reminds us of how little she cares for her lovers. The hunger for blood and for power takes precedence over her feelings, however strong they may have been, for her companions.

The central love triangle isn't the only relationship explored in the film, though there aren't any HEAs to be found. The young girl Miriam is grooming to become her next protégé/companion, Alice (Beth Ehlers), is viewed as a potential romantic and life partner for Miriam once she comes of age. Her parents have largely abandoned her, and under the guise of being music teachers, Miriam and John have welcomed Alice into their lives, treating her with affection that she certainly seems to believe is more akin to love. She thinks of the couple almost as surrogate parents, since her own family is so distant and cold. As such, her trust in the vampires makes her an easy and convenient target of John's anger when he discovers his eternal life doesn't also mean eternal youth. He murders the young girl in the hope that her blood will restore his youthful appearance, and perhaps also because he knows Miriam is grooming Alice to be her next companion, so whether out of jealousy or compassion, he makes the decision to end her life rather than condemn her to a miserable existence in thrall to Miriam. Sarah's boyfriend, Tom, tries to persuade her to escape from Miriam's seductive embrace once he starts to suspect that her fascination with John and his companion has become more than professional curiosity. He can't determine what's wrong with Sarah after her first sexual encounter with Miriam; he just knows she's changed (code, perhaps, for her queer awakening as much as her imminent vampirism). He's both upset that she's acting strangely and worried that he can't help her, and he wants her to take a blood test. His concern and attempts to win back Sarah echo John's attempts to get Miriam to cure his inevitable aging. Both men are shoved to the side by their respective female partners as the women come together and directly or indirectly cause the deaths of John and Tom.

As for the relationship between Miriam and Sarah, well . . . there's no HEA here either. Though the original version of the film ended with Sarah killing herself, rejecting Miriam's vampiric gift and the hunger it sparked in her, the studio wanted to keep things open-ended and tacked on a rather nonsensical shot of Sarah in London, taking on her own vampiric companions in Miriam's place as the head of a small coven of blood drinkers. The ending robs Sarah of her agency and makes her sacrifice seem in vain, which is too bad. She's a fascinating character and Sarandon does great work here, transforming Sarah from a no-nonsense, uptight woman of science to an uninhibited and powerful fledgling vampire; there's a scene where she's walking down the street after her encounter with Miriam, and even though she's not physically changed, her body language and mannerisms create an entirely different persona, one that Sarandon would translate into powerful, sexy women many times throughout her career.

Speaking of women who transform . . . Lucky McKee's 2002 debut, *May*, stars Angela Bettis as a shy and traumatized young woman who just wants to be loved and seen. May Canady is a young woman with a lazy eye, and in flashbacks we see that her mother (who seems to be emotionally manipulative if not outright abusive) has taught May to hide herself, covering her eye patch with her hair and providing her with a doll (who is never allowed to leave its case) in place of any real friends. In the present day, an adult May is a quiet veterinary assistant, solitary and longing for some true companionship. She spends her days sewing up animals at the vet hospital, and her free time sewing her clothes. (It's nitpicky of me, but as someone who sews, that's the one thing in this movie that really bothers me: She never operates the sewing machine correctly!) May fixates on Adam (Jeremy Sisto), a mechanic she watches from afar, and whose hands she finds incredibly beautiful. It's not explicitly mentioned in the film, but May's focus on people's body parts rather than their identities as whole people is a natural outcome of her mother's obsession with May's eye. The sense that a person can be rejected for one small aspect of their appearance seems to have conditioned May into compartmentalizing the people she meets into pieces, instead of seeing them as whole beings. This may also explain the queerness of the film (more on that in a minute); as with vampires, viewing people not as full creatures in their own right, but only as objects that can be broken down into segments explains why it doesn't matter to May whether the connection she's seeking is male or female.

May finally gets up the courage to talk to Adam, and they seem to hit it off. Adam is an aspiring filmmaker, showing May his short romantic horror film about a couple engaged simultaneously in a romantic clinch and a literal feast, as they writhe together and take bites out of each other. Since May doesn't have any real sense of what people are supposed to do in relationships, having only seen her neighbors groping each other in the elevator, she becomes aggressive with Adam, which leads to him rejecting her and telling his friends she's a little unhinged. Poor May has no idea how to react, and she rebounds by giving in to the advances of Polly (Anna Faris), the receptionist at the animal hospital. Polly is a hedonist, looking for sexual excitement wherever she can find it, and is quick to invite May into her life. But May wants more than just a one-night stand and is soon devastated by Polly's callous and dismissive behavior when she moves on to another beautiful woman named Ambrosia (played by Nichole Hiltz). All this rejection becomes too much for May—even the cat she's watching over, Loopy, doesn't seem to want anything to do with her. That ends up being the last straw. May breaks, killing Loopy and setting in motion the final act, where she follows her mother's advice from the beginning of the film: If she can't find friends, she'll make her own. From the pieces of the people who have spurned her.

The indie vibe of the film really helps sell the story, and for a good portion of the running time, audiences could well be thinking they are watching just another quirky, hipster movie about slightly strange but endearing characters. Jeremy Sisto plays Adam as a brooding almost bad boy who wants to be more dangerous than he really is, and Anna Faris's Polly is both vapid and affectionate in a way that fits the manic-pixie-dream-girl trope so popular at the time. The slow-burn meet-cute and subsequent adorable/awkward first dates are very reminiscent of late '90s slacker comedies. Even though we get glimpses of the horrors to come, Angela Bettis as May almost makes you believe she's too timid or broken to ever snap and go on a murderous rampage. But rampage she does. *May* is a precursor to the "elevated" horror that has since become a touchpoint for so many filmgoers in everything from *Jennifer's Body* (more on that later) to *Promising Young Woman* and *Midsommar*. The female protagonists in these films are celebrated for their reclamation of their autonomy, and the violence they perpetrate is often seen as a rejection of the misogynistic slashers that came before them (at the expense of realizing that they're perpetuating that same violence, but that is perhaps a conversation for later).

The queerness of *May* feels nonchalant, which is quite refreshing. There's no sense that May is questioning her sexuality throughout the movie; she's much more concerned with finding love and connection regardless of gender. I love that no one else in the story seems to be hung up on this aspect either. Polly is unapologetically queer but there's no big statement, and both she and Adam say, "I like weird" and basically leave it at that (obviously they don't end up liking weird as much as they think given how things pan out for them, but still). The love scenes between both May and Adam and May and Polly are shot similarly—the audience gets the sense that either pairing is fine, and ultimately the intention is for viewers to feel as though May deserves love from someone, anyone at all. Best of all, May's villainous turn doesn't hinge on her queerness, which is a wonderful change from many horror films and suspense thrillers where the villain's sexuality is shorthand for deviance and explains their murderous intentions, a harmful trope that still pops up occasionally even though it feels quite tired and overdone.

Karyn Kusama's *Jennifer's Body*, written by Diablo Cody, does feature a queer villain, but the 2009 film is *so* not about a queer person struggling with their sexuality and snapping (Carmen Maria Machado has a great essay about this film in *It Came from the Closet*[8]). Jennifer Check (played by Megan Fox) is entirely in control of her body and her sexuality, even before she's transformed into a man-eating succubus. She's the quintessential hot girl, and she knows it. So does her BFF, Anita "Needy" Lesnicki (Amanda Seyfried), a self-proclaimed nerd (one of those nerds who just takes off her glasses to transform into a pretty girl, so common in teen rom-coms). Needy loves spending time with Jennifer, even blowing off her boyfriend Chip (Johnny Simmons) when Jen asks her to come to a concert at the local dive bar to see her favorite new band, Low Shoulder. But when the bar catches fire and the band convinces Jen to leave with them, Needy goes home feeling betrayed by her best friend, who once again has left her for a boy. It's clear that even if Needy doesn't know it yet, she's got feelings for Jennifer that go beyond friendship.

When Low Shoulder tries to sacrifice Jennifer to Satan to seal their pact to become a successful indie band, they mistakenly think she's a virgin. Since she's most definitely not a virgin, she instead becomes possessed by a demon, and she needs to eat human flesh, preferably boys, to satiate her growing hunger. Jennifer's beauty and status as unattainable cool girl help her seduce everyone from the high school quarterback to the emo creative writing student who is friends with Needy. Then she rips them to shreds and eats them. She's unapologetic in her pursuit of bodies to eat, and perhaps this is partly due to her story being told to the audience via Needy's voiceover. Jennifer might actually be quite conflicted about her actions, but since this is Needy's story more than Jennifer's, we only see Needy's version of events. It's possible to read the movie as Needy's queer awakening, and as such there are shades of resentment as she reconciles her feelings for Jennifer with both her feelings for Chip and societal expectations of what teenage love and teenage girls should be.

While moments throughout feel a bit dated upon rewatch (did we really talk like this in 2009?), the movie is much more emotionally fraught than I had originally thought. Maybe it's because there was a lot less in the way of queer representation at the time, certainly from the female bisexual perspective. Though a number of horror films feature queer characters (usually villains, as you'll see in chapter 5), it's not often that we see both heroine and villain as queer, or at least queer curious. Needy's both drawn to and repelled by Jennifer and her unapologetic personality. Jen is direct where Needy is timid, decisive where Needy is unsure, and flits between flirty and mean depending on her mood. Jen's also a little jealous of Needy's connections with other people, including Chip. As her comfort with her demonic powers grows, Jennifer targets the boys who are close to Needy, taking them out so they're no longer obstacles to her and Needy's relationship. I don't know if Jennifer would admit to anyone, even to herself, that she has romantic feelings for her childhood best friend, but their connection is so strong they seem to be psychically linked, though this isn't explained in the movie at all (the audience is just expected to take this as fact).

This bond is what makes the film stand out in a sea of early 2000s horror. The decade started strong with some mainstream hits like *The Cell*, *Final Destination*, and *American Psycho*, but nine years in there was a glut of direct-to-video films like *Birdemic: Shock and Terror* and *Mega Shark vs. Giant Octopus*. And before I get angry messages, yes, there were good movies too (I love Sam Raimi's nasty *Drag Me to Hell* and Ti West's *The House of the Devil*), but by and large there wasn't a lot in the way of novel horror premises, and *Jennifer's Body* was a refreshing take on demonic possession. The fact that the film is both written and directed by women lends some legitimacy to the characterizations, and I think many women can relate to the teenage friendship shown here, with its tumultuous mix of super-close highs and alienating lows. I know I haven't talked much about the horror here, and though this movie is full of gore and murder, it's really focused on emotion and love rather than scares. Needy and Chip are in a sexual relationship for the first time, and it's a rather sweet romance that's taking place alongside Jennifer's transformation and the changes in her dynamic with Needy. There are a few tense moments, but this isn't so much a nerve-shredding suspense story as it is a poignant evaluation of figuring yourself out as a teenager and gaining agency over your life and your body. Unless you're one of Jennifer's targets, that is.

This film was definitely marketed to appeal to a demographic that I don't think fully appreciated the nuances of the film. Teenage boys were hardly the main audience for this movie, but it was advertised as a film where two very attractive young women make out. It's too bad, because the marketing and negative reviews (which are largely from straight men, so perhaps there's some unconscious bias at play) mean that *Jennifer's Body* didn't end up with a great reputation. It's only in the last few years as younger audiences, now grown up and rewatching, have reclaimed the film as an explicitly queer awakening that many critics are reevaluating their original positions. Imagine everyone's surprise when it turned out to be so much more about a love story between those two women, and how their relationship turns toxic when jealousy and insecurity creeps in. Not to mention the whole demonic possession thing.

While of course many other films have queer undertones or overtones, and explore sexuality and romance through a horror lens, I don't have room to explore them all here. In recent years, there seems to be a bit of a split between a regression back to very outdated views of gender and queerness (as in the camp counselor slasher *They/Them* where the focus on the violence perpetrated against the queer characters feels too close to actual violence they experience) to films that celebrate queerness, or at least treat queer characters as a fact of life that no one in the film really comments on because they've got bigger things (or monsters) to worry about. Movies with queer couples at their center, like M. Night Shyamalan's *Knock at the Cabin* (2023), an adaptation of Paul Tremblay's terrifyingly tense *The Cabin at the End of the World*, as well as explorations of trans characters, like Jane Schoenbrun's *I Saw the TV Glow* (2024), show horror audiences that queerness doesn't have to equal terror. Casting trans actors like Jamie Clayton as the new Hell Priest in the 2022 *Hellraiser* remake is a big step toward inclusivity that many horror audience members have embraced in search of newer, more expansive storytelling in the genre. It's a refreshing change. As more marginalized authors find success and acceptance in horror publishing (from Hailey Piper to Stephen Graham Jones to Paula Ashe), I hope Hollywood filmmaking isn't far behind and we'll be treated to more and more interesting takes on the same old tropes.

QUEER ROMANCE

The Haunting (1963, dir. Robert Wise)

TOP TROPES: Miss Lonelyhearts: Eleanor is a homebody who's never been in a relationship but longs for some romance. Her feelings for Dr. Markway aren't reciprocated, and his rebuff might be the catalyst for the increased paranormal activity at Hill House.

DARK MOMENT: Markway tells Eleanor she can't stay at the house, thinking that she's too unstable for their psychic experiments. He doesn't realize that pushing her away will bring about her downfall.

HEA? No. Eleanor's short and lonely life is cut short, but perhaps she ends up getting the one thing she wanted: a lifetime at Hill House.

The Hunger (1983, dir. Tony Scott)

TOP TROPES: Stalker Romance: Vampire Miriam sets her sights on the demure Sarah and will stop at nothing to turn Sarah into a bloodsucking companion to replace the dying John.

DARK MOMENT: Sarah awakens from her vampire frenzy and realizes that she can never stay with Miriam, who has turned her into a killer.

HEA? Not quite. Sarah kills Miriam but remains a vampire, and we see her from afar with a new companion.

Jennifer's Body (2009, dir. Karyn Kusama)

TOP TROPES: Monster Romance: Jennifer's transformation into a boy-hungry demon doesn't stop her friend Needy from being attracted to her, even if she won't admit it out loud.

DARK MOMENT: When Needy chooses her boyfriend Chip over Jennifer, the demon's jealousy marks Chip for death.

HEA? No. Needy realizes she has to kill Jennifer despite their strong bond. At least Needy gains some of Jennifer's powers, so she can avenge her best friend's death in a post-credits scene.

CHAPTER FIVE

SLASHERS

The Anti-Romance Film

When many people hear the words *horror movie* they immediately think of slashers. This subgenre has existed for a long time; masked serial killers are not a new thing. The slasher genre is much maligned, and not all the criticism is unfounded. Multiple films in the genre are full of misogynistic treatment of women. The penetrating, violating act of stabbing is sexual as well as violent in many of these movies. Though there are male victims, the majority of victims in slashers are women, and often women who are being punished by the killer for either specific slights or larger perceived affronts to the killer's view of the world. A large body of literature dives further into the psychology and sociology of slasher films and the treatment of women therein; of course Carol J. Clover's *Men, Women and Chain Saws* is one of the earliest, but Barbara Creed's *The Monstrous-Feminine* is a great counterpoint, as is Sady Doyle's (now Jude Ellison S. Doyle) *Dead Blondes and Bad Mothers.*[1] I won't go too far down this rabbit hole, because none of those books get to the heart of what I'm interested in exploring here: Are there romance elements in slasher films, or are these movies inherently anti-romance?

In 1980s North America, we start to see a backlash in certain segments of the population against the relative freedom of the late 1960s and early '70s. Though there had been a sexual revolution and women's liberation movement in North America, and in many countries around the world (on the heels of the Civil Rights Movement), the patriarchal power holders wanted to reinforce the social hierarchy and restore the "natural order" of things. The horror film is often held up as an art form that deals directly with societal fears and pressures. Sometimes it amplifies those fears and seeks a catharsis for its audience by grappling with uncertainty head on, finding a way through to the other side and acceptance of a sort (though the protagonists are always changed by their journey). On the flip side, the horror film and the villains within can be mechanisms to force protagonists back onto their proper courses, restoring and reinforcing the moral code of the era. This is where the slasher genre often sits. Occasionally, films play with subverting the audience's expectations, like Alexandre Aja's *High Tension* (2003), (which still leans quite heavily into stereotypes of mental illness and queer villains in a way that made it very much not work for me). But particularly in the 1970s and '80s, when slashers dominated the horror space, most of the mainstream films in the subgenre follow a strict set of guidelines.

Many argue that Alfred Hitchcock's *Psycho* (1960) is the first true slasher film, and Norman Bates's costumed killer is definitely the prototype for many of the slashers to come. But the very earliest slasher film I could find was a 1933 pre-code movie called *Thirteen Women*, produced by David O. Selznick and directed by George Archainbaud. The film details the lives and deaths of sorority sisters in Los Angeles, who write to a clairvoyant to find out their fortune only to hear from him that they are facing impending doom. The clairvoyant, under the sway of a biracial woman who was shunned by the sorority women while at college, is exacting her revenge on the popular women for their treatment of her. The genre certainly evolved from here, but the trappings of the slasher are all on display: the group of women marked for death, the mistreated killer out for revenge, and the lineup of kills, relentless if less bloody than in newer films. The pre-Code era allowed for more explicit themes, and *Thirteen Women* is no exception; the women in the film casually discuss their love lives and their sexual histories, and suicide is depicted in a frank (though not gory) way. Irene Dunne is great as always; here her character of Laura Stanhope is a single mother who is shown as being very loving and thoughtful to her child and her friends. It's a stark contrast to the villain of the film played by Myrna Loy.

Cast for her "exotic" looks, Loy's Ursula Georgi is out for revenge and will stop at nothing to get it. She uses her beauty to manipulate the men around her into helping with her plots, and her South Asian ancestry has supposedly given her occult powers of suggestion. The racial elements here are by far the most problematic of the themes in the film, as Ursula is unflinchingly portrayed as evil for wanting to dispose of the group of young white women who ruined her life when she was at school. In the climax, as she explains her motivation, she talks about how hard she tried to pass as white but that Laura and her friends dashed all her plans and hopes. I felt more than a little sympathy for her, even though she's clearly gone a bit far, having had a hand in murdering or driving to suicide a number of women at this point (as well as plotting to kill Laura's young son Bobby).

Ursula's trauma is the catalyst for her violence, and she pursues her quarries across the country, driving the sorority sisters to paranoia and suggesting they will kill themselves in letters sent by the clairvoyant, Swami Yogadachi (C. Henry Gordon). One woman, devastated by the recent death of her young daughter, shoots herself after meeting with Ursula on the train to Los Angeles. Did Ursula play a role in the young girl's untimely death as well? It's never confirmed but certainly implied. So many aspects of the film set up the genre of the modern-day slasher, and it's great to watch a film where the vast majority of the characters (especially the characters with agency) are women.

I'll go into more detail about *Psycho* in chapter 6, because I do think that it is a huge turning point in horror, shifting stories from atmospheric and implied scares to more visceral, blatant visuals. But *Psycho* also changed the focus of the horror film—rather than the villain being a shadowy, one-dimensional figure like the Creature in *Frankenstein* or an alien like the Blob, Norman Bates is a fully realized character. Until the shocking reveal, the audience is convinced that he's a victim too, trying to cover for his mother. The movie ends with a rather overblown expository monologue by a psychologist who explains away Norman's serial killer tendencies as a result of his latent desire to become his mother. But that monologue serves another purpose: It shifts the audience's perception of the protagonist yet again in a film where the protagonist changes over the course of the story. We identify with Norman at the end, as the psychologist absolves Norman of his crimes—Bates is too mentally ill to be aware of the evil he's committed, right? This shift to a villain as more than just a Bad Guy, as a character with a backstory and motivation, opens the door for more mythical, monstrous, and often more compelling villains who become more important than the interchangeable victims. In some cases that perspective shift goes too far, and countless sequels later the antagonist is stripped of their scare factor, becoming a character that spews one-liners while they dispatch cardboard characters in increasingly ludicrous ways. But I think it's fair to say that Hitchcock and director Michael Powell opened the door for viewing the killer in a more nuanced way, at least to start.

Powell's *Peeping Tom*, released in 1960 a couple of months ahead of *Psycho*, shows us the villain from the very beginning, leaving no mystery as to who is perpetrating the killing that begins the film. *Peeping Tom* centers on Mark Lewis (Karlheinz Böhm), a focus puller who aspires to become a director. He has been deeply traumatized by his father's psychiatric experiments, where Mark was subjected to various frightening scenarios and had his reactions recorded for study. His father wanted to find out how children reacted to fear and used Mark as a guinea pig, setting up increasingly terrifying situations without ever comforting Mark in any way. As a result of Mark's harsh and horrifying upbringing, he has become obsessed with trying to capture this sensation of fear onscreen himself and is making a "documentary" about fear. Said documentary consists of him filming beautiful women at the moment they realize they are going to die, and, of course, Mark is the one killing them. Mark is your typical serial killer type: quiet, unassuming, a little shy and awkward around women. He's seen as mostly harmless, and that's how he's able to exist without being looked at too closely. His day job is working at a large film studio, and in his spare time he photographs women in various stages of undress for a newsagent who's peddling smut on the black market. Mark's abusive father has created a monster, but it's a monster who is shown with more depth than the killers in many films leading up to this one. Powell's direction is incredibly effective here, forcing the audience to take on the role of voyeur and creating a closeness with the killer that is terribly unsettling. We see what Mark sees, and we watch these women as they realize they're going to die, and we can do nothing to help them. The lens distances us from the violence while simultaneously making us view it more intimately, in concert with the perpetrator. It's an uncomfortable feeling.

Peeping Tom is a horror film, no doubt, but there is, in fact, a strong element of romance in the movie. Mark meets a young woman named Helen (Anna Massey), who lives in the same building as Mark and is unaware that he's been watching her. Her compassion for Mark's upbringing and her anger toward his father prevents Mark from succumbing to his original urge to murder her. He can't stop his compulsion to kill completely, but he doesn't allow himself to follow his typical pattern with Helen. Instead, he substitutes other women for her as they grow closer. Helen, for her part, doesn't realize how deeply disturbed Mark is, and at first seems to think of him more as a friendly neighbor before realizing he's someone she's interested in romantically.

The romance part of the film follows a very traditional kind of arc. Helen invites Mark to her birthday party, but he's too shy to take part. She decides to invite herself up to his apartment and offers him a piece of her birthday cake, and in a different kind of movie, Mark's awkward deer-in-headlights expression when confronted with a woman he is attracted to would be endearing and denote the beginning of a foible-filled romantic comedy full of mishaps. Instead, he invites Helen to watch his film, thinking he'll record her reaction to watching the murder, but at the last minute, he decides to show her the footage of him as a child, almost as a cry for help. Her immediate concern for him baffles him, and it seems like Mark is struggling to reconcile this genuine, loving reaction with his learned behavior, expecting everyone to leave him as soon as he perceives them.

Once again, I think there's a hint of the I-can-fix-him sentiment prevalent in so many of these films where the killer is a possible love interest. Mark's skewed sense of the world has warped his perspective, and though he's attracted to Helen, he can't give himself over to the feeling. His father has associated romantic love (images of couples engaged in kissing sessions) with images of fear and trauma, so Mark cannot separate the two. Once someone is captured through his camera lens, they've essentially been marked for death, so he resists his compulsion to film Helen, someone he feels for much more deeply than the sex workers and film actresses he's been victimizing. Mark views Helen as pure, and thus she's saved from his violence—it's a trope that becomes more and more central to the slasher genre as the years go by.

I don't want to give the impression that Mark is nothing more than a wounded creature here. He's a deeply disturbed and dangerous man, and even though he knows what he's doing is wrong, he only once pauses in his plans to murder these women (with Helen). He can't or won't give up on his plans to go through with his ultimate goal of recording his own expression as he impales himself on the blade concealed in the tripod leg of his camera. The fact that he is aware of the depravity he is committing and still chooses to kill these women, and film those moments so that we as the audience are watching them from his perspective, leaves no room for misinterpretation. (If anyone ever tells you Mark Lewis is a good guy, just misunderstood . . . run.)

I don't want to spend much time on giallo, namely because I haven't seen all that many films in the genre. If you're unfamiliar, giallo films blend elements of crime and thriller movies, often featuring particularly artful violence and mysterious killers. They were popularized in the 1960s and 1970s by Italian film directors including Dario Argento, Lucio Fulci, and Mario Bava. I want to briefly mention Mario Bava's film *Blood and Black Lace* (1964). This is a stylish, stylized thriller that takes suspense elements that are front and center in *Psycho* and *Peeping Tom* and adds even more elaborate and upsetting violence, bridging the gap between the suspenseful but less bloody earlier slashers and the over-the-top, gore-filled films of the late '70s and '80s. Bava directed a number of horror films, but this one, taking place in a Roman fashion house, really set the tone for the more explicit mystery thrillers that would follow. There is also an element of romance throughout the movie, with multiple illicit relationships, scandals, and a central couple that incites the entire plot, though the audience doesn't know that at the outset. There is a lot to like here, and Bava clearly inspired many directors who came after him, with his grisly yet artistically shot murder scenes. I can't imagine that Sean S. Cunningham (the director of *Friday the 13th*) wasn't at least aware of *Blood and Black Lace*, since the killer reveal is a twist that is echoed in Mrs. Voorhees. Likewise, the masked killer in the film must have been partial inspiration for characters as varied as Rorschach in *Watchmen*, the Blank in *Dick Tracy*, and even Dr. Decker in Clive Barker's *Nightbreed* (brought to life by incredible horror director David Cronenberg).

The film begins with the murder of a woman named Isabella, who works in an Italian fashion house. Isabella had been keeping a diary full of secrets held by various employees—everything from abortions to secret affairs and drug addiction. As the killer dispatches various beautiful women, both the detective assigned to the case and the employees who are worried their secrets will get out search for the diary. There's a defined mystery structure, inviting the audience to solve the case alongside the detective; the opening credits feel almost like a police lineup, showing you all the characters so you can make some snap decisions about who looks suspicious. The more straightforward procedural plot is punctuated with sharp, vicious moments of violence where the women of the fashion house are stabbed, bludgeoned, dragged, and in one instance smashed into a furnace. I've seen a lot of horror films and have become somewhat desensitized to the violence, but I have to say that the first time I watched *Blood and Black Lace* I was a little taken aback by just how visceral some of these moments feel. The victims here are treated so dispassionately, thrown around like garbage, and I found it quite unsettling.

I know, I said there was a romance here. And there is, though it's not exactly a pleasant one. In a twist that admittedly I somehow did not see coming, there are two masked killers, not one, and they're working together (perhaps *Scream* drew some inspiration from this revelation). Cristiana, the head of the fashion house (Eva Bartok), and Massimo, comanager of the team and also Cristiana's lover (Cameron Mitchell), had conspired to kill Cristiana's husband, and Isabella was blackmailing them. In order to throw the detectives off the trail of Isabella's murder, the two decide to frame her killing and the subsequent murders as sexually charged frenzies. Cristiana must kill one more model to fool the detectives permanently, insinuating that said model was the real killer. But once she finishes the job, she discovers that her loving relationship with Massimo was much more one-sided than he had led her to believe. He's really only after her fortune, and throws her off the building. As in many horror films, though, if you don't see the body, the character might not be dead. Cristiana returns and shoots Massimo at the end of the movie, and though she technically wins, the credits roll as Cristiana sobs over her lover's body—everything in her life has fallen apart, and she's transformed by the violence that she both perpetrated and experienced.

So many moments in *Blood and Black Lace* very clearly influenced up-and-coming directors, and, as it is with many genre-defining pioneers, once you see the original iteration of a subgenre, you start to notice all the imitators. Bava's film showed audiences that you could add Grand Guignol–style hyperviolence to a mystery and create a new level of suspense for audiences hungry for a more visceral viewing experience. The emergence of the Italian giallo films opened the doors for a whole host of directors, as well as studios like Hammer, to run wild with explosive, bloody deaths and more explicit themes in their horror films. It would take a few years, but independent North American directors would take that extreme violence of the giallo films and expand it even further, pushing the line to see how far audiences would go with them in movies like *Black Christmas*.

Bob Clark's *Black Christmas* was released in 1974, and is widely considered the first North American slasher, though it of course did not get the recognition director John Carpenter would with *Halloween* a few years later. Clark (who went on to direct *Porky's* and *A Christmas Story*) centers the film around sorority sisters who live together in a large house near their university campus (the house is still there in Toronto) and have been dealing with a rash of obscene phone calls from someone they've deemed the Moaner. The young women in *Black Christmas* are enjoying their independence away from their families and are learning to navigate the world, and these obscene phone calls really rattle most of them. Barb (played beautifully by Margot Kidder), a rather brash and no-nonsense member of the sorority, is fed up with the calls and finally snaps, berating the caller and seemingly triggering the wave of violence that follows right before the women start leaving for the Christmas holidays. Her impulsive behavior upsets one of the young women, Claire (Clare Harrison), who breaks off from the group to pack. If you're at all familiar with slasher films, you know that's a bad move.

What the sorority sisters don't know is that the mysterious menace is actually already inside their house. We see, in true giallo style, the POV of this unknown creep as he spies on everyone at a holiday party, then climbs up to the top floor and hides himself in the attic. He is constantly muttering to himself, which lends him a very unsettling aura (Who is he? What is he doing here?) and links him to the Moaner calls from the very beginning: The audience is never wondering whether this guy is bad news or not. We know. When he hides in Claire's closet behind some dry-cleaning bags, the dread creeps in. Claire's death by asphyxiation is quick but definitely not painless, and the killer drags her up to the attic to hide her body while viewers wait to see when she'll be discovered.

The film is fairly rote from that moment on, the tension building as the main characters (including Andrea Martin, Art Hindle, and Olivia Hussey) begin to realize something bad has happened. Throughout the story the audience is reminded of the violence in the world these people inhabit, with mentions of dead children and rape serving as reminders that it's not a safe place. The police are generally useless, aside from John Saxon's Lt. Ken Fuller, with the desk sergeant outright dismissing Jess when she calls to report the obscene phone calls. It's a bleak world, and the movie ends on an even bleaker note, with the killer still alive and undiscovered, and Final Girl Jess (Hussey) left alone and vulnerable.

What sets *Black Christmas* apart from many of its followers is that no one here is punished for a particular reason. The killer (who calls himself Billy, though nothing of his identity is ever confirmed) doesn't seem to make judgments about these girls in the way that sex positivity is punished in later slashers. He is an opportunist, killing everyone with the same abandon. And though there isn't a romance here per se, there is a thoughtful discussion about the end of a relationship and women's rights that is lacking from many other horror films of the time.

Jess reveals to her somewhat distant boyfriend Peter (Keir Dullea) that she's pregnant and is going to get an abortion. He's studying to be a concert pianist and isn't around much, and she doesn't want to be stuck with a baby when she has other dreams. Peter is incensed by this, and subsequently Jess ends their relationship, in quite a calm and rational way. Peter, for his part, threatens her and tells her she can't go through with the abortion, and his rage leads the police (and Jess) to suspect that he may be the one behind the murders. He isn't, of course, but when he breaks into the basement to find Jess after she's locked him out and escaped the real killer, she beats him to death with a poker. His threat of violence and his attempt to control her convinces Jess that he must have been behind the murders, and honestly, who can blame her? Jess's actions here set the stage for all the Final Girls to come, as she takes back her agency and defends herself in any way she can. Rewatching *Black Christmas* after having seen so many of its imitators is a completely new experience; the audience can so clearly see how many slashers have taken inspiration from this movie (John Carpenter apparently began thinking about *Halloween* after a conversation with Clark).

After Bava and giallo, and *Black Christmas* in 1974, *Halloween* (1978) really kind of blew the doors off and kickstarted a massive surge in slashers that would dominate the horror landscape, at least in terms of the wider pop culture impact, for years. In addition to being a taut, suspenseful genre piece, *Halloween* solidifies many of the rules and tropes that would become signature slasher elements over the course of the next decade or so. Though it's not one of my personal favorites, there's no doubt that Carpenter's stylish and atmospheric thriller holds a massive place in horror history, and the character of Michael Myers (in all his various iterations) is iconic, as is Jamie Lee Curtis's Laurie Strode, the ultimate Final Girl. There's no romance at all to be found here, however; Laurie makes it out alive by being the only one not romantically involved, perhaps because she doesn't have the distraction of a boyfriend to hamper her escape plans.

In 1980, Sean S. Cunningham's *Friday the 13th* mixed the over-the-top kills of giallo films with the lives of typical American teenagers and solidified the new language of slasher films. It's hard to remember what these early slashers looked like, especially those that have gone on to become franchises full of trite, comically over-the-top kills and ludicrous dialogue. (Anyone who's seen Jason Voorhees smash a cryogenically frozen head into tiny pieces in *Jason X* knows how far from the original these movies have strayed, but there's no denying there are still moments of fun.) Revisiting the first film in the series reminded me how tense slashers can be. Jason isn't even the villain in *Friday the 13th*. He's the victim who sets up the entire story: a young boy who drowns while his camp counselors were too busy having sex and partying to pay attention to a child who couldn't swim well. Years later, his mother (Betsy Palmer) is still grieving, and when she learns that the camp where she lost her child is getting ready to reopen, she knows she must intervene and shut it down using any method at her disposal. Of course, the audience doesn't learn any of this until the end of the film, in what is revealed as a major twist. I can't imagine many viewers would have expected the killer to be a middle-aged woman (in a great sweater, by the way) when they sat down in the cinema.

Pamela Voorhees is avenging her son, and she does so unflinchingly and with brutal efficiency. The camera switches to Pamela's perspective as she hunts her prey, unsuspecting teenagers who are excited to be on their own (a "cool" adult named Steve is their only supervisor) and getting the camp back in shape. Using this point of view as Pamela stalks her victims is effective, both obscuring the identity of the killer and putting the audience in the character's position; like in *Peeping Tom,* we're asked to view the murders in a much more visceral way, as if we take some responsibility for them. The familiar soundtrack that threads throughout the film is actually Jason's voice in Pamela's head: "Kill her, mommy" translates to "ki-ki-ki-ma-ma-ma," and the refrain haunts Mrs. Voorhees and the audience as it runs underneath the scenes shot from Pamela's point of view. This eerie sound, much like John Carpenter's incredibly spare score for *Halloween*, set these new slashers apart from older films, with their full orchestral scores, and ushered in a leaner, bleaker vision. The iconic sounds of the film franchise also give a nod to composer Bernard Herrmann's *Psycho* and the dissonant strings that made up that other instantly familiar music. The throwback to Hitchcock's film reveals one of director Sean S. Cunningham's biggest influences, but the murder scenes—bloody, violent, and close up—are reminiscent of the Italian giallo influence of Mario Bava and Dario Argento.

Any hint of romance in *Friday the 13th* might as well be a death sentence. The couple who shares a quiet scene on the beach before a storm and then heads to their cabin for a lovemaking session? Murdered. The woman who suggests strip monopoly to pass the time? Butchered. In *Halloween* many of the teen victims are sexually active too, exploring their newfound freedoms, but overall the film is subtle in its condemnation of them. *Friday the*

13th, on the other hand, feels more exploitative and vicious in its punishment. The men who are killed tend to be dispatched efficiently, and the women are handled in a more visceral, brutal fashion, perhaps because Pamela is projecting a little of her own self-loathing onto them? Her inability to find care for Jason prompts her to bring him with her to the camp where she's working, and she's so busy that she relies on the teen counselors to be responsible caregivers. It's reasonable to assume that she holds a substantial amount of guilt for not being able to care for her son and keep him safe.

In stark contrast to the proto-slashers of the 1960s, these new films were decidedly anti-romance. Any confident, sex-positive behavior was a sure sign that the killer would notice you. This was doubly true if you were a woman. The wave of '80s slashers became increasingly misogynistic, featuring women who seemed to exist only to take off their shirts and be killed in escalating violence. There was no romance here, no sincerity or emotion; women were objects, either ready to please their partners and be punished for it or sacrificed to the villain—unless they were pure and virginal. Then they might stand a chance, whether it's because the killer took pity on them or was fascinated and fixated on their lack of sexual experience, giving them the chance to restore the moral code that their counterparts had breached. To survive in a slasher as the Final Girl, you must hold on to your virginity and resist both the love interest and the monster.

The lack of romance in the slasher film also speaks to an inherent avoidance of sincerity—people who expressed real feelings in slashers were usually presented as characters to laugh at. It's a very 1980s capitalist rejection of the hippie ideals of the '70s; peace and love were thrown out in favor of money and sex (seen in more mainstream films like *Wall Street* as well as horror). Shy and sensitive characters in slashers were easy marks. Dreamers with their heads in the clouds usually came down to earth when the killer decapitated them. The sense that society needed to wake up and get back to the "real world" was a direct repulsion of the idea that we could rebuild the world into a place where racism, classism, and sexism no longer existed. There's been a resurgence of this pushback against sincerity in recent years (very online behavior), where "cringe" is considered the ultimate insult and protagonists are expected to be snarky, sarcastic, and never, ever sincere. Gita Jackson wrote a fascinating article on one aspect of this style of writing for *Vice*, "When Joss Whedon Was Our Master," and though I don't think he's solely to blame for the return to the anti-sincerity of the 1980s, he certainly helped.[2]

At the same time as this hater sentiment took over the slasher movie, an even more explicit fear of the Other permeated the genre. Obviously, much of horror from its very beginnings deals with this idea that the Other is alien, full of menace and malice. This Other has been used as a metaphor for societal pressures and fears about immigration, or civil rights, or women's liberation, or really anything that threatens the status quo. And in the '80s slashers, one of the societal anxieties that was exposed over and over was worry over queerness and gay rights. With the AIDS crisis looming and yuppie conservative values the norm in Canada and the US, queer characters either died or were doing the killing. They were to be punished or reviled, depending on the film, but they were rarely unsuspecting or innocent victims. Part of this treatment of queer men in particular was in line with the misogyny of the time; gay men who were portrayed as effeminate or flamboyant were treated as less "male," and therefore needed to be disposed of. Many slashers ended with a Final Girl, but often this girl had to take up male-coded (phallic) weapons or shrug off her feminine persona in order to dispatch the villain. For much, much more on this, I do recommend Clover's seminal *Men, Women and Chain Saws*, even if I don't agree with everything she has to say. (And for a thought-provoking essay on the lack of Final Boys in horror, you should check out Stanley Swindling's "Where Is the Final Boy?").[3]

Many of the slasher films of the late 1970s and 1980s explored the fear of the Other through a queerphobic, transphobic lens. Rather than incorporating romance as a way to explore a deeper understanding of the Other, these slashers were anti-romance and anti-Other. Sex was punishable by death in films from *Friday the 13th* to *Chopping Mall.* In addition, many of the victims in these films were queer coded, and a large proportion of slasher villains were portrayed as mentally unstable, sexually frustrated, or dysfunctional. The epitome was Robert Hiltzik's *Sleepaway Camp* (1983), featuring a homicidal young trans girl punishing sexually promiscuous teens.

I won't write too much about this film, because much better people have written many more compelling pieces about it than I can (two examples are Viet Dinh's "Notes on *Sleepaway Camp*" in *It Came from the Closet* and Alice Collins's *Bloody Disgusting* essay on the film[4]). It's a contentious movie for many—there's queer representation in the form of both Angela (the trans girl at the center of the film) and her gay father. The film begins with young siblings Peter and Angela at the lake with their father and his lover. When Angela is killed in a boating accident, her brother Peter is sent away to live with his rather abusive and mentally unstable aunt, who desperately wants a girl child of her own. So, Peter became Angela, and Angela, played by Felissa Rose, lives as a girl throughout the rest of this film as well as in the sequels. There is some debate over whether Angela is forced to transition or whether her aunt, as abusive as she was, simply unlocked Angela's latent transgender identity. (For more, read Sean Abley's rebuttal.)[5] But being a product of the 1980s, where there was much less information available widely about the trans experience, the film is not great at exploring any of this with sensitivity or thoughtfulness. *Sleepaway Camp* is set up as a typical summer camp slasher, with added transphobia. As is common in slashers of the era, the killer is depicted as insane, but is Angela mentally unstable *because* of her transness, or despite it? There's no nuance here, and no unpacking of these ideas, of course. Instead, the film ends with a (shocking for the time period) reveal of Angela standing naked on the beach, a giant knife in her hand, screaming a kind of otherworldly scream. It's an arresting image, and *Sleepaway Camp* is still an important film within the slasher landscape.

The slasher era didn't end completely after the 1980s, but the actively anti-romance, promiscuous-teens-punished-by-death movies petered out over the next few years, as Hollywood moved on to create different kinds of slasher movies. For the purposes of this book, we'll leave slashers here and get back to movies that feature different takes on romance within a horror framework.

CHAPTER SIX

DEEP DIVE

Is Hitchcock Horror, Romance, or Both?

Alfred Hitchcock is known as the master of suspense, and he's one of my favorite classic film directors, creating some fantastically memorable scenes and characters. One of my absolute favorite sequences in all of cinema is in *North by Northwest*, when Leo G. Carroll, the spy handler, explains the reasons behind the espionage operation they're asking Cary Grant to help with, and the entire speech is drowned out by the roar of airplane engines. Hitchcock knew the importance of pulling the audience into the story in such a way that the plot details don't really matter if the rest of the film is compelling through acting, music, and shot composition.

While a great many of Hitchcock's films are of the thriller persuasion, he dabbled in other genres as well. Over the course of his long and varied career, he directed films that explored everything from spies and political thrillers to romance to dark comedies. He also made three films that I consider either horror or at least horror adjacent: *The Birds*, *Psycho*, and *Vertigo*. *Frenzy* deals with a serial killer in rather graphic fashion for the year it came out (1972), but I think it reads more as straight-up thriller than horror, since much of it is told from the perspective of a man who is wrongfully accused of the murders, unlike a horror film where the audience is put in a place of tension and discomfort and fear of the unknown. All three movies discussed here not only embrace horror elements; they also feature strong romance cues.

Before we dive into the films, though, a note on Hitchcock and his behavior behind the scenes. It's no secret that Hitchcock was both a fantastic director and an awful person to many women in his life. He fetishized women, particularly his icy blondes, and when they spurned his advances, he was often rude or worse, sometimes assaulting them by groping or attempting to kiss them without their consent. Tippi Hedren, who starred in two films for Hitchcock, went on to describe such an experience with him in her autobiography during the filming of *Marnie*, but his terrible treatment of her began during her first film, *The Birds*. In the climactic scene, Hitchcock forced Hedren to deal with live birds for the filming, instead of the mechanical ones that were initially proposed, and she is really being pecked and attacked in the scene. The crew threw live birds at her, inflicting real injuries and once coming dangerously close to hurting her eye. Filming the scene took five days of production (for only about a minute of finished film), and Hedren was deeply traumatized by the experience, much as her character Melanie was.

In light of the revelations surrounding Hitchcock's treatment of not only Hedren but other women in his professional life (ranging from inappropriate comments to outright sexual assault), it's difficult to watch this scene (and others) and not feel uncomfortable. Much as we need to acknowledge the many romance novels that perpetuated dangerous tropes like dubious consent, exoticizing and fetishizing non-Western cultures, and, let's face it, outright rape in earlier works, there's also no sense in hiding the problematic aspects of powerful figures in the film industry, from directors and producers to actors and agents. So, while Hitchcock played a pivotal role in horror romance, I'm not romanticizing the man himself.

Psycho (1960) is, arguably, Hitchcock's most influential and most famous film. It regularly holds a place on best-of lists, and it changed the movie landscape in so many ways, from graphic depictions of violence onscreen to plot twists to theaters making sure film audiences were seated before the opening credits began rolling (so as not to spoil the shocking twist at the beginning). Much has been written about the production of the film (see Stephen Rebello's *Alfred Hitchcock and the Making of Psycho* among others), so I don't think I need to go into many of those details here.[1] But here's the lowdown: The film is based on Robert Bloch's book of the same name, which was in turn inspired by real-life serial killer Ed Gein, who murdered at least two women and desecrated the bodies of many more in order to create a "woman suit" of human skin. Hitchcock's film was a huge pivot from his previous production, *North by Northwest*, which was a slick spy romance starring Cary Grant, Eva Marie Saint, and James Mason in beautiful Technicolor. Hitchcock used his *Alfred Hitchcock Presents* crew to shoot *Psycho* in black and white with a short shooting schedule and a lower budget, and this lends a grittier, bleaker feel to the project.

Though *Psycho* is definitely a horror movie, there is romance here as well. Marion Crane (Janet Leigh) is involved with Sam Loomis (John Gavin, and the inspiration for Donald Pleasence's Dr. Loomis in the *Halloween* franchise). Marion and Sam's relationship is framed as illicit; the film opens with the two of them in a hotel room, clearly post–romantic interlude, with Marion in her undergarments, though the couple is not married. A bit of a scandalous start, and it sets the audience up to prepare for something a bit wilder, a bit more extreme than a typical romantic thriller. Still, since spoilers were much less readily available in

1960, most people who saw the movie in the theater wouldn't have known it was anything but another Hitchcock suspense film for the first third of the runtime. Marion impulsively steals some money from her boss so she and Sam can move on and start a proper life together, and the film follows her as she goes on the run, very straightforward thriller fodder. Right up until she arrives at the Bates Motel, looking for a place to stay.

Though the chemistry between Leigh and Gavin is not terribly strong (perhaps due to the fact that John Gavin is just okay), there is something both compelling and unsettling about Anthony Perkins's Norman Bates and his attitude toward the frank and direct Marion once they meet. He seems very friendly—almost too friendly—and he clearly has something to hide. But since Marion does too, the scene of the two of them in the Bates Motel parlor, as they eat a quick meal together, feels a bit like a dance, neither wanting to give away their secrets while trying to seem as normal as possible.

Of course, it's difficult to know for sure how audiences would have felt when watching the film for the first time, but I know when I first saw this movie, I thought perhaps the twist was that Marion would leave Sam to take up with the shy and awkward Norman. It's clear here that Norman is attracted to Marion, and that is reinforced when we see him spy on her through a peephole into her room as she changes. Clearly, not romantic from Marion's perspective! Norman doesn't seem to have a grasp on real love in any way; his relationship with his mother has completely skewed his sense of love and romantic relationships, and he turns his loneliness and yearning for connection into frightening violence.

Once Marion is killed, the rest of the film veers completely into the horror genre, setting up so many iconic moments that have been copied throughout the media landscape. But the romantic elements served as both a way to draw audiences into this very dark story and to trick them into feeling a sense of security; after all, if Marion Crane is the love interest, how could she possibly be killed so quickly and so violently?

TOP TROPES: Forced Proximity: Marion is stuck in the motel with Norman, and the initial scenes with him are played in such a way that the audience could be convinced that she would be able to save Norman from his controlling mother.

DARK MOMENT: Well, murdering the woman who showed you a bit of kindness and understanding definitely seems like the darkest possible moment.

HEA? No one ends up happy here. Sam and Marion's sister Lila discover that Norman is in fact the killer, Marion is dead in the lake near the motel, and Norman is (according to the psychiatrist's very exposition-heavy monologue at the end of the film) completely subsumed by his mother's controlling personality.

Though it received middling reviews upon release in 1958, many critics now consider Alfred Hitchcock's *Vertigo* his masterpiece.[2] The story of a private eye who finds love, loses it, and mysteriously finds it again is an emotional, intense exploration of obsession and how far a person will go to reclaim the life they lost. It's very romantic in so many ways, but is it horrific? Let's dig in.

The story opens with an incredibly tense first scene, with Jimmy Stewart's Scottie chasing a suspect across rooftops in San Francisco. The chase reaches its climax with Scottie slipping and hanging on to the roof for dear life while his partner falls to his death. This traumatic experience results in Scottie's debilitating vertigo, and he retires from the force. But he needs work, so takes a job for an old school friend who needs his wife followed because, he says, he's afraid she wants to hurt herself. Scottie begins following Madeleine, played by Kim Novak, and it's easy to see why he's so drawn to her (much to his best friend Midge's dismay—she's been in love with Scottie for a long time). Madeleine is beautiful and melancholy, spending hours driving around San Francisco and contemplating a painting that seems to haunt her. Scottie's pursuit of Madeleine, first as a quarry, begins innocently enough. But he is slowly captivated by this woman and how mysterious and alluring she is. When she falls (jumps?) in the water at the Golden Gate Bridge, Scottie rushes to save her, and from that moment, there's no turning back. He's fully committed to following her down a dark path.

The film at this point reads very much like a romantic mystery: How can Scottie keep Madeleine safe from whatever is seeking to cause her harm (whether that's an external force or inner demons)? Madeleine is drawn to Scottie as well, and the two work together to uncover the secrets haunting her. But when the two of them end up at a Spanish mission, things get much darker. Madeleine climbs the bell tower, and Scottie tries to follow, but his vertigo prevents him from reaching her in time, and he watches her fall to her death. The scene is brilliantly shot by Hitchcock, using a dolly zoom that has become so iconic it's called the Vertigo effect and has been mimicked in countless films, including, perhaps most famously, in Steven Spielberg's *Jaws*, when Chief Brody sees the shark for the first time.

Madeleine's tragic death utterly breaks Scottie, and we see the aftermath of the police investigation and court case. Scottie is absolved of blame, but he remains catatonic and despondent, and a brokenhearted Midge visits him in the hospital to no effect. Barbara Bel Geddes's portrayal of Midge is such a beautifully tragic character here, realizing she'll never have her friend back, much less be able to move forward romantically with him. Once Scottie's released from the hospital, the film takes a very dark turn.

In my opinion, the second half of *Vertigo* is more psychological horror than mystery. The romantic elements are slowly stripped away, but not before Hitchcock plays another cruel trick on the audience (and on Scottie). Scottie can't believe his eyes when he notices a woman almost identical to his beloved Madeleine walking down the street. She tells him he's mistaken, her name is Judy, but Scottie is so taken by her, he asks to see her anyway. Little by little, Scottie tries to transform Judy into his lost love, buying her new outfits and changing her hairstyle. Scottie's punishing, smothering treatment of Judy, who bears much more than a passing resemblance to Madeleine, borders on truly terrifying to many women watching the film. Many of us know (or have experienced firsthand) this kind of controlling, jealous, obsessive behavior from a romantic partner. Judy is gaslit into changing her clothes, her hair, her personality to fit Scottie's rigid vision of his ideal woman.

Why does Judy go along with it? Well, she is in fact Madeleine, and she still has feelings for Scottie. She falls deeper and deeper into the lies and deception she can't seem to pull herself out of, and seems to give in because she wants to fix everything and make a life with him. There is a flashback of exposition explaining Judy's role in the deception (a rather elaborate murder plot that, like *North by Northwest*, doesn't really matter), and from that moment on, the audience is waiting for the revelation, to see how Scottie will react when he finds out how he's been manipulated. One of the reasons Hitchcock is called the Master of Suspense is because of the way he draws out the tension, keeping the audience on their toes as they anticipate the worst. But in *Vertigo*, we're not only anticipating the worst: We're hoping somehow that Judy will be able to save Scottie and herself, and that the two of them can move on from the past. This same tension building is often used in romance fiction to heighten the emotional stakes for the characters; will they get together, or stay together even though one of them (or both) have made mistakes? (For a great shout-out in a horror romance novel, check out Clay McLeod Chapman's *Devil Inside*, which has a chapter that takes place in a second-run cinema where the midnight movie is, fittingly, *Vertigo*.)[3]

Ultimately, though, the happy ending is not in the cards for Judy and Scottie. He figures out the deception and in the final act becomes even more awful. He whisks Judy away to the same Spanish mission and forces her up the stairs to admit she's been lying to him. Even though Judy has succumbed to his every whim, she still ends up dead (and Scottie is cured of his vertigo, free to harass the next woman he obsesses over).

TOP TROPES: Other Woman: The labyrinthine film features not only the other woman in Midge, but also in Scottie's vision of the fictional Madeleine spurring him to manipulate Judy's appearance. Secret Identity: Judy first pretends to be Madeleine, then pretends to be herself before pretending to be Madeleine again. The concept of identity constantly shifts in *Vertigo*.

DARK MOMENT: Scottie sees Judy wearing Carlotta's necklace (which Madeleine owned) and realizes that she's the same woman he thought he lost.

HEA? Scottie misses out on an HEA twice, once with Madeleine, and again with Judy, and the woman ends up dead.

So, *Vertigo* being a horror (or horror-adjacent!) film might feel like a bit of a stretch for a lot of folks. But there's no arguing that *The Birds* (1963), Hitchcock's follow-up to *Psycho*, is anything but horror. Deeply unsettling, this adaptation of Daphne du Maurier's story details a world where birds of all kinds suddenly decide to start attacking humans. But the story doesn't start there; after all, horror is when we go from comfort to tension, remember? Hitchcock does a wonderful job of setting the scene and half convinces the audience that we're in for a much different film in the opening.

It opens with Tippi Hedren, the newly minted Hitchcock It Girl. He'd been trying to find a replacement for his beloved Grace Kelly after she fell in love with Prince Rainier of Monaco and retired from the cinema, and he hadn't felt that either Vera Miles in *Psycho* (who got pregnant before she could appear in *Vertigo*) or Kim Novak (Miles's replacement) were quite right. Hedren, a model who hadn't appeared in movies before Hitchcock discovered her, was beautiful, poised, and most importantly, new to the industry and willing to please. She's delightful in the film's first act as Melanie Daniels, a bored and capricious socialite who's been told she needs to grow up after being caught getting up to no good overseas. She meets Mitch, a self-important lawyer played by Rod Taylor, who pretends to mistake her for a salesperson in a pet store, but he's well aware of her reputation. It's a total meet-cute, setting up the audience to expect a romantic story full of silly hijinks and one-upmanship. After the misunderstanding, Melanie impulsively decides to buy the lovebirds that Mitch had been looking for at the pet store and bring them to his younger sister at their house in Bodega Bay. On the way across the bay, Melanie is attacked by a random seagull, setting up the sinister plot device.

The rest of the film quickly descends into various levels of nightmarish weirdness. Melanie is stuck with Mitch, his mother, and his younger sister (played by Veronica Cartwright, a horror veteran who's played major roles in *Alien*, *Invasion of the Body Snatchers*, and *The Witches of Eastwick*, among others) in the small town, as increasingly large numbers of birds begin turning on the humans around them. Some incredibly tense moments follow, including a couple of scenes that will stay with me forever (the multiplying birds on the playground equipment and the rapid jump cuts zooming in on the farmer's plucked out eyes, in case you were wondering). But the reason these frightening scenes work *so* well is that Hitchcock knows there must be some emotional investment from the audience, especially when the actual events are so random and inexplicable.

The love story that blooms between Melanie and Mitch is a classic rivals-to-lovers story. They're prickly toward each other at the start, but they are both drawn to each other, despite their fairly obvious flaws and the fact that they should probably never get together. They need to overcome other external conflicts as well (aside from the birds, of course), including Mitch's overly protective and reserved mother (played by the wonderful Jessica Tandy) and his ex-girlfriend who still has feelings for him, played by Suzanne Pleshette in a heartbreaking small role. Mitch is clearly intrigued by the confident and playful Melanie, and he seems to recognize the deeper layers of hurt and loneliness that Tippi Hedren keeps bubbling just under the surface of her performance.

The emotional beats in the story start out light and romantic and gradually become deeper and more fraught as the situation outside becomes more frantic and people are killed by the birds. As Melanie, Mitch, and his family try to stay safe inside his family home, the film comes to its truly unsettling climax. Melanie hears a noise upstairs, and contrary to what every audience member is thinking, she decides to investigate on her own. She opens the attic door and realizes that hundreds of birds have pecked their way into the attic. Poor Melanie is swarmed and viciously attacked until Mitch comes to her rescue in a scene that is visceral and frightening. The fact that Hitchcock used only ambient sound in the film (no score at all) makes things even scarier, as we only hear the fluttering and chirping of birds and Melanie's slowly fading cries for help.

Mitch rescues Melanie, who is deeply traumatized, and the newly formed found family leaves the house, where they see malevolent flocks of birds perched all over the house and the surrounding area. Hitchcock leaves us with a very ambiguous ending, and we're never sure if the birds take over the world and kill everyone, or whether the small group of humans is able to escape. But the romance remains—Mitch has welcomed Melanie to the group of women whom he loves, and he will try to keep the three of them safe.

TOP TROPES: Rivals to Lovers: Melanie and Mitch start off on the wrong foot with Melanie's pranks annoying Mitch, but circumstances force them to band together. Found Family: Melanie's personal life feels lonely and she's happy to be welcomed into Mitch's life, even though it takes his mother a bit of time to accept her. Meet-Cute Misunderstanding: A ridiculous set of circumstances set up the couple; this is a mainstay trope in romantic comedies and serves to set audience expectations for a very different (and less unsettling) kind of film here.

DARK MOMENT: Well, obviously birds attacking and murdering people all around you is pretty dark. But I think the darkest moment for the couple's relationship is when Mitch seems to be taking his mother's side against Melanie, causing her to break down.

HEA? The two end up together at the end of the movie—though Melanie is injured and catatonic, and we're not quite sure when the birds are going to murder everyone. But they're together, so I'm going with kind of.

CHAPTER SEVEN

VAMPIRES

Sex, Death, and Twilight

From *The Vampire Lovers* and *Daughters of Darkness* in the '60s and '70s to *The Lost Boys*, *Near Dark*, and *Lifeforce* in the '80s, all the way to *Twilight,* Robert Eggers's *Nosferatu*, Ryan Coogler's *Sinners*, and Luc Besson's new *Dracula* remake, vampires are at the forefront of the horror romance subgenre. I think it would be utterly impossible to talk about horror romance without mentioning vampires. I tried to keep most of the vampire films to this chapter, but they're everywhere, largely because the vampire is one of my favorite monsters. Alluring and eerie, the range of vampire types and films reflect the diversity of vampire tropes. But I think in almost every case, it's true that the vampire is an inherently romantic creature, and the act of drinking blood and transforming victims into helpless familiars who do your bidding certainly has some sexual connotations.

That's not to say that all vampires and vampire films are romances; some vampires are monstrous, treating their human victims more like cattle to be bred for food than people whom they desire for more than just sustenance. Films like John Carpenter's *Vampires* aren't terribly interested in the love lives of the creatures at the heart of the films. And in movies like *From*

Dusk till Dawn, the vampires are almost secondary to the plot, and there's not much in the way of emotional development between human and monster. But there is an added layer of titillation in many vampire storylines, whether it's strictly the vampire deriving pleasure from their victims or vice versa or both. Paranormal romance features so many vampire characters (and it's not just because of *Twilight*, though that book and movie certainly played a part in growing the paranormal romance genre). In addition to giving general romantic vibes, vampires can be seen as inherently queer characters. They don't tend to have any qualms about who their victims, thralls, and familiars are, and they are often content to claim anyone who catches their eye, regardless of gender, age, or relationship status. In some of the films I talk about here, romance is more of a subtext or an underlying feeling rather than a full-on HEA, but in a few movies we do in fact get a real love story. Toxic? Perhaps. Dubious consent issues? Possibly. But there's romance.

The Hammer Frankenstein films may be viewed through a queer lens (see *The Curse of Frankenstein* in chapter 4), but sexuality of all stripes is much more overt in Hammer's vampire flicks. Obviously, Dracula is a character whose entire modus operandi is to take advantage of his victims, holding them in a kind of sexual thrall even in the most chaste versions of the story. The Hammer productions hit on a formula that worked incredibly well for them, featuring buxom women and arresting vampires, anchored of course by Christopher Lee's iconic performance in seven of their vampire movies. But Hammer made sixteen vampire films in total, and the second one (and proper sequel to *Dracula*), Terence Fisher's *The Brides of Dracula* (1960), only mentions Dracula's name twice.

The film opens with a young woman traveling through Transylvania forests on her way to begin her teaching assignment at a remote girls' school. Marianne Danielle, played by Yvonne Monlaur, is a typical Hammer heroine: wide-eyed, innocent, and positively oozing sex even as she's covered from head to toe (in an absolutely fabulous wool hooded coat). She ends up stranded in a village when her coachman leaves without her, and the viewers can tell from the start that something more sinister is going on. It's not long before the severe Baroness Meinster (Martita Hunt) shows up and very graciously tells Marianne she can stay at the castle before being sent on her way to the school. Marianne, rather naively, accepts without any reservations, and she arrives at the Castle Meinster to discover the baroness hasn't been entirely truthful. Her son, the baron, has been locked up in the rooms below Marianne, and she can't help but be drawn to him. In a less horrific story, this would be the moment where true love sparks. But of course, it *is* a horror film, and the baron is not what he seems.

Marianne vows to help this handsome young man escape from his bonds, since it's clear to her that the baron's mother has been lying and is confining her son so she can control his lands. Marianne seems powerless to resist her attraction to the baron, played by David Peel with an arrogance that rivals the billionaires that populate so many modern romance novels. As Marianne walks away from him, ready to sneak through the castle to find the key that will unlock his chains, the camera lingers on his face: The audience sees his expression transform ever so slightly, a smirk that indicates he's not as helpless as he lets on. Marianne helps him escape, and the baron takes his revenge on his mother, murdering her before he flees into the forest. Marianne runs off, not sure what exactly took place, and ends up collapsing in the same woods before Dr. Van Helsing (played by Peter Cushing) finds her. Then the story really gets going.

I won't recap the entire film here, but suffice to say that the baron is, of course, a vampire, one of Dracula's disciples. Van Helsing has been studying vampires since the death of Dracula, and when he finds Marianne and brings her to the village, he discovers that there is another vampire on the loose that he must defeat. The remainder of the film oscillates between the baron and the doctor as they circle each other, with Marianne as the central figure for both of them. The baron finds Marianne, now at the school, and proposes marriage, which she for some reason accepts; I guess the murder of his mother wasn't enough to put her off. Marianne's new friend Gina (Andrée Melly) is jealous of Marianne's new beau, but she doesn't have long to wait before the baron comes to her room at night and drains her blood, turning her into another one of his brides, which include girls from the village and his former servant Greta. Van Helsing eventually prevails, though not before he is bitten by the baron, and in a gruesome scene for the era, must brand himself and cleanse the wound with holy water to prevent the vampire's curse.

Romance makes *The Brides of Dracula* work as a film: Though obviously contrived, the romance cues offer the audience an easy way to deal with Marianne's lightning-fast acceptance of the baron despite the obvious red flags flying around him. Whether it's entirely organic or due to the vampire's powers of persuasion, we don't think much about the speed with which Marianne throws herself into the situation; we've seen these kinds of love-at-first-sight scenarios play out so many times it seems normal. The other women in the film, the true brides, lose their humanity and become nothing more than acolytes of the baron, there to do his bidding and recruit others to his harem. Van Helsing does his best to keep Marianne safe while the baron toys with them both. Whereas Lee's Dracula simply takes the women he desires as prey, the baron seems to want his victims to want him, playing with their affections and forcing them into submission. This is a much more insidious kind of vampire, the kind of monster that feels very close to home for many women who've fallen for the charms of a creep.

The Vampire Lovers (1970) is perhaps the most explicit of the queer horror films of Hammer's legacy. (Maybe the idea of lesbianism through the male gaze of director Roy Ward Baker was more acceptable than the homoerotic undertones in the Frankenstein films.) In *The Vampire Lovers*, the main character is loosely based, of course, on the character from Sheridan Le Fanu's seminal vampire novel, *Carmilla*. The vampire antagonist uses various names throughout the film, alternately identifying as Marcilla, Carmilla, and Mircalla (I'll call her Carmilla here for ease of reading). No matter her name, she's a centuries-old vampire who kills indiscriminately but prefers to seduce young women. Played by Ingrid Pitt, one of Hammer's favorite gorgeous scream queens, Carmilla finds ways to insert herself into various wealthy families and slowly befriends, then feeds on, the young women in the household. Her first victim in the film, Laura, is plagued by nightmares where she's being attacked by a giant cat and keeps waking with puncture marks on her breasts (said breasts are, of course, photographed in a rather objectifying way, in line with Hammer's typical focus on beautiful and seductive women). I think what sets *The Vampire Lovers* apart is that it features more than just the horrors of vampires and animal attacks.

Though Carmilla's attempted seduction of Laura is quite obviously intended to titillate, it's clear that some emotional romance cues are at play as well. Carmilla seems to be genuinely interested in her new friend at first, and the sapphic romance stereotype of a stronger, confident woman seducing a more innocent woman who hadn't perhaps thought of her sexuality as being fluid is very much on display here—not only with Laura, but with Carmilla's next victims, Emma (Madeline Smith) and her governess Mademoiselle Perrodot (Kate O'Mara). I like the focus on this rather unapologetic villain in Carmilla; she's definitely a monster, but as with some of the other Hammer films, the focus is more on her than on the supposed heroes of the story.

The monster here isn't meant to be feared right away; she draws her victims in with her sensual nature, and the audience is equally entranced. I think that's a quality that engages the viewer in a very different way, and it has seen a resurgence in popularity in recent years, particularly in fiction. Dark romance (comprising several subgenres, like mafia stories, stalker romances, and even serial killer romances) is about bringing an innocent (usually female) character into a dangerous and exciting world. Though audiences were generally not given an HEA in the 1960s and '70s for these kinds of stories, since the monsters must be destroyed for their transgressions, the new iteration of the dark romance trend has allowed for more open-ended conclusions, and even sometimes features the heroine fully embracing their own dark side to stay in their relationship. As well, it's taken a while for mainstream publishers to embrace LGBTQ+ romance in fiction, but today there are certainly more and more publishers and authors exploring everything from sapphic dark romantasy to m/m hockey romance.

This trope of the subtle, seductive (and ultimately corrupting) vampire comes up again and again, especially in movies that feature a little more romance than the more action-heavy, bloody vampire movies. One of the most fascinating portrayals of this trope for me is Delphine Seyrig's performance as Elizabeth Báthory in 1971's *Daughters of Darkness*, directed by Harry Kümel. This is another lesbian vampire movie, similar to *The Vampire Lovers* (other great examples of this subgenre include *The Velvet Vampire*, also from 1971, and *The Hunger*). The film opens with newlyweds Valerie (Danielle Ouimet) and Stefan (John Karlen) on a train in Belgium. They're on their way to Stefan's British family home ahead of their move to the United States, and they end up at a hotel that's mostly empty (the tourist season is at an end) before their trip to England. At the hotel, they encounter a gorgeous and mysterious woman, Elizabeth, and her assistant Ilona (Andrea Rau). Elizabeth had hoped to stay in the honeymoon suite, and when she learns it's occupied, she takes the room next door and makes an effort to spend time with the couple, seemingly fixated on the two even as Ilona seems a little uncomfortable with the whole thing. Valerie and Stefan's relationship is not exactly full of newlywed bliss, as it turns out: They admit to not being in love, and in one scene Stefan isn't able to perform sexually, not that Valerie cares much. So, it doesn't take long for the couple to become interested in the intriguing and gorgeous Elizabeth and Ilona, whose relationship is definitely more than just business. One night, they listen to Elizabeth's story of the legend of her namesake, Elizabeth Báthory, who murdered young women and bathed in their blood. Valerie finds the story shocking and revolting, but Stefan is visibly excited by the violence. Elizabeth's corrupting influence has begun its work on the unsuspecting couple, allowing the two to reveal their true natures to each other.

The romance in this movie feels more like a facade than anything true and deep. Valerie and Stefan seem hopelessly in love at the start, but in reality, they are together for the wrong reasons. A phone call to Stefan's "mother" reveals that the person he's been hiding from is actually an older man, clearly coded as a gay man. His real connection to Stefan is never fully revealed—perhaps he is another of Stefan's lovers, and that's why he's so angry that Stefan got married. Stefan turns violent and sadistic toward Valerie after the call, as he takes out his hurt and anger toward "Mother" on his new wife. The film features a rather brutal beating and rape scene that I was not expecting in a film advertised as an erotic horror film. As the focus turns from the newlyweds, Ilona is realizing that her relationship with Elizabeth is coming to an end, and she's heartbroken that her love is no longer reciprocated. She is being cast aside by her lover, and it's clear that Elizabeth's tale of obsession with young women isn't just a folk story.

These two rejections, of Valerie and Ilona, signal the shift in the dynamic of the film. As Ilona and Stefan come together out of spite, both spurning their lovers for each other, Elizabeth prepares to take Stefan's place, and her dazzling presence affects

Valerie like a flame for a moth. Valerie seems helpless to resist the seductive nature of Elizabeth, and actor Seyrig, with her exquisite costumes and devastatingly beautiful face, is incredibly hard to resist. Seriously, this woman is absolutely the perfect person to play the ultimate vamp.

All the relationships in *Daughters of Darkness* are of the messy variety; the movie reeks of eroticism but lacks actual romance. The relationship stories wouldn't be out of place in a 1970s melodrama, or even an '80s soap opera. Well, except for the murders occurring in the town. And the blood. But the reason this film has achieved cult status, beyond the seriously stunning Delphine Seyrig, is that these relationships feel tragic and fraught and so, so compelling. You watch in horror as Valerie and Stefan fall apart. And then again as Ilona meets a stupid, tragic fate. When Valerie and Elizabeth decide they're better together, it feels inevitable, almost as if Elizabeth has seduced the audience alongside Valerie. Of course Elizabeth would get what she wants. She's always gotten what she wanted. The first time I watched this movie, I was so surprised by the ending, and I almost don't want to give it away. It feels like such a '70s ending: bleak, unexpected, and yet exactly what should happen, and definitely not an HEA. If you haven't already seen it, I highly recommend this movie. It's stuck with me since that first watch.

Many of the art-house horror films of the 1970s came from Europe and filmmakers like Jean Rollin, Dario Argento, and Nicolas Roeg. But North American directors and producers were breaking away from the studio system and making unapologetic cinema of their own. The relative freedom and financing for provocative, fresh films introduced audiences to new voices and new ideas. Producers Jack Jordan and Quentin Kelly were searching for the next Black horror movie on the heels of William Crain's *Blacula* (1972), starring William Marshall as an African prince bitten by Dracula. They tapped Bill Gunn to write and direct *Ganja & Hess* (1973), but the film was mostly ignored in the US at the time, even after it was selected for the Cannes Film Festival's Critics' Week. I rewatched it recently and it is a stunning, strange exploration of love, religion, and sacrifice.

Gunn plays a pivotal role as George Meda, a newly appointed assistant to Duane Jones's Dr. Hess Green. Jones is perhaps best known for playing Ben in George Romero's seminal *Night of the Living Dead*, and he is just as captivating here. The slightly aloof Professor Green is studying an ancient African tribe called the Myrthians, and the voiceover at the beginning of the film sets the stage: Hess is stabbed three times with a tribal knife and afflicted with an addiction to blood. The movie jumps around in time, going back to reveal just how Meda stabs Hess. Once Meda kills himself, the story skips ahead. We see Hess hunting and killing people, sticking to those of lower socioeconomic status in order to stay away from his upper-class neighborhood. Out of the blue, he gets a call from Meda's wife, Ganja (Marlene Clark), who's searching for her missing husband. She tells Hess she's coming to stay with him to wait for Meda to return, and thus the stage is set for the real story: the relationship between Ganja and Hess.

Clark's portrayal of Ganja is, in short, incredible. She is gorgeous and she knows it, and she has spent her life looking out for just one person: Ganja. It doesn't take long for her to strike up a romantic relationship with Hess, and the two end up married after a seemingly whirlwind romance (though because of Gunn's elastic interpretation of time, we don't truly know how long they are together). The two of them feel like equals throughout the film; we don't see many of the stereotypical "romance" elements like meet-cutes, miscommunications, or climactic declarations of love. Instead, when Ganja discovers that Hess has been keeping Meda's corpse in the cellar to drain of blood, she says, "Everyone is some kind of freak." For someone like Ganja, who has always had to find a way to survive despite her hardships, becoming a vampire isn't a dealbreaker. It's a way to take control of her life, and Hess becomes a true partner for her in a way that I don't think Meda ever was.

The two vampires seduce and murder more victims, but even as Ganja embraces the life she is building with Hess, he begins to falter. Hess's addiction to blood is a source of shame and guilt, and he looks for ways to release the two of them from the cycle of violence he's conjured. He discovers that the only way to release them from the addiction to blood is to stand in the shadow of the cross. Hess tries to convince Ganja to follow him into death, but she refuses. The end of the film shows Ganja smiling in Hess's mansion, watching her first victim (who is now reanimated and presumably also a vampire) run toward her. She's no longer beholden to any man, with Meda gone and Hess destroyed; Ganja has harnessed the power she's been given and seems to be ready to continue her life as a vampire with a new companion.

This isn't exactly a typical horror romance, but I think Gunn's film is still relevant and important today *because* it doesn't follow typical story beats. There are some stunningly beautiful shots, and the nonlinearity of the story imparts a captivating fever-dream quality to the narrative. Sam Waymon, who plays a reverend and friend of Hess in the film, also created the dense, layered score, and its haunting juxtaposition of chanting, animal sounds, and gospel music adds to the strangeness of the movie. Ganja and Hess are characters that defy easy stereotypes; they feel more dimensional and complex than many of the era's depictions of both Black people and male and female partners. At a time when the power dynamics between couples onscreen often skewed heavily toward one gender or the other, a relationship that feels equal is truly interesting to see.

Though *Ganja & Hess* was treated poorly at the time, with the producers recutting and rereleasing it as an exploitation film to capture drive-in audiences, it has since been reevaluated as an important exploration of the Black experience.[1] Spike Lee's

2014 remake, *Da Sweet Blood of Jesus*, helped to renew interest in the original, which is now restored and well worth tracking down. (If you're interested in reading more about Gunn and his film, check out Donato Totaro's essay in *Offscreen.*)[2]

As I mentioned previously, in North America (and much of the West), the 1980s became more conservative socially and politically. Vampires once again became code for more transgressive relationships, particularly queer relationships, instead of just sex itself. Big-budget vampire movies like *The Lost Boys* (1987), directed by Joel Schumacher, were ostensibly teen-friendly popcorn flicks, but it's hard to rewatch this movie now and miss the very clear queer signals being broadcast. On the surface, Jason Patric's character Michael is attracted to a mysterious woman named Star when he and his brother Sam (Corey Haim) move to Santa Carla, California. Star (Jami Gertz) and her brother Laddie (Chance Michael Corbitt) are part of a group of teens who at first glance seem to be your typical raucous youth, but of course they turn out to be vampires. Michael is lured to this group of vampire punks by Star, who is used as bait by David to capture the attention of young people who feel like they don't quite fit in with the rest of the status quo in the California beach town. Kiefer Sutherland plays David, who seems to lead this vampire coven, and as much as Michael is interested in Star, he is even more compelled by the dangerous David. Michael becomes more and more drawn into the life and culture of the vampires and distances himself from his brother, Sam, and mother, Lucy (Dianne Wiest), who symbolize "family values." Sam teams up with some other young teens who believe in the paranormal and together they try to bring Michael back from the dark side.

When I first saw this movie as a young teenager, the queer subtext was very much not on my radar (the endlessly memed shirtless saxophonist was not a thing!); I was much more interested in the romance between Star and Michael. But on rewatch, it's so clear that they are not the couple that is most interesting to the filmmakers—Star's character is quite two-dimensional and really is little more than window dressing, a symbol for heteronormative relationships rather than a real person who is offering and looking for a real connection. David, on the other hand, is an incredibly compelling and highly nuanced foil for Michael. He's not just looking for Michael to join his crew. He's looking for someone to be his equal, someone with whom to cement a true partnership instead of just another friendship. Michael is seduced by the idea of vampirism, drinking David's blood and flying around in David's embrace. He starts to act differently, raising suspicion with his brother and his mom. Much of this transformation feeds into many of the stereotypes and anxieties of the gay panic of the 1980s, when the AIDS crisis brought ideas of homosexuality into mainstream conversations and worried suburban families who thought they were losing their kids or their partners to a different lifestyle. Sam uses Michael's guilt about abandoning his family to help convince Michael to come back to a more traditional, heterosexual life by rescuing Star and her brother from the wild and, let's face it, more interesting, David.

David and Michael aren't the only ones with romantic chemistry in *The Lost Boys*, and the other pairing in the film is a really interesting take on the vampire angle. Lucy (played to harried perfection by Wiest), is recently divorced and moving home to live with her father. She's not looking for a relationship and is more focused on trying to keep her boys happy and stable after what must have been a tumultuous time. She finds a job working at a video store (oh how I miss video stores) for a guy named Max (Edward Herrmann). He's a Nice Guy, though seasoned romance enthusiasts will recognize his "just friends" energy as that of a man trying to make a move out of the friend zone and into Lucy's good graces. The B-plot (or maybe C-plot) of the film is the burgeoning relationship between Lucy and Max, whom Sam initially suspects of being a vampire too but changes his mind when he realizes that none of the tricks for revealing a vampire's true nature work on Max.

It turns out that Sam's original accusation is correct. Not only is Max a vampire, he's the *real* head of the vampires. He told David to turn Michael, then Sam, so that Lucy would agree to be transformed into a vampire mother for his pack of Lost Boys. The idea of a vampire trying to forge a family, instead of just claiming individual victims as whims take them, is an interesting and rather uncommon one (a theme echoed in Anne Rice's *Interview with the Vampire*, which had been written at the time but not yet made into a film). Though elements of sex and seduction still feature in this movie, the overarching idea that family is the most important thing, eclipsing romantic relationships, feels like a very 1980s conservative way of thinking. *The Lost Boys* is an example of a horror movie that explores the transgressive nature of vampirism, queerness, and the Other but ultimately retreats into the comfort of the known. It's a safe film, where the audience knows there will be temptation, and maybe even some danger, but that ultimately everything will turn out okay for the main characters. Even if (especially if) that resolution reaffirms the status quo that many '80s horror films strove for.

Stuck between the artsy stylings of *Daughters of Darkness* and the pop-centric, stereotypically '80s vibe of *Lost Boys*, Tobe Hooper's *Lifeforce* (1985) asks, what if vampires are really space aliens? It's a question that I admittedly never thought needed answering, but this movie is such a unique and strange take on the vampire trope that if you get a chance, you should definitely take a look.

The movie opens with the doomed crew of the *Churchill*, an international team of astronauts (led by Steve Railsback as Colonel Tom Carlsen) from the US and the UK, as they come across a massive spaceship hidden inside Halley's Comet. While exploring the ship, they find hundreds of bat-like alien creatures and three humanoid figures, one female and two male, all in what appears to be a coma-like state. The crew take the humanoid creatures back to the *Churchill*, but shortly after, the space agencies on the ground lose contact with the ship and a recovery team is sent to find them. When they find the vessel, they realize that the crew is all dead save Carlsen, but the aliens remain in stasis. They're brought back to Earth, and that's where things begin to go sideways. One by one, the aliens awaken and begin draining the lifeforce from their victims, just as vampires do but without the blood (the practical effects showing the draining of characters' essence, however, are incredible). For some reason, these space vampires spend quite a long time unclothed, and, of course, the unsuspecting humans who encounter the aliens, particularly those who meet the female space vampire (played by Mathilda May with an otherworldly presence), are powerless to fight back due to the utter shock of seeing a nude woman wandering around the space exploration facility.

You're probably thinking, where's the romance? (Actually, you're probably thinking this movie sounds a little bizarre, and that's definitely the case.) When Carlsen arrives in London, we discover that he has somehow developed an incredible bond with the female space vampire (in the credits, she's simply known as Space Girl). He's so captivated that he shared some of his lifeforce with her, and their bond leads him to give up the rest of his crew to the Space Girl, allowing her to drain their lives away. Their connection isn't really explained, but love works in mysterious ways. The Space Girl, for her part, seems a little less interested in Carlsen when she first arrives on Earth. She is happy to suck the life out of anyone she encounters, at least until Carlsen arrives.

The space vampires not only drain the life from their victims, but a few hours after they seemingly perish, the husks come back to life with lifeforce-draining powers of their own, passing along this strange vampirism like a plague. This behavior leads to a full investigation by Peter Firth's Colin Caine, an SAS colonel who's trying to contain the threat and find out how to overcome what is turning into a city-wide epidemic. Which also leads to my favorite exchange of the film, when Caine is interrogating one of the men who was first attacked by the Space Girl:

> **COLONEL COLIN CAINE:** Tell me again how the girl overpowered you.
>
> **DR. BUKOVSKY:** She . . . was the most overwhelmingly feminine presence I have ever encountered. I was drawn to her on a level . . .
>
> **COLONEL COLIN CAINE:** Was it sexual?
>
> **DR. BUKOVSKY:** Yes. Overwhelmingly so, and horrible. Loss of control.[3]

This idea that men are both entranced by this beautiful woman and horrified by her is a common trope in horror films, so much so that it has a name: the monstrous-feminine. You can read the original book by Barbara Creed or 2020's *Re-Reading the Monstrous-Feminine* for more on this from an academic perspective.[4] But essentially, horror films often depict women's sexuality as terrifying, and women are typically seen as either virgins or whores. Female monsters are constructed in these films, and they usually fall into various tropes, including archaic mother, monstrous womb, and vampire, among others. Of course, not every movie that involves a female villain fits these guidelines, but when Creed's book came out in the '90s, there was certainly a vast catalog of films she could pull from to argue her case, particularly when it came to horror directed by cis men. *Lifeforce* fits into that category for sure. Though there are two male space vampires, they are very much background characters and are barely given any lines, let alone motivation or conflict to overcome. The Space Girl is both the catalyst for the story and the crux of it, as Carlsen tries to resist his compulsion to join with her and help her drain the energy from the entire world (or at least the entire city of London).

The romance in *Lifeforce* is of a toxic nature. Mostly. Of course, Carlsen knows this woman/alien is not good for him, or for the world at large. But he can't help but gravitate to her even though she's "bad." For her part, the Space Girl says that since he willingly gave her some of his own energy, their bond is unbreakable, and he must feel the same way. It combines the fated-mates trope (where characters don't necessarily like each other, but they can't stay apart) and seduced-by-the-dark-side trope, both of which are common in the publishing world. A romance that you know intellectually is no good for you is a thrilling kind of proposition, and one which fits quite nicely in the horror/romance genre. How far would you go to keep love alive? How much would you destroy or let rot in order to pursue your relationship? Obviously *Lifeforce* looks at these questions from a less-than-philosophical angle, clearly more focused on the special effects and (especially in the latter half) the big explosions and car wrecks. But there is a different emotional struggle within Carlsen as he grapples with whether he can put an end to Space Girl's siphoning of humanity. Ultimately, Carlsen chooses to remain attached to the space vampire, stabbing himself and her with a giant sword, which causes his own lifeforce, bound with hers, to rise up to the waiting spaceship in the comet. A bittersweet ending but one where the couple remains entangled in their relationship even after physical death on Earth.

So, the 1980s give us space vampires in *Lifeforce* and California pop-punk vampires in *The Lost Boys*. The romances in both these films end in some version of an HEA, though one could argue that there are unresolved aspects in each case. But these aren't the only vampire movies of the era—movies like *Vamp*, *Fright Night*, *Vampire's Kiss* (featuring a truly wild Nicolas Cage performance), and *Transylvania 6-5000* all feature bloodsuckers with varying degrees of sensuality, but most of these are a little more comedic in nature. For a truly great, angsty vampire film full of yearning (as well as copious amounts of blood), we need to look at Kathryn Bigelow's incredibly awesome *Near Dark* (1987). It's not the easiest movie to track down (or at least it wasn't at the time of writing), but it's so worth making the effort, as I think it's probably the best of the 1980s vampire bunch.

Released shortly after *The Lost Boys*, *Near Dark* was perhaps not as widely seen (it made $3.4 million during its first run versus $32 million for *The Lost Boys* two months prior, according to Box Office Mojo). But in terms of impact, it's definitely as influential if not more so than Schumacher's more mainstream movie. A gritty western infused with nihilistic vampires and gore, Bigelow's film focuses on a found family of vampires who travel the country to find victims, since they can't feed on the same person more than once. Jesse and Diamondback (played by Lance Henriksen and Jenette Goldstein, respectively) act as de facto parents of the group, and Severen, Mae, and Homer (Bill Paxton, Jenny Wright, and Joshua John Miller, respectively) are the younger members of the coven. When Mae meets Caleb Colton (Adrian Pasdar), the two hit it off, and instead of Mae simply draining Caleb and moving on, she feels a connection to him, and she ends up turning him into a vampire because she wants him to stay with her. This is *not* what the rest of her vampire family wants, however.

Caleb is given one week to make his first kill and join the clan for good, but he finds it difficult to go through with murder. He wants to stay with Mae, but her dark side is too much for him. Unfortunately, since Caleb has been turned, he can't go back to his family (the vampires in *Near Dark* are damaged by sunlight, as they are in many vampire tales). He waits for Mae to drink blood, then feeds from her (so technically he's still heavily involved in murdering these victims, but I guess he doesn't think it's so bad if he's not the one actually doing the killing). This behavior doesn't exactly endear him to the rest of the vampires, but Mae seems as enamored of Caleb as he is of her, and she fights for him to remain part of the group.

After some harrowing violence (Bill Paxton is the catalyst for much of the mayhem, particularly the terribly bloody bar scene), Caleb finally splits from the group when his younger sister Sarah (Marcie Leeds) is targeted by Homer, who looks like a child himself. With the other vampires pairing up, with the exception of Severen, Homer wants a partner of his own. But the abduction of Sarah is the last straw for Caleb; no matter how much he thinks he loves Mae, he can't give up his true family. His father finds him and gives Caleb a blood transfusion, which miraculously cures his vampirism. Realizing that he has a way to save Mae and his sister, Caleb fights the vampire coven and manages to dispatch Severen. Mae decides that Caleb and his family have become more important to her than the vampires, and their cruelty in kidnapping Sarah solidifies her opinion. She helps Sarah run away from the vampires at great physical cost, hiding from the sun as best she can until she finds Caleb. He gives her a blood transfusion as well and she's cured, and the two of them are able to begin again, this time as humans.

There is so much romance here, from the first moment that Caleb and Mae meet to their final embrace. As well, Jesse and Diamondback's partnership is essentially a long marriage, and they clearly care for each other and support one another through hardship and trauma. Homer longs for romance, so much so that he immolates himself when he tries to chase Sarah, only caring about possessing her, not the harm he's causing himself. But back to Caleb and Mae. The romance here is intimate and vulnerable, and the giddy new love feeling is quickly replaced with deep emotion. Mae giving her wrist to Caleb to drink from so she can help him circumvent the rules he's been given and sustain himself is shot so beautifully, a stand-in for a more traditional love scene.

Though *Near Dark* is quite a gritty, violent imagining of vampire lore, Bigelow is great at injecting some beauty and hope here too. The dusty Western landscape, with wide open spaces (even the vampire hideout in a giant warehouse is a stark contrast to the cramped cave of *The Lost Boys*) gives the film a mythic quality. These are monsters, sure, but also heart, which has led to the film's resurgence as an acclaimed entry in the genre. Pasdar and Wright show the audience a connection that feels true even when it's beset with obstacles. And there's an actual HEA here! The two are changed, transformed by their ordeals, but come through their trials stronger and more committed than before. It's a great way to cap off the discussion of the '80s vampire trend.

There were a few more big vampire movies in the '90s, but I'm going to leave them aside for now. They're part of the gothic trend of the 1990s that was pivotal for me and my appreciation of both horror and romance, so I want to discuss them apart from the rest—see chapter 9. For the most part, vampires, at least the super romantic kind, were a little quiet for a while in pop culture after that '90s boom. That is, until Stephenie Meyer created a phenomenon that would have lasting impact on romance publishing, even if it didn't spark quite as big a trend on the movie side of things. I'm referencing, of course, the massive success of *Twilight*. The romance between young Bella Swan and sparkly Edward Cullen took publishing by storm, inspiring countless imitators and launching a franchise that was a cultural touchstone for a generation of young women. (I'm just slightly too old to have fallen under its spell the first time around.)

The gist of the story in the first book and film, directed by Catherine Hardwicke in 2008, is as follows: Bella Swan (Kristen Stewart) has moved to Forks, Washington, to live with her father after her parents' divorce. She meets Jacob Black (Taylor Lautner), an Indigenous teen, who seems to have a rivalry with

Edward Cullen (Robert Pattinson) and his mysterious family. Edward is very cold to Bella, and his standoffishness only intrigues her further. Jacob warns Bella against Edward, and she learns that his family is unwelcome on Jacob's land, but she's still not quite sure why. After Edward defies physics on more than one occasion to save her, Bella decides to do some research, and she suspects Edward is a vampire. He confirms his identity to her, and tells her that though he's incredibly attracted to her (he finds her scent irresistible), he can't pursue a relationship with her because they're too different. Of course, things don't end there. Bella and Edward fall in love, and she's introduced to the Cullen clan, who have mixed feelings about her—they don't want to have their secret exposed. The Cullens are portrayed as "good" or "safe" vampires; they only consume animal blood, and they never take human victims. So, they're dangerous but in a way that is much more palatable to an audience of largely impressionable young girls, who devoured this book as well as the three sequels voraciously (the series has sold over 160 million copies to date). Bella is threatened when new, more vicious vampires arrive in town, and one of them, James, wants to hunt her. She escapes to her mother's house in Arizona, and the Cullens come to her rescue again. Edward defeats James and prevents Bella from becoming a vampire by removing the vampire venom from her wrist after James's attack. Though Bella asks Edward to turn her into a vampire, because she's so in love with him, the movie ends with Edward refusing, as James's partner waits in the shadows to plot her revenge (obviously setting up the stakes for the sequel).

Twilight takes the gothic vampire romance in a different direction than many of the films here. It's not so much a vampire film with a love story as it is a romance story with vampires. And while I don't think *Twilight* had much of a lasting effect on horror in film, it *did* lead to a trend of YA (young adult) and teen film series that lasted for much of the first decade of the

2000s. Book series like *Divergent*, *The Hunger Games*, and *Maze Runner* all launched a host of derivative follow-ups as well as a new set of teen heartthrobs, but the horror connoisseur was much more likely to look down their nose at the vampires in *Twilight* (there's a discussion to be had about the dismissal of romance and stories aimed at and told by women in the wider patriarchal society in North America, but that is beyond the scope of this book). Still, there's no denying the series was a massive success. And it had an *enormous* impact on romance publishing, with lasting repercussions today.

The books and the film both opened the door to more supernatural tales in the romance world, and readers were hungry for stories of (mostly) women getting caught up in a strange and otherworldly love story with a (usually) dark and handsome mysterious man who is harboring a magical or evil secret. Fascination with vamps definitely helped fuel these paranormal romance novels that were popular in the 1990s and 2000s, and there have been a number of indie authors bringing this paranormal romance back to the forefront, with the category showing up on acquisition reports and in traditional publishing houses once again. Publishers raced to find the next Stephenie Meyer, especially as her original YA readership grew older and wanted more adult stories. Meyer is arguably one of the catalysts for the aging up of YA novels in general, which is still pushing young readers out of the market and is making it increasingly difficult for both YA and middle grade authors to find space on the shelves next to books that are ostensibly YA but are aimed at an older "crossover" audience.[5]

The other trend that came out of the *Twilight* phenomenon is the advent of fan fiction as a legitimate avenue for writers to break into the publishing industry. Fan fiction is not new; fans have been riffing on popular stories as far back as the 1800s, and the Star Trek fandom popularized the modern fanfic back in the 1960s. But the ease of writing and publishing stories digitally on sites such as Archive of Our Own and Wattpad (or even on your own blog or Tumblr page) brought forth an explosion of stories that not only used the original media as inspiration but also built on each other, creating an entire ecosystem of self-published fiction writers who didn't need a traditional publishing contract to build a readership. They also didn't need to worry about gatekeepers of traditional publishing, and as such began to write darker stories within a fandom's universe that wasn't edited or toned down (as is evidenced by *Fifty Shades of Grey*, a *Twilight* fanfic, which helped grow erotic fiction into a much bigger category than ever before).

Twilight's impact on the romance genre was staggering, and we're still seeing it decades later: Indie publishing and self-publishing are thriving, authors are being approached by agents and publishers seeking out new voices, and the appetite for dark romance, like stalker romance, or kinkier stories, has never been higher. Even the massively successful romantasy category owes a debt to *Twilight*; as one of my editor friends says, when we're looking for compelling love triangle narratives, we need a Jacob, an Edward, and a Bella. Personally, I don't count *Twilight* as one of my faves, since much of the romance itself is a little suspect (it's hardly young love when one part of the couple is a hundred-year-old vampire) and arguably a little toxic. In addition, the representation of Indigenous peoples in these stories is highly problematic, particularly in the sequels. But there's no denying the impact of the series on the romance genre.

In the first part of the twenty-first century, vampires continued to show up pretty frequently in films like the action-horror *Underworld* series (which I'll touch on later), *Van Helsing*, and *30 Days of Night*, along with quieter vampire stories like *Let Me In*, *Only Lovers Left Alive*, and *A Girl Walks Home Alone at Night*. But *Twilight* was certainly the biggest vampire romance; many of these other movies were more interested in big action sequences or avoided using the term *vampire* at all, aiming for a more artsy approach. On TV, shows like *The Vampire Diaries* and *True Blood* married vampire politics with more explicit soap-opera style love stories and reinforced the vampire's place as the most sensual of monsters. Vampires are currently back on trend, veering between more action-heavy movies, with recent releases like *Renfield*, *The Last Voyage of the Demeter*, *Abigail*, and *Morbius*, and more romance-focused vampire stories that crop up, like 2022's *The Invitation* and Robert Eggers's retelling of *Nosferatu* (more on these in chapter 12). On the publishing side of things, vampires are certainly not going anywhere; some amazing recent vampire stories explore the many, many facets of the monster (two of my faves are Johnny Compton's *Devils Kill Devils* and Hailey Piper's *All the Hearts You Eat*[6]). For now, we'll leave the vampires here and come back to them shortly in chapter 9, with the revival of the gothic horror story.

VAMPIRES

Lost Boys (1987, dir. Joel Schumacher)

TOP TROPES: Love Triangle: Michael moves to a new town and falls in with a very wrong crowd when he meets the beautiful Star, but the person he's really drawn to is the dark and brooding David, the perceived leader of the vampire gang.

DARK MOMENT: Michael finds out his love interest Star only approached him to recruit him to the vampire clan, and that even though she has feelings for him, she's doomed him to a life of vampirism unless he can break the curse.

HEA? Yes. Michael and Star defeat the head vampire and become human again.

Near Dark (1987, dir. Kathryn Bigelow)

TOP TROPES: Love at First Sight: When Caleb meets drifter Mae, he's instantly drawn to her and decides he'll follow her anywhere, even if that means joining her vampire family.

DARK MOMENT: Mae betrays Caleb, distracting him so the other vampires can kidnap his younger sister.

HEA? Yes. Caleb figures out how to cure Mae of her vampiric nature and the two recommit to each other as humans.

CHAPTER EIGHT

Deep Dive

The Two Davids: Horror Romance from Cronenberg and Lynch

Some directors become so synonymous with a style or genre that their names become adjectives. *Hitchcockian* for labyrinthine mysteries and spy thrillers. *Cronenbergesque* for science fiction and body horror depicted with a clinical, detached eye. And *Lynchian* for cryptic, often frustratingly opaque exercises in dream logic and art-house imagery. We've looked briefly at Hitchcock and his exploration of genre blending in films like *Vertigo* and *Psycho*, but now we'll turn to the two Davids: Cronenberg and Lynch.

In the 1980s, in contrast to the anti-romance slasher films that were popping up all over the place, there were still some filmmakers making films that were both horrific and romantic. Though I wouldn't say these two directors were striving for Happily Ever Afters that could always be tied up nicely by the end of their films, both David Lynch and David Cronenberg expanded their styles and produced some incredible movies in the 1980s that played with both horror and romance. Their boundary-pushing films, which didn't always resonate with critics, have nevertheless stood the test of time, and both directors have made movies that are considered classics of the speculative genre. We'll look at some of their most well-known (and most romance-adjacent) films: Cronenberg's *The Fly* and *Dead Ringers*, and Lynch's *Blue Velvet* and *Wild at Heart*.

Most people probably wouldn't put *romance* and *David Cronenberg* in the same sentence, unless they were talking about the *lack* of romance in Cronenberg films. The director has made movies across a wide variety of genres over the years, but much of his early work is in horror and science fiction. Romance doesn't seem to play a large role in many of these films, particularly his earliest trifecta of *Shivers*, *Rabid*, and *The Brood*; the films don't shy away from sex, but Cronenberg avoids romantic tropes or undertones. In 1986, Cronenberg's remake of 1958's *The Fly* pivots to something much different from his previous work: monster romance. How do we get from the horrors of *Rabid* to, well, horror of a different kind in *The Fly*?

Rabid's main character, Rose, is separated from her partner, Hart, at the beginning of the film after a motorcycle accident. When they find each other, it's decidedly not a reunion romance. *The Brood*, written and directed when Cronenberg was in the middle of an acrimonious divorce, is full of visceral rage following the collapse of a marriage, and Cronenberg explores how it manifests in murderous ways.

Videodrome's dysfunctional and twisted "romance" isn't exactly a love story for the ages. Max, the main character in the film, is pulled into a dark and obsessive relationship that certainly doesn't feature a Happily Ever After. Max meets Nicki, a mysterious woman who pulls Max deeper into the dark world of Videodrome. There is a distinct lack of emotional and romantic connection, though they pursue a sexual relationship. The lines between sex and violence blur as the story progresses, ultimately leading to horrific consequences (you have to see it for yourself).

David Cronenberg's early films typically explore sex and the body in an unflinching, albeit clinical, way. But when we look a little closer, we can see that as his work progresses, Cronenberg begins to examine relationships with more emotional depth. In particular, *The Fly* tells an incredibly romantic and tragic story. When Mel Brooks (yes, that Mel Brooks, of *Young Frankenstein* fame), decided he wanted Cronenberg to direct the remake, I don't know if he was expecting such an emotional film. The romance elements are often overlooked by critics who focus on the body horror, which is, admittedly, hard to ignore. One of the first horror films in the 1980s to explore deeper romantic connections rather than shallow sexual trysts in the midst of murder and mayhem, Cronenberg's 1986 remake adds an emotional layer that solidifies the monster romance trope.

The Fly follows very standard romance beats in the opening act. The couple's introduction wouldn't be out of place in a more contemporary, mainstream romance where opposites attract. Veronica "Ronnie" Quaife (played by Geena Davis) is a smart, funny journalist who falls for Jeff Goldblum's enigmatic scientist Seth Brundle, and the two strike up a believable partnership (helped by the fact that the two actors were romantically involved off screen at the time). Cronenberg gives us two protagonists who really feel like equals, and the audience becomes emotionally invested in their romance early on as they grow closer. This of course makes their inevitable downfall that much more tragic.

In romance, there's always a conflict that presents itself and threatens the main couple. Sometimes it's external, like a rival for one of the partners. In other stories, the main conflict is internal, whether it's commitment phobia, past trauma, or in Seth's case, jealousy. Seth's work is his driving motivation, and the distraction that Ronnie brings into his life—a distraction that could be wonderful if he gave himself over to it fully—is ultimately what leads to his downfall. Ronnie and Seth find love while working together (another great romance trope), then the conflict sets in. Seth, jealous over Ronnie's old boyfriend, decides to test the teleportation device himself when Ronnie leaves to meet with her ex, a magazine editor and professional colleague. Not noticing the fly that sneaks into the device, Seth seals his messy, tragic fate.

The Fly was released in 1986 near the height of the AIDS crisis in North America. Many critics and audience members equated Seth's agonizing transformation into a human/fly hybrid (or Brundlefly) with those afflicted with AIDS, and the parallels are easy to see. Seth's slow metamorphosis is horrifyingly realized onscreen: It's visceral, wet, and, well, disgusting. But Cronenberg has said in past interviews that he doesn't feel as though *The Fly* has anything to do with AIDS specifically.[1] He argues that all love stories end in tragedy, especially if you don't believe in an afterlife. One partner will always leave behind the other, either quickly and without warning or slowly and painfully. Ronnie and Seth could be any pair of young lovers who have to reckon with an unexpected disease or accident.

The reason *The Fly* remains so compelling is that Ronnie truly loves Seth. She stands by him for better, for worse, in health and horrible sickness. There's a little bit of Florence Nightingale syndrome in the film, that I-can-fix-him vibe again. But there's more going on here. Ronnie can't help but love Brundlefly, even as he becomes more terrifying. *The Fly* is one of the first movies to show a woman who isn't unwillingly seduced or compelled through magical means to stay with the monstrous hero. Ronnie knowingly and defiantly returns to Seth even when she knows they can no longer be together the way they were. The film ends with Ronnie shooting Seth, ending his suffering. But hers remains. At least she'll have a larval fly to remember him by.

Sure, Cronenberg doesn't exactly craft a Happily Ever After for Ronnie and Seth, but there's no denying that *The Fly* delivers a compelling, emotional, and highly romantic story. Perhaps, as

Cronenberg says, all romances end in tragedy. At least Ronnie and Seth were able to find love together, if only for a little while.

TOP TROPES: Working Together, Surprise Baby, Jealous Ex

DARK MOMENT: Seth's run-in with a fly in his teleportation machine causes his DNA to combine with the insect's, turning him into a horrifying mutant fly and preventing Ronnie from being with him.

HEA? No. Ronnie is forced to shoot the Seth/fly hybrid before he kills more people.

While *The Fly* proved that Cronenberg could, in fact, create believable emotional connections through romantic relationships onscreen, his next film, *Dead Ringers*, didn't continue that exploration of romance. Or at least not in the way that mainstream audiences may have been looking for. The film is often described as detached and cold.[2] But romance tropes are definitely at play here, and while there is a chilling or removed quality to the film, I think the romance is there. It's just not between the characters you'd expect.

Jeremy Irons plays dual roles as Beverly and Elliot Mantle, twin gynecologists treating fertility issues at their clinic in Toronto, Canada. The two brothers are externally identical, but internally their personalities couldn't be more different. Elliot is confident, ruthless, and commanding, while Beverly is shy, sensitive, and withdrawn. Bev spends much of his time with the twins' patients as they struggle with various gynecological problems, and Elliot is outgoing, promoting the pair's work and accepting awards for the both of them. In addition to sharing accolades and research methods, the twins share women: Elliot sleeps with them first, and when he grows tired of his conquests, he passes the women off to Beverly, who assumes his brother's identity. This dysfunctional and, let's face it, predatory behavior comes to a halt when Claire, played by Geneviève Bujold, enters the twins' clinic.

It begins as a typical romantic relationship for the men, with Claire unknowingly becoming part of a throuple. But Beverly develops an attachment to Claire that the twins are completely unprepared for. This love triangle threatens the deepest relationship the doctors have ever known: the connection each one feels for the other. On the surface it seems like Bev and Claire are the romantic pairing in *Dead Ringers*, but I would argue the central emotional bond is between the brothers, which gives the film even more disturbing context. Loosely based on a true story of twin gynecologists who were found dead and decomposing in their luxury apartment, Cronenberg's film imagines the ties between the men as ultimately unbreakable. Their codependent, toxic relationship is full of enablement, jealousy, and depression, but it's also full of longing and compassion. Jeremy Irons does a stellar job of showing us two wildly different characters, and his ability to create such depth and nuance carries the film to its disturbing and heartbreaking conclusion.

I don't want to mislead anyone: While the film does have romance elements, albeit twisted and distorted ones, it's definitely not missing the horror. This movie feels more in line with some of the so-called "elevated horror" that came to the forefront in the 2010s; there is very little in the way of gore or grotesquerie onscreen, save for a few key moments. But I think anyone who's ever had a uterus would agree that the sequences in the operating room and in the clinic are some of the most uncomfortable moments on film, even without seeing much in the way of blood and guts. The images of monstrous gynecological tools and pained expressions on patients' faces are more than enough to make many audience members uncomfortable, and Cronenberg is unflinching in showing the twins' often cruel and callous treatment of their female patients as they spiral out of control.

This is a modern gothic, all moody lighting and sharp angles, with family legacies and sordid ethical violations coming to a head in a melancholy and almost inevitable way. The oppressive interior environment of the film (very few shots take place outside) heightens the feelings of paranoia and claustrophobia as the two brothers move closer to each other and farther away from everyone else in their lives.

Though Cronenberg sets up Beverly and Claire as the relationship we're meant to root for on the surface, it's clear that by the end of the film, there's no way the twins can live separate lives. Beverly seems to be the weaker twin at the outset, but Elliot is equally bound up in his love for his brother, enabling him and slowly trying to "sync up" with him in an attempt to reconnect. Any chance Beverly might have had for happiness with Claire becomes impossible as he leaves her and dies in the arms of his loving brother.

TOP TROPES: Opposites Attract, Secret Twins, Love Triangle

DARK MOMENT: Bev calls Claire while she's away and mistakes her assistant for another lover, causing him to spiral out of control.

HEA? Well . . . not really. Claire leaves the twins as Beverly's drug problem causes him to lose control, and though Bev reaches out one last time after Elliot is killed, he realizes he can't live without his other half.

David Lynch offers his audience very little overt explanation, usually preferring to sit in silence rather than answer questions about what his films mean, something that I'm sure must be maddening to interviewers (and highly memeable for people on social media). But that's not to say his movies are without meaning. I would argue (and have done so many times!) that Lynch films are some of the most sincere made by an American filmmaker. Beneath their nightmarish surfaces, there is a profound love and respect for the human condition. And unlike many of his counterparts, Lynch frequently adds elements of outright romance to his films, heightening the emotional payoff for his audience. Though romance and romantic relationships play roles in much of his work, from *Eraserhead* to *Dune* to *Twin Peaks: The Return*, I'll focus on two of Lynch's earlier films here: *Blue Velvet* and *Wild at Heart*. Neither of these films is strictly horror per se, but they both feature horrific moments and definitely include the discomfort and tension that is so prevalent in horror movies.

Although Lynch began his film career in the weird and surreal with *Eraserhead*, unlike many directors, who crossed over from indies into mainstream movie production, Lynch didn't work with big studios for long. When Mel Brooks (yes, that same Mel Brooks!) tapped him to direct *The Elephant Man*, many critics assumed that the director had left the dream logic and meandering storytelling behind, but I disagree. Although *The Elephant Man* is a fairly linear story, there are telltale Lynchian signs throughout. His approach to the character of John Merrick defied the studio producers, who wanted a comedic film, and he directs John Hurt with incredible empathy and sincerity, while still creating an atmospheric and sometimes haunting vision. Lynch could have easily stuck with the mainstream studio system, even after his production of Frank Herbert's *Dune* fell far short of expectations. While there has been a recent push to try and revisit Lynch's *Dune* in the face of Denis Villeneuve's remakes, audiences overall remain puzzled and frustrated by the sprawling and sometimes confusing film, though personally, I give it full marks for the incredible set design and the audacity it took to try to bring such a rich world to life.

Blue Velvet, Lynch's first film after the much-maligned *Dune*, is a postmodern masterpiece, blending genres and styles in a way that was perhaps ahead of its time in 1986. Though much of Lynch's work can be considered horror or horror adjacent, *Blue Velvet* is also firmly a romantic piece, with Jeffrey and Sandy even getting a Happily Ever After (or at least a Happy For Now) ending.

Jeffrey Beaumont (Kyle MacLachlan) comes back to the small town of Lumberton and instantly falls into a mystery featuring a severed ear. This eventually leads to sneaking into singer Dorothy Vallens's apartment, and things get strange and horrifying from there. Lynch makes sure we, the audience, are able to insert ourselves into the story, and we become voyeurs in much the same way Jeffrey does. We're dragged along into a violent and terrifying world as Jeffrey is pulled further away from the light of Lumberton, and the promise of beauty and security in his love interest, Sandy Williams (Laura Dern), toward the grimy underbelly of the town where Frank Booth reigns.

Isabella Rossellini's portrayal of Dorothy is incredible, a masterful interpretation of a broken, desperate woman. Perhaps part of her comfort in the role is due to her romantic partnership with Lynch when they were making *Blue Velvet*, but it's quite clear that Rossellini knows what she's doing. Her performance is magnetic, and it's easy to forgive her for dragging Jeffrey into a dangerous, unpredictable world. The juxtaposition of the virginal Sandy and the sexual Dorothy is echoed throughout many films that straddle the horror and romance genres (from *Island of Lost Souls* to *Cat People* to *Crimson Peak*, although the roles are somewhat reversed there).

The horror in the film primarily stems from Dennis Hopper's wild and unpredictable Frank, who terrorizes everyone around him. As the audience, we're first introduced to him through Jeffrey's eyes, as he witnesses Frank's abuse of and assault on Dorothy while he hides in her closet. Suddenly, we're watching a film that has turned from a noirish mystery into something much more vicious. Jeffrey seems to forget about Sandy and the promise of a stable, romantic life as he finds himself ensnared in a cycle of violence and sex that is far darker than anything he's experienced before. Jeffrey seems helpless to resist, and the longer he spends with Frank and Dorothy, the more he, too, becomes prone to violence. Lynch not only shows us the dark side of people; he also does a tremendous job making the audience *feel* the characters' emotional states. Watching a Lynch film is to absorb that sincerity with which he crafts his scenes and internalize it. He makes us complicit in the characters' actions in a way that is terrifically uncomfortable (perhaps one of the reasons his films are so polarizing). Many directors, especially in the 1980s, would shoot sex scenes like those between Jeffrey and Dorothy or Dorothy and Frank in a way that objectified these characters, treating them as playthings for the titillation of the viewer. Lynch, on the other hand, gives us visceral, awkward, *honest* cinema here—we're not meant to be aroused; we're meant to be horrified.

While there is a central romance in *Blue Velvet*, the movie takes quite a roundabout route to get to Jeffrey and Sandy's happy ending. Sandy has a boyfriend, Mike, when she meets Jeffrey, though it becomes clear to the audience (especially those with even a passing knowledge of romance) that Mike is not meant for her. The spark between Jeffrey and Sandy from the first moment he sees her is obvious. The two grow closer as they work to discover the origins of the severed ear and how it relates to the enigmatic Dorothy Vallens. The scenes between actors Kyle MacLachlan as Jeffrey and Laura Dern as Sandy here are both touching and romantic, and Lynch gives the audience a lovely couple to root for. This only makes Jeffrey's foray into Dorothy and Frank's dark world even bleaker.

Sandy chooses Jeffrey and his flawed but earnest character over her wooden boyfriend Mike. It would have been easy to have Sandy be strictly a jealous young woman, a naive "good girl" who is the catalyst for Jeffrey's more "adult" relationship with Dorothy. But Sandy is in fact the reason Jeffrey ends up in Dorothy's apartment in the first place. She leads Jeffrey to the darkness on the other side of town, almost a match for Dorothy's siren. Then she shows genuine concern and care for Dorothy when she appears, dazed and broken, in front of Jeffrey's house. Sandy treats Dorothy as human, and her behavior spurs Jeffrey into breaking the spell Dorothy (and Frank) have cast over him, paving the way for his return to the bright, if artificial, idyll of Lumberton.

Ultimately, *Blue Velvet* defies genre expectations. It's a fabulous film, but Lynch is only getting started here. His subsequent films explore the space between love and violence, hope and despair in even greater detail, from *Wild at Heart* to the mind-bending twists of *Lost Highway* and beyond.

TOP TROPES: Other Woman, Solving a Mystery, Jealous Ex

DARK MOMENT: Jeffrey leaves Sandy to embark on a BDSM-fueled nightmare trip of violence and chaos with Dorothy and Frank.

HEA? Yes. Sandy and Jeffrey are together at the end of the film, enjoying each other's company and putting the past behind them. Probably.

Wild at Heart is more a surreal romance than anything else, a fever dream of sex and violence. Laura Dern is mesmerizing once again, this time as Lula, who is head over heels in love with Nicolas Cage's Sailor. The two go on the run through a Wizard of Oz–fueled nightmare of a road trip. This could easily veer into ultraviolent, campy territory à la *Natural Born Killers*, but Lynch grounds the pair's relationship in real affection for each other even as the world around them spins out of control.

Though the story here is perhaps less capital-*H* Horror than many other films in this book, there is definitely horror. Willem Dafoe's Bobby Peru is a frightening, out-of-control character, similar to Dennis Hopper's Frank. His assault on Lula is truly unnerving, and he's one of those Lynchian characters who exist in their own weird universe. The violence in the movie is often shockingly vivid and random, beginning in the first ten minutes of the movie and popping up all over the place as Lula and Sailor travel across the country. The lovers-on-the-run trope is a hugely popular one in romantic suspense stories, and Lynch doesn't hold back, sending danger upon danger after the couple, who just want to settle down and be happy somewhere. Even as the audience roots for Sailor and Lula to escape the grasp of Lula's mother, Marietta (played by Dern's real mother, Diane Ladd), there's no avoiding the fact that Cage's Sailor is himself an unhinged, terrifying guy who has no problem subjecting people around him to stomach-churning mayhem. The entire vibe of the movie is one of chaos; Sailor and Lula are so madly, wildly in love with each other that the world around them spins further and further out of control but they don't seem to really care; they've only got eyes for each other.

The movie hinges on Laura Dern's performance (much like Lynch's later magnum opus, *Inland Empire*). Dern is certainly up to the task. She imbues Lula with both an innocence and a kind of world-weary wisdom that comes from dealing with so much trauma in her life before meeting Sailor. She doesn't fit the traditional perception of a virginal romance heroine, for sure. But that perception is so often a mistaken one; romance heroines are much more nuanced and layered than many people unfamiliar with the genre believe. And Dern does an exceptional job here of portraying a character who has been battered by life's circumstances but is still optimistic and looking for the love she knows she deserves.

Nicolas Cage's Sailor certainly fits the bad-boy stereotype, dialed up about a hundred notches. There is a real sense that this character has done some bad things, even before the audience sees him doing anything. But Lynch convinces us that deep down, Sailor is worthy of Lula's love, and that while the ends don't necessarily justify the means in every instance, Lula is able to forgive Sailor's flaws, and in turn, so should the audience. There's a little more room in darker romance stories to explore how terrible the hero can become before the audience can no longer root for them to find love, and Lynch pushes that boundary in almost every one of his films. Just as Jeffrey's willingness to hit Dorothy before having sex with her in *Blue Velvet* threatens to alienate some viewers from wanting Jeffrey to achieve an HEA with Sandy, Sailor's repeated forays into violence might prevent the audience from seeing how this man can appeal to Lula. But as in *Blue Velvet*, and arguably in all his films, Lynch builds such sincerity and honesty into the characters that by and large they are forgiven and earn their happy endings.

TOP TROPES: Lovers on the Run, Touch Her and Die

DARK MOMENT: Sailor gets out of jail, tells Lula she will be better off without him, and walks away.

HEA? Yes. Sailor realizes (with a little help from the Good Witch) that he shouldn't turn away from love and returns to Lula.

CHAPTER NINE

SECOND-CHANCE ROMANCE

Return to the Gothic

Most of the movies in this chapter are from the 1990s, a magical era when big studios were paying big money to release lavish, elaborate retellings of classic horror tales. But gothic is not necessarily period costumes and shadowy castles. I think of gothic as being stories where the revelation of family history and secrets bring about (risk bringing about) the downfall of the main characters. Gothic tales often take place in isolated areas, or at least the characters are being isolated from their surroundings. The crumbling estates of classic gothic films are stand-ins for the protagonist's crumbling psyche, and unreliable narrators, mysterious shadowy figures, and startling revelations abound. Films like David Cronenberg's *Dead Ringers* and Paul W. S. Anderson's *Event Horizon* take gothic themes and push them to contemporary or futuristic settings.

One contemporary take on gothic with a bit of a twist is 1968's *Rosemary's Baby*. This horror romance doesn't exactly have an HEA (though maybe someone is happy at the end of this film . . . we'll discuss it); it starts out as a love story and devolves into an incredibly tense, paranoia-filled fever dream anchored by a stellar performance from Mia Farrow. Based on Ira Levin's novel of the same name, and directed by Roman Polanski (convicted sex offender Roman Polanski, I feel I must mention), this is a beautiful, stylish film that centers on a young newlywed couple, Rosemary and Guy Woodhouse, played by Farrow and John Cassavetes, respectively, who move from their modest apartment into an incredible building in New York City (the exteriors were shot at the Dakota, the famed NYC apartment building where John Lennon and Yoko Ono lived). Guy, an actor, is hoping to get his big break, and Rosemary begins the film as a bubbly, social woman who is excited about her future with her husband. Obviously, things go wrong.

Guy and Rosemary meet their neighbors, Minnie and Roman Castevet (Ruth Gordon and Sidney Blackmer), when the young woman who is staying with them falls to her death. The older couple invites the Woodhouses to dinner, and they agree, even though Rosemary thinks they're a bit weird. But after Minnie and Roman befriend them, good things begin to happen for the newlyweds. Guy gets a starring role in a play after the lead mysteriously goes blind, and with his newfound success, he tells Rosemary he thinks they should have a baby. It's 1968, and as a young wife without a job, becoming a mother is a goal that most women are told they should aspire to, so of course Rosemary agrees. Minnie and Roman are strangely very invested in this endeavor, and Minnie is pushy, foisting old home remedies on Rosemary to help her get pregnant. And now things *really* start to go wrong.

In a scene that makes my blood boil every time I see it, Rosemary wakes up after a strange nightmare where she was sexually assaulted by a monstrous figure, and she finds scratches all over her. Guy tells her he didn't want to miss baby-making night and therefore decided to continue having sex with her unconscious body. This is so incredibly maddening, and I think it's even more infuriating because it was considered completely acceptable behavior at the time. This, for me, is where the loving marriage that has been portrayed so far really goes off the rails. Rosemary soon finds out she's pregnant, and she's both excited and suspicious, as bizarre things keep happening around her. Ultimately, she discovers that she's been unwittingly impregnated by Satan himself to fulfill a prophecy from a devil-worshipping cult headed by the Castevets.

So why am I including this movie (as great as it is!) in this roundup of gothic horror romances? It definitely doesn't fit a typical romance plot; in fact, it starts just as many romance stories are ending, after the wedding. But some common romance elements are here, subverted to wonderful effect. Instead of the older couple down the hall helping to bring the two leads together by showing them how beautiful long-lasting love can be, Minnie and Roman work at separating Guy and Rosemary, first by appealing to Guy's vain self-interest by helping him get the part in the play, then by convincing him that being the earthly father of Satan's child will bring him more glory than any acting role. As Rosemary begins to grow more suspicious and worried about what's going on around her, the story again leans on well-known romance tropes; could Guy be cheating on Rosemary, and that's why he's acting strange? Could he be preparing a big surprise for her and that's why he's being so secretive (a very common romantic comedy trope)?

These are elements of the gothic; just like the narrator in *Rebecca* is investigating Maxim de Winter and piecing together the puzzle of Rebecca's life, Rosemary is struggling to unearth the conspiracy surrounding her and her baby. Using these tropes is a way for the audience to infer certain outcomes based on what they're used to seeing as resolutions to the common plot points, which makes the reveal of the baby Antichrist that much more shocking. As for a Happy Ever After . . . I don't know that Guy and Rosemary will be able to stick together after the credits roll, but Rosemary can't resist the pull this baby has over her, and the film ends with her picking up her infant and seemingly embracing her new role as the mother of the devil. Hopefully she's happy with her new position.

Now we get into the good stuff, the reason, in fact, that I was inspired to write this book in the first place. The 1990s was a time of both looking at the past (given the advent of the new millennium) and looking ahead, to a future that felt both very far away and frighteningly close as we barreled toward the year 2000. Most importantly for me, the 1990s was the decade in which I became a teenager and started to form my own ideas and opinions about movies and art. I'd always loved watching films, but the '90s was when I started going to the theater with my friends (and, say, sneaking into PG-13 movies like *Batman Returns* because the usher wouldn't let me in). As a teen with a bit of disposable income, movies were a fantastic escape, and I loved both new films and older ones, as I haunted the video store shelves looking for new-to-me treasures from the "5 movies, 5 days, 5 dollars" shelves. I mentioned in an earlier chapter the effect that *The Phantom of the Opera* had on me at twelve; seeing that spectacle and feeling all the angst of the Phantom, Christine, and Raoul unlocked a fascination with brooding antiheroes and beautifully dramatic fashion that hasn't left me. But the thing that pushed me from becoming a theater kid to becoming a goth teen (aside from the fear of performing in a high school production of *Little Shop of Horrors*) was the Hollywood revival of lavish, gothic productions of classic horror.

The 1990s returned the gothic to its period film roots, with some notable exceptions. Columbia/TriStar (later TriStar) released a trio of remakes of classic monster tales: *Bram Stoker's Dracula*, *Mary Shelley's Frankenstein*, and *Mary Reilly*, a retelling of *Dr. Jekyll and Mr. Hyde* from the point of view of a maid in Jekyll's household who becomes romantically entangled with both the doctor and his unhinged alter ego. Though there are romantic elements in most versions of these horror stories, the '90s films were much more overtly sexual (though not explicit) than much of the previous catalogue, largely because the moviegoing audience was generally more open to seeing sexual relationships onscreen than during the '30s through the '60s, when earlier versions of these stories were being filmed. As an aside, I (and others) would argue that the films of the 1990s and early 2000s in general were sexier and more relaxed in their depictions of (cisgender, heterosexual) sex than many films being made now, as the North American market has become more and more puritanical, but I'd probably need a whole other book to write about that phenomenon (you can read more about it in R. S. Benedict's piece for *Blood Knife*, "Everyone is Beautiful and No One Is Horny"[1]). In any case, there was an appetite for sensual, gothic stories, at least for some audiences, and as a teenager who was slowly becoming more and more interested in weird, horror, and goth culture, I was in my element with these movies. These big-budget studio films mined stories audiences were familiar with and added big star power with the likes of Tom Cruise and Brad Pitt (*Interview with the Vampire*) and Julia Roberts (*Mary Reilly*), as well as teen heartthrobs like Keanu Reeves and Winona Ryder (in *Bram Stoker's Dracula*). These movies are definitely more romantic and sensuous than the body horror of 1980s David Cronenberg or the more overt sexuality of David Lynch films like *Blue Velvet* or *Lost Highway*. That doesn't mean happy endings, but audiences get a few more heaving bosoms and breathless kisses along with their gore.

The 1990s reaches peak vampire saturation, at least until *Twilight* comes along. With *Interview with the Vampire* and *Bram Stoker's Dracula*, we see two very different yet similar vampire romances. Though *Interview with the Vampire* (1994), directed by Neil Jordan, does not make this explicit, Anne Rice's book plays up the queerness of the tumultuous relationship between Lestat (Tom Cruise) and Louis (Brad Pitt) (and the AMC television adaptation leans into this as well). Louis is a reluctant vampire to start, but Lestat, forceful and charismatic, brings

Louis over to darkness, and the two develop a toxic rollercoaster of a relationship. For a time, they are able to form a family of sorts with the tragic child vampire Claudia (played brilliantly by a young Kirsten Dunst), but the tensions in their relationship, as well as the introduction of a love triangle with Antonio Banderas as the vampire Armand, lead to the destruction of the romance.

In contrast, *Bram Stoker's Dracula* (1992) is a pinnacle of gothic romance. Dracula searches for his beloved over centuries, finally finding her again as Mina Harker. Gary Oldman brings all his charm to young Dracula, telling Winona Ryder he's crossed oceans of time to find her in a way that made teenage girls of the goth persuasion (that's me!) swoon. Though the romance is largely absent from the original novel, Coppola's version commits to the love story, and you almost want to root for the tortured vampire to run away with his reincarnated soulmate.

But back to *Interview with the Vampire*. The movie opens with a mysterious stranger telling his story to a reporter played by Christian Slater. The journalist is clearly very skeptical of the outlandish tale he hears, of a young plantation owner in Louisiana in the 1790s, Louis de Pointe du Lac, who is found by a charming man, Lestat de Lioncourt, following the death of Louis's wife and unborn child. Lestat tells Louis he can sense his dissatisfaction with life and offers him a solution: be transformed into a vampire. Louis agrees, but although he seems to have a moment of clarity where he changes his mind, the die is cast, and he's destined to become immortal like his progenitor. Lestat and Louis become companions, living together in New Orleans, while Lestat tries to coax Louis into embracing his new powers and his thirst for blood. Lestat, for his part, relishes the thrill of the hunt and the ultimate submission of his victims as he drains them. Louis doesn't seem to feel the same. In fact, Louis is almost as miserable as a vampire as he was when he was still human. But he can't bring himself to leave his mercurial, charming, abusive maker. (I didn't say the romance here was necessarily healthy.)

The two go on for decades, sometimes loving and caring for one another, sometimes bitterly resentful of their relationship. Finally, Lestat thinks he's found a way to keep Louis from leaving him. During the plague that has found its way to the city, Louis drinks from a young girl whose mother has died and left her alone. In an effort to give Louis a reason to stay and enjoy his undead existence, Lestat impulsively turns the girl into a vampire. Claudia becomes the couple's de facto daughter, and Louis, Lestat, and their "child" spend a few decades as a mostly blissful family unit. Louis truly loves Claudia and knows he could never leave Lestat now that she's part of their lives. This is such a longstanding trope in romance, where one character (usually the secondary love interest and/or villain) attempts to win back their former partner by revealing there's a secret baby. But just as in those romance novels, the ploy to keep their relationship intact doesn't hold up.

Being ten for the rest of your life—the rest of eternity—isn't something Louis and Lestat considered when creating Claudia. As she matures and grows internally, she becomes increasingly aware and frustrated by the realization that she will never grow up, never be able to have a romantic relationship. Dunst does a wonderful job of bringing a wiser, wearier persona to the role, and you really can believe she's a tired and angry woman imprisoned in the small body that never changes (the scene where she realizes she can't even cut her hair is a heartbreaker). As Louis begins to understand that even his found family can't stay intact—much like his original family unit—depression and bitterness set in once more. Claudia plots to kill Lestat, and Louis eventually helps her out of love for his daughter rather than hatred for Lestat. (If you can't tell, Louis is a bit of a sad sack for much of the film. Apparently, Brad Pitt hated the endless night shoots and was legitimately a little depressed while making the movie, which adds to Louis's air of despondence.) Louis seems to grieve for his relationship even as he's still not fully free of it;

his brooding follows him to Paris, where he and Claudia have escaped the abusive man in their lives and are welcomed to the Theatre des Vampires when they meet Santiago and Armand by chance.

Louis is drawn to Armand, an elusive, sensual vampire who leads a coven of melodramatic monsters. They perform at the theater in Paris, putting on a titillating and dangerous show for the audience, who of course think that the murder on stage is just for show. Hiding in plain sight, the Parisian vampires offer Louis and Claudia another way to exist, and Louis is plainly fascinated by the enigmatic Armand, who, in turn, is entranced by Louis and offers him and Claudia a home in Paris. Unfortunately, everything falls apart when Santiago (Stephen Rea) reads Louis's mind and suspects that he and his daughter have murdered their maker, a crime in the vampire community. Armand, trying to save the two, tells Louis to send Claudia away so she'll be safe, and asks Louis to stay in Paris to learn more about the ways of being a proper vampire, promising to keep Louis from harm if he agrees. Though Louis does send Claudia away, she understands it's not only for her safety. She can see that Louis is just as interested in Armand as Armand is in him. The two part on bad terms, and tragically that's the end of their relationship. The Parisian vampires abduct Claudia and her new vampire companion Madeleine, and they sentence them to death for murdering Lestat. Louis finds Claudia's remains turned to ash after she's been left to burn in the sun. Armand tries to offer comfort, but Louis is bereft, doomed to wander the streets alone after losing everyone he's ever cared for.

So, definitely no HEA here. These vampires, Louis in particular, are depressed and lonely, and whatever moments of joy they experienced together are fleeting. Lestat, for his part, seems vibrant and charming on the surface, but as the movie ends and he turns the reporter Daniel Molloy (Christian Slater) into a vampire, he confesses he never chose to be a vampire, to be a monster. His choice was taken from him, so in turn he has removed other's agency. The vampires here are all bitter, sad, and eager to inflict suffering on each other. But there was still romance and love to be found, if only for a short time.

In contrast to the melancholy stylings of *Interview with the Vampire*, *Mary Shelley's Frankenstein*, directed by Kenneth Branagh, is all manic energy and histrionics. Fresh off the success of Francis Ford Coppola's *Bram Stoker's Dracula* (we're getting there, I promise!), TriStar Pictures enlisted the British director to adapt another classic monster movie and put a fresh spin on it. It still takes place in the 1800s, but the stylings and pacing of the 1994 version are starkly different from those of the original 1930s Universal picture. Branagh stars as the young Victor Frankenstein here, and the development of his romance with Elizabeth (Helena Bonham Carter), his adopted sister (a bit weird but, of course, more common at the time), is front and center. Elizabeth and Victor are happy together for a time, but lurking throughout the film is the central idea that Victor is, more than anything else, obsessed with the idea of conquering death. His mother died when he was young, and that event has been the catalyst for everything else Victor's done in his life. Branagh portrays Victor as an idealist, someone who believes that the ends justify the means, no matter how grisly the means are. His drive to reverse death and create life out of nothing leads him to John Cleese's Shmael Augustus Waldman, who has seemingly figured out how to manufacture life, though his notes are merely theoretical. Waldman warns Victor and his companion Henry Clerval (Tom Hulce) not to attempt his experiments—they could unleash a monster upon the world.

Shortly after Victor and Henry approach Waldman, Waldman is murdered by a patient, and the crime affords Victor the opportunity to assemble the body parts he needs to carry out his plans. While he's immersed in his laboratory and experiments, poor Elizabeth waits and worries. The obsessive man she finds in Victor is not the inquisitive man she fell in love with, and his passion for science begins to outweigh his passion for her. Victor, for his part, thinks he's got everything under control, not realizing that his work-life balance is very much out of whack.

When the Creature (Robert De Niro) is finally brought to life, the sequence is full of electricity. Not only that, but in keeping with the more sensual storytelling of '90s gothic, it features a shirtless Kenneth Branagh in black leather pants. He runs around, turning valves, unleashing electric eels, and trying to animate the amalgam of bodies he's crafted into a sentient being. The romance here might be that of a director for himself, as Branagh seems more interested in showing Victor in a flattering light than he is in showing off the doctor's work. But these beauty shots, featuring Branagh with flowing locks, sweaty chest, and feverish obsession on his face, was textbook Romance aesthetic with a capital *R*. Victor wouldn't be out of place on a '90s-era clinch cover, though he'd probably be embracing Elizabeth instead of laboring over a dead (or undead) body.

The Creature hews much closer to Shelley's original character here; he is a bit of a philosopher and a far cry from Karloff's stoic, stiff creation. He learns to speak and feel love, and then anger and jealousy. The Creature discovers that his maker has abandoned him, and the betrayal he feels is akin to so many romance novel openings, when the main character finds out their partner isn't who they say they are. The Creature is trying to find a family, and Victor is definitely not a family kind of guy. When he finally understands how Victor has spurned him, he lashes out, killing those close to Frankenstein (like Victor's younger brother). Victor discovers the Creature is on the hunt after he abducts the doctor and tells him he must create a companion monster since Victor himself can't provide the Creature with a loving relationship with a "regular" person. The Creature offers Victor the dead body of the Frankensteins' maidservant Justine, who had recently been wrongfully hanged for crimes the Creature himself perpetrated. Victor can't go through with his promise to give the Creature a friend of his own, and flees.

Rather than focusing on the Creature's needs, Victor leaves to marry Elizabeth, perhaps hoping that he'd be able to put his experiment behind him and spend time on quieter pursuits. But that's not the case. In a rather horrific display, the Creature surprises the newlyweds on their wedding night and rips out Elizabeth's heart. A distraught Victor knows he only has one option: He must revive Elizabeth, no matter the cost. And the cost is high. He attaches Elizabeth's head to Justine's body in the hope of being able to bring the love of his life back to him, but the Creature wants Elizabeth for himself. It's a bit of a love triangle, except that Elizabeth doesn't want to be involved with either of these men, alive or undead. Elizabeth's realization that she's been transformed into a hideous, undead creature is heartbreaking, and rather than choose her suitor, she sets herself on fire instead. Again, another ending that is far from an HEA.

The formula that was so successful with Francis Ford Coppola's vampire adaptation didn't work quite so well in Branagh's picture, though it still resonated with audiences. The next TriStar picture in this same gothic horror realm did not perform up to expectations. Stephen Frears's *Mary Reilly* (1996) differs from the previous two films first by not mentioning the monster in the title, and second by deciding to tell the story from a very different perspective. The titular Mary, played by Julia Roberts in a role that feels incredibly counter to her typical lighthearted persona (especially back in 1996), is a housemaid in the quiet household of Dr. Henry Jekyll. You may remember Jekyll's name from a host of other adaptations (or from earlier in this book), and if you do, you'll know that things aren't what they seem here.

Mary herself is a quiet, traumatized young woman, having been hired into service since she was a young child because her father was an abuser who locked her in a closet with rats. Mary is timid but seems to have captured the attention of the doctor, played by John Malkovich as a man of science, similar to Branagh's Victor Frankenstein. His secretive work in his laboratory intrigues the entire household, particularly Mary, who is not only interested in the doctor's experimentation, but in the doctor himself. Jekyll has obviously not been taking care of himself, since (as many in the audience probably know) he's secretly been taking a serum that transforms him into an impulsive, rage-filled monster called Edward Hyde. The fact that Malkovich plays both characters with very minimal makeup is reminiscent of Spencer Tracy's work in his adaptation of the Jekyll and Hyde story. I was kind of shocked at how distinct the two characters are; Malkovich as Hyde just absolutely oozes sex, whereas Jekyll is so restrained, even though he's still clearly enamored of Mary. The story is full of sidelong glances and small gestures, similar to Merchant and Ivory romances like *The Remains of the Day*. Jekyll seems fascinated by the scars and obvious suffering Mary has endured. He wonders if she would have wanted her father to take medicine to remove all his anger and abusive tendencies. Mary, of course, is far too gracious and forgiving to wish for that, and said she'd made peace with her father even if she didn't want to see him again. The attitude intrigues Jekyll and perhaps gives him hope that his experiments and his struggles with Hyde reappearing can be saved or at least forgiven as well. Again, if you're familiar with the story, you'll know that Jekyll is sadly mistaken.

The overarching tropes in *Mary Reilly* are extremely gothic in nature; this story is all about the sins of the past coming to light and the secrets that have been buried resurfacing. The family curse extends to both Mary and the doctor, since they are both trying to push past the horrors in their lives—Mary has been more successful on that front, while Jekyll is still trying to cage his mistake, with mixed results. As Hyde grows more powerful, and encounters Mary more regularly, she is both repelled by and drawn into his presence (though how no one realizes he and Jekyll are one and the same is a little baffling; Malkovich is great at playing two roles, but they're still very similar in looks, at least). Though they remain mostly chaste throughout the film, and Mary thinks it's Jekyll she's in love with, it's Hyde she fantasizes about, and Hyde who kisses her. Of course, the story can't end in anything but tragedy, as Hyde must be destroyed (and with him, Jekyll), but Mary does gain a sense of self and peace that she didn't have when we first met her, so there's an HEA of a sort.

There's a bit of a Beauty and the Beast/alpha-male situation here, where Mary is emotionally or intellectually drawn to Jekyll, but because the two of them are so bound by cultural norms and the decorum of the time, Hyde's lack of inhibition allows Mary to give into her feelings of lust and excitement in a way that Jekyll can't compete with. This feels very like the cyclical trope in romance publishing of a (usually young, usually virginal) woman who is helpless in the face of a much more direct and forceful (and sometimes a little scary) man, whether he's a gruff rancher, a mafia boss, or a straight-up serial killer. There's certainly a readership who wants to vicariously experience a "dangerous" relationship, and the love story in *Mary Reilly* fits the bill in the dynamic between Hyde and Mary, where she, at least subconsciously, seems to understand that Jekyll is there all along, and that's who she's really in love with.

Since we're looking at dangerous relationships, I think we're finally ready for quite possibly my favorite horror romance (especially of the gothic variety) of all time: *Bram Stoker's Dracula*. Francis Ford Coppola's epic is bold, bloody, and extremely romantic, and as previously mentioned, this film is a touchstone for me. It was released in 1992, just as I was just getting into my teens and discovering romance and horror, and I truly couldn't name you a more devastatingly romantic movie for many years after I first saw it. Not only is the movie a story of an almost otherworldly love story that spans centuries, it's also a fantastic vampire story that, of course, takes inspiration from what is probably the most well-known vampire novel of all time. I will fully admit that my perspective on this movie is quite skewed; it's simply one of my top ten and I don't think I can be completely objective about it, but that's okay! Maybe by the end of this section, I'll even be able to convince you that Keanu Reeves was the perfect actor to play the hapless Jonathan Harker.

Gary Oldman plays the titular Dracula, and he transforms himself into multiple personae throughout the film: the bloodthirsty and virile warlord waging war on the Ottoman Empire, the ancient lord of his decrepit Transylvanian castle; the suave and seductive count in Victorian London, and even beast-like bat and wolf forms. Dracula is transformed into a vampire when he returns from war to find that his beloved Elisabeta has killed herself after being tricked into believing Dracula has been killed in battle. Since she is no longer welcome in Heaven as a suicide, Dracula renounces God and drinks blood, transforming him into a vampire who vows never to rest until his love is avenged.

The stakes are set very high from the start: After all, it's not every spouse who would declare war on a deity when their partner dies. Soon enough, we find Jonathan Harker, a solicitor, traveling to a mysterious castle to facilitate a real estate acquisition for Count Dracula, after the original solicitor, a Mr. Renfield (Tom Waits), had a nervous breakdown. I'm not going to recount the entire plot for you, of course, but here are the essentials: Dracula sees a photograph of Jonathan's fiancée, Mina Murray, and recognizes her as Elisabeta (both are played by Winona Ryder). Dracula eventually travels to London to find his presumed lost love, and along the way seduces Mina's friend Lucy Westenra (Sadie Frost) as well (who has a number of suitors). Jonathan, along with Lucy's beaus, enlist the help of Dr. Van Helsing to save the women from the dangerous and lustful Dracula, but Lucy dies, and Mina becomes enamored of the vampire and must be saved from him and from herself.

There's plenty of blood and suspense throughout, but the crux of this film is the romance. Though previous iterations of the Dracula story don't shy away from the seductive nature of the count, very few versions also explore the role the women play in those seductions. In many cases, the audience is reminded that the victims of Dracula are being compelled against their will into complying, and his powers of hypnosis are what force the women to fall under his spell. Though Dracula does still harness the power of suggestion with his seduction of Lucy, Mina at least is allowed more agency, and as such, the power dynamics feel a little less wonky.

That's not to say there aren't a few slightly queasy moments in the story. Prince Vlad's first meeting with Mina feels very off-balance, as he's acting on his previous connection with Elisabeta but Mina thinks of Vlad as a complete stranger. His repeated attempts to engage her in conversation (and later, an embrace) are rebuffed, and rightly so, because at this point, he's just a random guy to Mina. But she begins to realize that there's something more going on under the surface, and even though she's engaged to Jonathan and tells Vlad she's uninterested, she can't help but continue to see him. The opener with Vlad and Elisabeta sets up the audience to root for the couple even though when we next see Winona Ryder she's playing someone else's love interest. This is a common romance trope: that a couple is destined to be together, whether it's because they were lovers in a former life or because the universe has decreed that nothing will come between them. So even though we learn Jonathan and Mina are engaged, Coppola doesn't take long to remind us that Dracula has never forgotten his love, and that Mina bears a striking resemblance to her (the ink spilling on Mina's portrait to imitate her long, dark hair is a bit on the nose, but the film is nothing if not over the top). When Jonathan is confined to

Dracula's castle, seduced and then drained by the three female vampires (called Dracula's brides, though in this version we don't learn much about them at all), the metaphorical door is open for Prince Vlad to travel to London and insinuate himself into Mina's life. Of course, she doesn't know at this point that the vampire is also the one responsible for Lucy's affliction, which further complicates matters.

Something that struck me on rewatch is the fact that everyone is much more open in their relationships here than I remembered. As mentioned, Lucy's suitors don't seem to harbor any jealousy or ill will toward one another even as she vacillates between them, and when Jonathan is reunited with Mina, she's made aware of his infidelities with Dracula's brides, but she doesn't seem to be bothered (perhaps that's because she's already in love with Vlad at this point). Even at the end of the film, when Mina chooses to go with Dracula into the Transylvanian church, leaving Jonathan outside, there's no rancor on his part; in fact, he encourages Mina to go. We never get a resolution of Mina and Jonathan's story, because theirs isn't the central romance.

Beneath the trappings of gothic romance, with stolen kisses, dark secrets, and breathless embraces, there's a rather pure emotional core to the story. The love triangle between Vlad, Mina, and Jonathan doesn't offer much in the way of drama from a romantic perspective, partly because Jonathan never seems to be fully committed to anything. Many critics chalk that up to Keanu Reeves's acting style, but I think he's perfectly suited to playing a man who isn't yet ready for the task he's been given, and is uncomfortable in his own skin, a bit of a fish out of water not only in Transylvania, but even with Mina.[2] She's the one who initiates their physical contact and the one who is pushing for them to be married so they can consummate their vows. Her prim demeanor is betrayed when Lucy discovers Mina's hidden copy of *Arabian Nights*, with its sexual illustrations that clearly excite both young women. Though Vlad introduces himself to Mina first, as their relationship blossoms, she is very much the one who asserts that she wants to renounce the world around them and give in to the darkness of vampirism ("Take me away from all this death" is one of my favorite lines). When she asks to be transformed, Vlad agrees at first, then pulls away, saying, "I love you too much to condemn you." Mina knows what he is, knows he's the monster who killed Lucy, but wants to be with him anyway, saying, "Our love is stronger than death." That's the crux of it, right there. The two are bound together, their connection spans decades and violence and pain and longing, and he is comforted at the end by the fact that the two of them will find each other once more, in the next lifetime if not in this one. If that's not horror romance, I don't know what is.

While in my mind there's no beating *Bram Stoker's Dracula* for the sheer spectacle of it, there are a couple of gothic horror romances that I think deserve honorable mentions at least before I move to more contemporary-set films: *Sleepy Hollow* (1999) and *Crimson Peak* (2015). Both of these movies are visual feasts with gorgeous costuming and cinematography, and both marry the traditional elements of romance stories with darker horrific themes. The two films sit on either side of a rather fallow period for not only gothic stories but period films altogether. Whether it's because of an increasing reliance on computer-generated special effects rather than tangible artifacts that actors can interact with, or the audience's boredom with looking to the past, between 1999 and 2015, there weren't many films with an 1800s setting. But there have been a few entries in the period horror genre since *Crimson Peak*, including Robert Eggers's *The Witch* (2015) and *Nosferatu* (2024), Scott Cooper's *The Pale Blue Eye* (2022), and Guillermo del Toro's own *Frankenstein* (2025), so maybe del Toro was just slightly ahead of the curve.

Tim Burton's retelling of the Legend of Sleepy Hollow is not a true gothic tale; the story is very much American folk horror and is more of a grisly turn-of-the-century detective story, but when it was released in 1999, it seemed to echo the trappings of the period piece horror films that had been regularly released throughout the 1990s. And it certainly features a strong romantic element in addition to the sinister danger of Christopher Walken's bloodthirsty Hessian (the headless version is played by Ray Park, who's probably most well-known for his role as Darth Maul in the *Star Wars* prequel *Episode I—The Phantom Menace*). Johnny Depp, a frequent Burton collaborator, plays Ichabod Crane, a rather odd detective who relies on cutting-edge science to enhance his powers of deduction, much to the dismay of the police force in New York. Crane is sent to upstate New York to investigate a series of beheadings as a way to get him out of the magistrate's hair for a while, and he uncovers a conspiracy that extends to all the powerful families of the small town.

He also discovers a young woman named Katrina van Tassel, played by Christina Ricci. The two are immediately drawn to one another, and Crane enlists Katrina to help him peel back the layers of secrecy he finds when trying to investigate the murders in the town. A skeptic, Crane doesn't believe the townspeople when they tell him that the person responsible for the killings is actually the reincarnated spirit of the Headless Horseman, a Hessian mercenary whose taste for violence resulted in a rash of vicious killings during the Revolutionary War. He was eventually beheaded and buried near the town, and the residents of Sleepy Hollow are convinced that the Horseman has somehow found a way to come back to life and dispatch the founding fathers of the area as revenge. The detective, of course, disagrees, since there's no scientific explanation to be found, and he enlists a young man, Masbath (Marc Pickering), to apprentice with him as he tries to solve the case.

The romance here is fairly engaging, hitting many of the traditional romance tropes. Katrina and Ichabod couldn't be more different; Crane, a man of science and investigation, is a stark contrast to Ricci's van Tassel (a character Ricci herself happily proclaimed is a rather one-dimensional princess type without a lot of depth), who secretly is a practicing witch of the good magic variety.[3] Their meet-cute is wholesome, with Katrina accidentally grabbing Ichabod while blindfolded. And the relationship has plenty of ups and downs stemming from miscommunication and withholding of information (a pet peeve of mine but nevertheless a staple of the romance genre). Still, there's what feels like a real emotional connection, as Katrina feels as though she must save this man from his past trauma as well as the current danger of the Horseman.

As the mystery deepens, revealing more and more about the sinister nature of the origins of the town of Sleepy Hollow, so too does the relationship between Ichabod and Katrina grow stronger. Each reveal and clue discovered in the murder case is echoed in a revelation or emotional breakthrough between Katrina and Ichabod, which builds the love story in parallel with the suspense. This is a technique we often use when we're editing romantic suspense stories so that we can ensure the pacing feels right—too much suspense and not enough romance, or vice versa, throws off the reader altogether; they'll be unsatisfied with both the mystery and the emotional plot. Burton does a good job here of layering tension, both romantic and otherwise, to keep the audience engaged. Ultimately, the plots converge in a climax that both explains who's behind the murders and allows Katrina and Ichabod to profess their love for one another after a dark moment of distrust between the two of them.

Filmed in England both on soundstages and in a small village that was constructed for the film, *Sleepy Hollow* very intentionally harkens back to the Hammer films of the 1960s, with their artificial sets and over-the-top (for the time) horror. Everything is highly stylized, from the desaturation of the cinematography calling back to black-and-white films like Bava's *Black Sunday* (a touchstone for Burton during the making of this movie) to the twisted and macabre Tree of the Dead where the Horseman bursts out of the ground to claim his next victim. There are some marvelous set pieces here, and it's definitely one of Burton's most horror-forward films, with blood and gore painting the entire film in a way that I had honestly forgotten when I came back to rewatch it. In my mind, it was a much tamer, much more romantic film than the gruesome (and sometimes darkly funny) mystery that I found it to be more recently. It's a fun take on the supernatural period piece. But it's nowhere near as full-on gothic as Guillermo del Toro's gorgeous *Crimson Peak*.

Del Toro, an enthusiastic lover of the gothic in both literature and film, intended his 2015 movie to be an homage to the giants of the gothic genre, with clear references to the wonderful Hammer films as well as earlier Hollywood gothics like *Rebecca*, with its young protagonist thrust into a family estate mired in suspicion and a somewhat less happy marriage than she originally anticipated. *Crimson Peak* is firmly seated in the pantheon of true gothic tales: The story centers on a family full of dark secrets that come back to haunt them, and is positively dripping with dread, tension, and, of course, romance. The film opens with a young woman in the snow, blood on her hands, as she tells the audience that ghosts are real. It's a striking image, and it sets the tone for the rest of the movie. We see in flashback the woman's childhood and the death of her mother from cholera, and then we find out why this young woman believes in ghosts: She sees them. Her mother comes back with a cryptic warning: Beware of Crimson Peak.

Mia Wasikowska stars as Edith Cushing (a perfect name, harkening back to one of the Hammer greats, Peter Cushing), a young woman who aspires to be a writer—near the beginning of the film (now 1901), we see her getting feedback from an editor that her ghost story needs more romance. It's a rather fitting way to start, and del Toro clearly understands the origins of the gothic here. Edith, for her part, has no time for love, despite her friendship with Dr. Alan McMichael (Charlie Hunnam), who very clearly feels more strongly for her than she does in return. Alan's affections go unnoticed, and Edith seems perfectly content to move through the world as a loving daughter and hopeful writer, until Baronet Sir Thomas Sharpe (Tom Hiddleston) and his sister Lucille (Jessica Chastain) arrive in town. Thomas is soliciting investment funds from Edith's father, Carter, and his businessmen friends. Thomas and Lucille live at Allerdale Hall in England, an estate resting on top of red clay mines, but the mine is no longer functioning, and Thomas needs money for his machine to revitalize the mining industry. Edith meets Thomas and is instantly intrigued, much to her father's chagrin. He doesn't trust the Sharpes, even going so far as to hire an investigator. But love works in mysterious ways, and even though there are hints that Thomas and Lucille are not quite what they seem, Edith is enamored of Thomas. When her father is brutally murdered, she accepts Thomas's proposal and the two move back to the Sharpe family estate.

Allerdale Hall is a gloriously decrepit mansion, sinking into the red clay mine and dilapidated in so many ways. There's a giant hole in the roof, the elevator has a mind of its own, and the staircase is slightly crumbling. But Edith is determined to give her marriage to Thomas a fair chance, and even makes overtures to the standoffish Lucille, trying to win her over. There's a hint of Mrs. Danvers in Chastain's performance, an undertone of disdain and disapproval that she's unable to hide. Still, Edith thinks she's making progress as she settles into her new life, drinking Lucille's special tea to keep warm and trying to find a way to get Thomas to fulfill his marital duty (he's also a little standoffish, preoccupied with his machine and getting the mine up and running). All is well until Edith begins seeing ghosts again.

Del Toro does a fabulous job here of ramping up the feelings of unease and dread as Edith explores the estate and discovers more and more mysteries that she must solve. The spirits, as decayed and decrepit as the house they occupy, are wonderfully executed, all tattered rags and oozing menace (and a little melancholy). It's not long before we begin to suspect that the ghost might actually be trying to help Edith figure out what secrets the Sharpes are holding back. As Edith uncovers more layers to the mystery, her relationship with Thomas deepens as well, and they finally make love when they're snowed in away from the mansion. Unfortunately for Edith, their marital bliss is soon ended, as she finds out that there may have been previous Mrs. Sharpes that Thomas and Lucille have been hiding.

Meanwhile, the plucky Alan has been pursuing the investigator that Mr. Cushing had hired, trying to find out what secrets were shared with Edith's father before his untimely death. What he discovers is kept hidden from the audience at first, building up the tension as Alan decides he needs to make his way to Allerdale Hall to share his new information with Edith. For her part, Edith has continued her own investigation, helped by the ghosts who keep pointing her in the right direction. She finally discovers wax cylinders, and when she plays them on the gramophone, she (and the audience) find out that Thomas has most definitely been married before, and the last wax cylinder has an even more sinister warning: The previous wife, Enola Sciotti, thought she was being poisoned by the Sharpes once they took her money.

In and of itself, this sordid mystery would be more than enough to place *Crimson Peak* well within the gothic sphere: The secrets, the love story, the crumbling atmosphere are all hallmarks of the genre. But del Toro adds one more layer that catapults the film into the top echelon of gothic stories: incest. Yes, when Edith searches for Thomas to confront him about his past secrets, she finds something even more disturbing. She walks in on Lucille and Thomas, locked in an embrace, and Lucille reveals that she and Thomas have been romantically involved since they were young and confined to the attic. Their mother was a cruel woman who isolated the children from the outside world, and so they found comfort in each other. Edith is, of course, shocked and horrified, and is about to leave when Lucille pushes her over the balcony. Alan arrives to save Edith, but he's attacked by Lucille and Thomas, who pretends to kill Alan and hides him in the mine. Thomas has finally realized that he loves Edith, and when he tells Lucille they should all run away together, leaving Allerdale Hall and the past behind, she kills him, just as she had killed their parents. Edith escapes, rescues Alan, and they make their way to the surface; Edith is able to defend them both from Lucille's final attack. Lucille becomes a ghost, haunting Crimson Peak with the rest of the ghosts she created.

The plot seems outlandish and over the top when you write out all the points in a row, but that's the appeal of this story, and gothics in general. The melodrama, the heightened sense of place and of character: all are elements that enhance the atmosphere of the story and compel the reader or the viewer to deal with the emotional fallout of the secrets that have been weighing on the (often doomed) participants. Del Toro once again does a phenomenal job of creating a world that viewers can sink into, much like Allerdale Hall is sinking into the crimson clay. There's a texture in his films that is certainly enriched by his love of practical effects, and Tom Sanders's stunning set design and Kate Hawley's gorgeous costuming further expand on the world these characters inhabit (for a wonderful exploration of the costumes in the film, read Cat Dippell's *Victorian Visual Culture* piece[4]). In addition to creating some truly suspenseful and horrific moments, del Toro understands that the heart of the gothic is the love story, and even though love is not always enough to save the day or end in an HEA, the romance must be emotionally resonant, or else the rest of the story kind of falls apart. As someone who works primarily in a romantic genre that is layered with other genre elements (namely horror), I talk a lot with authors about balancing these elements. Luckily, *Crimson Peak* pulls off this interplay incredibly well.

Sadly, after del Toro's beautiful film, there isn't much else in the way of gothic films for a while (a couple of thrillers, a couple of vampire stories, but nothing that would hit the heights of the '90s revival). Whether because of audience fatigue, the fact that period pieces were more expensive to produce, or the dramatic shifts in the entire filmmaking landscape over the last five or ten years, there has been a dearth of grandiose tales of murder, romance, and paranormal frights. I'm hopeful there will be another resurgence (Robert Eggers's *Nosferatu* and del Toro's *Frankenstein* are leading the charge), but for now, we'll leave the gothic behind for something a little lighter.

RETURN TO THE GOTHIC

Interview with the Vampire (1994, dir. Neil Jordan)

TOP TROPES: Toxic Love: Human Louis is pulled into a centuries-long, extremely volatile relationship with the petty but sensual Lestat, whose vampire embrace leads to nothing but drama, misery, and extremely awful behavior.

DARK MOMENT: Claudia, the vampires' surrogate daughter, convinces Louis to murder Lestat so they can break free of his grasp.

HEA? No. Louis is finally able to rid himself of Lestat, who continues to search for a new human to join him in undeath.

Sleepy Hollow (1999, dir. Tim Burton)

TOP TROPES: Fish out of Water: Detective Ichabod Crane arrives in the village of Sleepy Hollow to solve a murder but instead uncovers a sinister conspiracy with the help of the beautiful and mysterious Katrina Van Tassel.

DARK MOMENT: Ichabod pushes Katrina away because he thinks she's using black magic to carry out the murders in Sleepy Hollow, and Katrina is thrown into danger.

HEA? Yes. Once Ichabod realizes Katrina is a good witch, he defeats the evil woman behind the mayhem in Sleepy Hollow and the two reunite.

Crimson Peak (2015, dir. Guillermo del Toro)

TOP TROPES: Marriage of Convenience: Edith falls head over heels for Thomas and agrees to marry him and move to the ominous Allerdale Hall. Little does she know that Thomas has married her for money, not because he loves her, and his dark past will catch up with them when they arrive at his crumbling mansion.

DARK MOMENT: Edith finally uncovers the truth about Thomas's incestuous relationship with his murderous sister, Lucille, and must fight for her life.

HEA? Yes, but not for Thomas and Edith; luckily, the lovesick Alan comes to Allerdale to rescue Edith from the clutches of Lucille and Thomas, and they leave for America together.

CHAPTER TEN

GRUMPY/SUNSHINE

Horror Meets Rom-Com

As you can tell from the title of this book, I love movies that throw different genres together and create fresh and interesting combinations. A great many of the films I've mentioned so far feature the kind of serious, melodramatic love stories that make up a large portion of the romance genre. But there's another kind of romance that I've mostly ignored until now: the rom-com. Romantic comedy is a subgenre of romance that mixes sweet (or raunchy) love stories with comedic hijinks of a cute or boundary-pushing nature, depending on the story. From the vaudevillian antics of Abbott and Costello meeting various Universal monsters to my favorite zombie movie, *Shaun of the Dead*, adding romantic elements to horror comedy has been popular in various forms for a long time.

The 1950s begins a major demographic shift in the way horror films are produced and marketed. Before the 1950s, cinema was often separated into children's movies and adult movies. Much like the huge shift in publishing when the young adult category took off, films became segmented further, with movies like *The Blob* grabbing the attention of teen audiences.

1958's *The Blob* is a wonderfully weird movie that married the sci-fi focus of the era with the tropes of popular teenage delinquent movies of the time, where teens (or at least adult actors playing teens) were the main characters and were pitted against the police, their parents, and the establishment. The teens in *The Blob* are definitely not teenagers; Steve McQueen stars in his first big role, and he's twenty-seven (and kinda looks it). Still, his charm and take-charge attitude help elevate this movie from a silly B movie to a slightly less silly B movie. The plot is very simple: The main characters, Steve and Jane (Aneta Corsaut), are enjoying some alone time up at the local lookout spot. He's been pursuing Jane for a while, as he knows she's the one for him, and McQueen pours on the charm. He sounds so sincere and even wounded when Jane asks him whether she's the only one he's ever tried to kiss that we almost believe him. A meteor falls just outside of town and it contains an amorphous, murderous substance, which catches the attention of an old man who lives up in the hills. That substance begins to take over the town, one person at a time, and the teens are the first to warn everyone. Naturally the police don't believe them, since they've clearly gone to the lookout spot to make out. But the romance is forgotten pretty quickly as everyone grapples with this alien goo.

The Blob is a simple special effect, but it looks rather impressive. Using trick photography and stop-motion, filmmaker Irwin S. Yeaworth Jr. convinces audiences that this jello-like substance is capable of grabbing onto an unsuspecting victim and absorbing them into its oozy shape, a shape that grows with each new body. There are some rather gruesome scenes here, when the Blob first attacks the old man, then attacks the doctor and nurse in town after Steve and Jane try to help the old man. It's not as horrific as the 1988 sequel, which features some of the most disgusting special effects of the 1980s as far as I'm concerned, but it's still pretty grim for 1958.

One of the best things about this version of *The Blob* is that the filmmakers allow for room in the story to take a break from the killer Blob. Spending time with the characters, especially Steve and Jane, shows the audience the emotional journey the two are taking together as they realize that this alien they've discovered poses a real threat. The rising stakes heighten the emotions the characters feel; whereas Jane was hesitant and skeptical about Steve's feelings toward her at the beginning of the film, the more time they spend together, the more she relies on him and starts to fall for him as they play house in a way, taking care of a dog together and then Jane's younger brother. By spending extra time focusing on Steve and Jane, the story feels much more organic, and the couple share some lovely moments that make the shift toward the more mundane aspects of the plot make sense.

The Blob subverts some typical teen drama tropes as well, like that of the police versus the teenagers, which was a tremendously popular theme in many of the teen films of the period. Here, though, the dynamic is a little different, as one of the police officers seems to really want to make friends with the teens instead; he lets them off with a warning after they drag race, and he is the only one who believes Steve and his friends when they are trying to warn everyone about the Blob. The teens in the film are trustworthy, and the authority figures are incompetent. This portrayal allows the teens in the audience to relate more closely to the protagonists, and that's one of the reasons these teen movies started to become so successful. Filmmakers began to recognize that the audience would want to see versions of themselves onscreen, with their own troubles and relationships, and that featuring teen protagonists would tap into a market that felt new.

As young people came of age, they flocked to movies made more explicitly for them, featuring young and beautiful actors, a little bit of romance, and jump scares made to get your date to cuddle up. These films feature younger protagonists, often at odds with their parents, who get caught up in sinister plots or are stalked by mysterious creatures. Unlike many trends that would come and go quickly, teen horror has pretty much been around since these early days, with recent films like *M3GAN*, *Five Nights at Freddy's*, and *Lisa Frankenstein* all nodding to these original young adult movies.

Independent filmmakers like William Castle also get their start at the end of the 1950s, ushering in a looser and slightly edgier style of moviemaking. Castle opened the door for the king of B movies, Roger Corman, as well as the first Hammer horror films that would go on to be hugely popular (and equally titillating) in the 1960s. Some of the tropes and themes that dominated these B movies appear in earlier films, like 1953's *House of Wax*. But the lurid, often revenge-soaked tales of men driven mad by women who wronged them or society that shunned them really take off at the end of the 1950s and early 1960s.

William Castle made some films prior to becoming known for his over-the-top antics, but in 1959 he released two films (starring the amazing Vincent Price) that cemented him as a horror movie icon: *The Tingler* and *House on Haunted Hill*. While neither of these films is an outright horror romance, I think both are hugely influential to the genre as a whole and, maybe even more importantly, the marketing of these films created a massive shift in the way audiences went to the cinema. Castle wanted going to the movies to be a fully immersive experience, and he partnered with theaters to create events. While the stories about Castle have likely become exaggerated into legends over time, he did rig certain seats at the cinema with vibrating motors for early screenings of *The Tingler*. When the monster got loose, certain seats would vibrate, making the audience member sitting there feel as though the monster had leapt off the screen and into the crowd.

Why the gimmick? The biggest factor was certainly the advent of television. Between 1948 and 1955, television ownership in the United States grew from 1 percent to 75 percent, so many people who had relied on the cinema for their entertainment viewing found that they were able to watch programming from the comfort of their own homes.[1] To compete with the convenience, movie studios came up with a variety of ideas to entice folks back to the theater, ranging from incredibly silly things like Smell-O-Vision to impressive technical feats like CinemaScope and Technicolor. Since some of these technologies were incredibly expensive, movies were costing more money to make, and studios were taking fewer risks (the same thing has happened in publishing at various times, as paper and freight increased in cost or fewer retailers were buying books). The lack of support for smaller films opened the door for indie producers who made movies cheaply, often with very common tropes and hooks that audiences could reliably enjoy.

The Tingler doesn't quite hold up, particularly when watching at home by yourself instead of in a theater. The screen fades to black and the audience is encouraged to scream so that they won't be killed by the title creature (if you can't release your fear through screaming, the monster will frighten you to death, the movie posits), and my empty living room is a poor substitute for a packed theater full of screaming teens, some of whom might be "shocked" by vibrating seats. But I think the bulk of the film is still quite compelling.

Vincent Price is delightful as always, playing Warren Chapin, a doctor and medical examiner. Though Price starred in a few horror or horror-adjacent projects prior to 1959, including *The Fly* and *House of Wax*, with *The Tingler* and *The House on Haunted Hill* he begins to cement his reputation as king of the macabre. He would go on to play creepy characters in dozens of horror films, and he used his distinctively ghoulish voice to great effect narrating books and voicing characters like Ratigan in Disney's *The Great Mouse Detective*. In *The Tingler*, he isn't really the villain, though he's definitely a morally gray kind of guy. He's obsessed with his research into the human reaction to fear, so much so that his wife

Isabel (Patricia Cutts) has decided their marriage is essentially over; she goes drinking and dancing with various men and comes home only to argue with Warren. The romance in the film falls to Warren's assistant, David (Darryl Hickman), and Isabel's sister Lucy (Pamela Lincoln). Their love story is a contrast to Warren and Isabel's loveless marriage, and I think serves as a shorthand to the audience; Warren might be less likely to play with dark forces if he had a woman like Lucy around, as she stops David from going too far down the rabbit hole of fear and manipulation that comes from trying to capture the Tingler.

While there have always been films that look honestly at romantic relationships, and explore both healthy and toxic marriages and partnerships, so-called genre films have been much less likely to do so. Warren's marriage to Isabel is full of lies, deceit, and backstabbing. Warren spends all his time working and ignoring his wife, and in turn she tries to find any opportunity to humiliate him and throw her wedding vows in his face, even engaging in a full-on make-out session with another man on their front lawn.

Though Lucy and David's relationship is relatively loving and healthy by contrast, the other romantic relationship we see in the film is even more dysfunctional than Warren's. Oliver Higgins (Philip Coolidge) meets Warren at the beginning of the movie, when Ollie comes to identify a body at the morgue. The scene is really more about exposition, so we can ignore the oddness of a man coming to identify a body ending up with inviting the medical examiner out for a drink. But it introduces Oliver and his wife, a deaf and mute woman named Martha (Judith Evelyn). Since Martha can't scream, when she sees blood and becomes afraid, there's no way for her to release her fear, and the Tingler inside her (we all have one, apparently) causes her to lose consciousness. Warren finds this fascinating and wants to test this woman, to see whether her lack of vocal cords means she is doomed to be scared to death.

Between Warren surreptitiously injecting Martha with LSD to induce fear, and Ollie doing whatever he can to rid himself of his wife, whose medical issues are too much for him to handle, Martha really gets treated horribly. Her fear-induced hallucinations, though, are a highlight of the film. Jump scares, and a splash of color in an otherwise black-and-white movie, must have added an extra layer of novelty and fun when audiences saw this in 1959. Until, of course, they realized that these frights are what send Martha to her death.

The '60s era is full of horror films that try all kinds of new tactics to pull in viewers, whether it's focusing on gimmicks, like William Castle; re-embracing the gothic, like Corman and Hammer; or tapping into social anxieties in big movies like *Rosemary's Baby*. Another kind of horror film arrives at the end of the '60s and early '70s: the horror comedy. Of course, Universal was making Abbott and Costello Meet the Monsters films back in the '30s and '40s, but there wasn't much in the way of deliberately silly horror films through the 1950s and most of the '60s (though a ton of films were unintentionally silly for sure, like *Tarantula* or *The Navy vs. The Night Monsters*). Corman and American International released a few films that skewed comedic, such as 1959's *A Bucket of Blood* and 1960's *Little Shop of Horrors*, but for the most part the horror movies that were coming out were earnest and committed to their premises, not winking at the camera or making fun of their subject matter. But then we start to see a shift toward slightly stranger and funnier stories, and one of the best known of these early horror/comedy mashups just so happens to all fit into the horror romance genre.

Robert Fuest's *The Abominable Dr. Phibes* (1971) isn't a romance, technically, but it *is* a love story, and it is so weird that I adore it (weird is my favorite kind of story). Vincent Price is perfect as Phibes, playing a man who plans revenge against the surgeons responsible for his wife Victoria's death on the operating table. His unending love for Victoria makes him sympathetic in some ways, and it's not uncommon for audiences to root for the lovesick Phibes even when he's downright evil. That probably has a lot to do with Price's incredible charisma, honestly; he's truly magnetic onscreen, and whether he was playing good or evil, audiences loved him.

Phibes took time to find its audience but is now a cult classic. It's true that this film won't win any cinematography awards; it was mostly shot on the 1920s-era sets at Elstree Studios in England, and you can tell, as everything looks just slightly better than a high school play that's been recorded by the eleventh-grade A/V club. And that's too bad because the costumes and the sets are delightful, and with a more skilled director I think the film would be even more highly regarded. Vincent Price does another fantastic job of embodying a strange, melancholy man who is so overcome with grief over the death of his wife that he vows to murder every doctor who took part in the operation that ended with her death. This is where I confess that the microtrope of weirdos avenging their dead loves is something that I just love, from *The Crow* to *Titus* to *The Northman* (which, of course, is really *Hamlet* in disguise). Price inserts such genuine anguish into his role, even while hampered by lavish costumes and bizarre props like the speaking device he must use, since his vocal cords were damaged in a car crash. Along with his silent and stylish assistant Vulnavia (Virginia North), Phibes dispatches the physicians in increasingly wild ways, from emptying bats into a bedroom to "shred a man to death," as the detectives put it, to a frog mask that grows tighter and tighter, crushing the man's head like a trap reminiscent of *Saw*, to blasting a man with a snow machine and turning him into a frozen corpse. It's silly but it's entertaining, and the parallel plot that develops between the detective investigating the murders and Dr. Vesalius, the head of the surgery department and Phibes's ultimate nemesis (Joseph Cotten) leaves the audience wondering whether Phibes will get away with it or whether the police will close in with help from Vesalius.

But if you strip away all the costumes and bizarre elements (like the clockwork band clearly played by human actors in masks), there is a poignant and tragic love story here. Victoria was the love of Phibes's life, and he can't go on without her. He spends much of the movie talking to her as if she's still alive, and he devotes his entire existence to avenging her. You can feel his heartbreak and rage, and like all grand, romantic tragedies, the audience can definitely relate to the desire to destroy the ones responsible for a loved one's death, if not the acts themselves. Though Phibes's wife is only ever seen as a portrait until the very end of the film, her presence is palpable from the moment she's revealed to the viewers. There aren't any standard plot beats like a meet-cute or love at first sight, but Phibes and Victoria do get an HEA of sorts, as Phibes drains his own blood and replaces it with embalming fluid so he can finally rest alongside his wife's corpse, which he stole from the cemetery. If that's not true love, I don't know what is.

The Love Witch was released in 2016, but it wouldn't be too out of place in the early 1970s. The film, written, produced, and directed by Anna Biller, borrows its aesthetic from the bright, kitschy era, and at first glance its sexual politics and gender biases as well. There has been much debate over whether this strange film qualifies as horror, but I think there's no question that it's a character study of a rather amoral woman who's murdered at least a few men in her pursuit of true love by any means necessary, tackling both horror and romance through a comedic lens. And though the story is told in bright pinks, florals, and psychedelic rainbows, a darkness permeates the film. It's a movie worth watching, even if you don't end up loving it.

Samantha Robinson plays the titular witch, a beautiful young woman named Elaine who tells us in voiceover that her husband left her, as we see the flashback of his dying body after drinking some sort of substance. From the start, the audience is aware that what Elaine believes and tells herself (and us) is quite disconnected from the reality of her situation. Having left her husband behind, Elaine is on a quest to find true love and is going to live in an apartment owned by Barbara (Jennifer Ingrum), a friend who happens to be a witch. A witch from the same coven as Elaine, run by Gahan (Jared Sanford), who has essentially brainwashed his predominantly female cult into believing that the only way they can find love and be happy is to give themselves completely to men and fulfill their every need while suppressing their own desires. Elaine parrots this philosophy to her new friend Trish (Laura Waddell), who seems a bit appalled at the throwback attitude; Trish is married to Richard (Robert Seeley), who is perfectly happy loving her for her true self (she says). Elaine reiterates that men are incredibly fragile creatures who need constant reassurance and nurturing, and that her mission is to provide everything for her future mate. All of this is told in a very matter-of-fact, completely unwinking way; *The Love Witch* presents the story very straight, without the snark or insincerity that would undercut the actors as they spout their dialogue. I kept waiting for the facade to fall away, and the curtain to pull back revealing the real premise of the film, but the veneer never cracks.

The whole film is about love and romance, though Elaine's idea of what they are is pretty outside the norm, and that's where the horror comes in. This might not be a gory or monster-filled story, but that doesn't mean it isn't unsettling or suspenseful, or just plain strange. Biller has stated that she thinks women will view the film very differently from men, and that men will be the ones to see it as horrific since Elaine is both luring men in and causing their deaths.[2] Women, on other hand, may tend to focus a little more on the emotional journey Elaine is taking, and can perhaps relate somewhat to her quest for romance. That is a rather essentialist take, and not every man or woman (not to mention nonbinary folks) will have the same reading of the movie, regardless of the director's intent. For me, Biller doesn't do enough to subvert the tropes that she sets up; I was never quite sure whether the filmmaker was sending up this idea of melodramatic period films or mythologizing that era. For my taste, there's a little too much focus on Samantha Robinson's excellent figure and not quite enough on deconstructing the incredibly damaged persona of Elaine. But as I said, the film is still well worth checking out as an alternative to some of the more straightforward horror rom-coms in this chapter.

As the '70s give way to the '80s, and the slasher subgenre takes over, many of those films—particularly later entries in the franchises—become a little silly, if not outright intentionally humorous. Freddy Krueger is most menacing in the first and second *A Nightmare on Elm Street* movies, but by the time we get to the fourth, he's a full-on comedian, serving one-liners and whimsical sight gags along with gruesome kills. The films become much less about horror and much more about everyone's favorite villains and how gross or over the top their murdering can be. While there was obviously an appetite for these things, critics tired of the derivative cavalcade of teen deaths more quickly than audiences did. Film studios did what film studios always do: try to ride the wave of slashers as long as possible. It wasn't until 1996's *Scream* that Wes Craven (the original creator of Krueger) returned to his scarier roots. Though elements of humor cut the tension in the film, and meta-commentaries on the ridiculous plot holes that were so often overlooked in earlier films in the genre, the first *Scream* is a much nastier and more vicious movie than the slashers that directly preceded it. There's not much in the way of romance, and the tried-and-true slasher tropes, like the Final Girl losing her virginity and still surviving, are subverted. The romance between the central characters turns out to be much more sinister than we expect at the beginning of the film. The prologue in particular, with Drew Barrymore slowly realizing the person she's talking to is scarier (and much closer) than she first thought, is a fantastically suspenseful sequence, and delivers a shock that audiences were certainly not expecting, akin to the scene with Janet Leigh in *Psycho*. Craven's *Scream* gives way to many more "serious" horror films along with its multiple sequels, and at the same time sets the stage for parodies like *Scary Movie* (for better or worse).

In many horror rom-coms, the scares take a backseat to the other tropes. The horror is more about the trappings and setting surrounding the story; there's no real attempt to disturb or frighten the viewer. This treatment of the genre often makes for love stories with a little less oomph as well, as the heightened emotions of the movie are either tamped down or played for laughs, which mellows the emotions and as such, dilutes not only the fear but also the romance. This is, in my opinion, a failing of much of the current, cynical societal pressure to avoid being "cringe." Sincerity is frowned upon, and audiences are frequently uncomfortable with even the slightest hint of real feelings in the story they're watching, so filmmakers need to add a joke, or a wink to the camera, or some other mechanism to allow the audience to distance themselves from the potential pitfalls of feeling too much.

Horror rom-coms like Edgar Wright's *Shaun of the Dead* (2004) subvert both romance and horror tropes—for some reason zombies seem to be a great theme for these types of films. The real romance in *Shaun of the Dead* is, of course, between Shaun (Simon Pegg) and Ed (Nick Frost), as is the case with all the Cornetto trilogy films, which are much more focused on the relationships between male friends than on the women who love them. Shaun is stuck in a dead-end job, not able to move forward and do anything good with his life. His roommate Pete (Peter Serafinowicz) is annoyed that Shaun is stuck in the past and spending too much time with Ed, Shaun's best friend from elementary school, who's even worse off than Shaun. At least Shaun has a girlfriend.

Liz (Kate Ashfield) is just as frustrated with her boyfriend as his roommate is. Shaun is forgetful, emotionally stunted, and shuffling through life like a . . . zombie. After Shaun makes one too many mistakes, Liz tells him she can't see him anymore. Shaun is devastated and Ed takes him out to their favorite pub, the Winchester, to drink away his heartbreak. And that's when things start to go south. Shaun and Ed wake up the next morning to find that, overnight, London seems to have become home to a zombie apocalypse. Shaun and Ed make a plan: go pick up his mum (whose husband has been bitten), drive to Liz's apartment and rescue her, and then they can all make their way to the Winchester to wait for this whole thing to blow over. Of course, nothing is that simple.

Shaun's mum, Barbara (played by Penelope Wilton and so named to reference the original zombie film, *Night of the Living Dead*) is married to Philip (Bill Nighy), her second husband, who was a bit hard on Shaun while he was growing up, at least from Shaun's perspective. Shaun, in turn, has never respected Philip as a father figure, and is conflicted about bringing Philip along after Shaun discovers he's been bitten fending off a zombie. That's the first hiccup in their plan. But Barbara won't leave without her spouse, and Shaun begrudgingly takes Philip along as the four set off for Liz's apartment. The conversation between Shaun and Philip as they drive along becomes an incredibly heartfelt goodbye as Philip realizes that the bite he's suffered is much worse than everyone originally thought. Nighy does a fantastic job of portraying a terribly British stiff-upper-lip type who finally shows some emotion and wants to end his relationship with his stepson on a loving note, and Simon Pegg's slow realization that he's losing a dad is played straight, a tone shift that works because of Pegg and Nighy doing some really fantastic character work.

Most of the relationships in this movie feel beautifully realistic. Liz and her friends David (Dylan Moran) and Dianne (Lucy Davis) genuinely care for one another even through their sniping and arguing, and the poignant moment when Liz finds out that David harbors more than just friendly feelings for her is emotional without being cloying (and gives his eventual demise an additional layer of poignancy, because he's never able to resolve his relationship with Liz or with Dianne). When Shaun finally arrives at Liz's apartment to save her, she won't leave without her two roommates, and they all team up to execute Shaun and Ed's plan of getting to the pub, even in the face of rapidly deteriorating circumstances. Shaun and Ed's relationship feels equally well realized, as does the tension between Ed and Pete, who loathes Ed's lack of drive and ambition. Shaun feels stuck in the middle and has some wonderful moments of genuine reflection amid the chaos of a zombie apocalypse.

The heart of the story, as mentioned, is Shaun and Ed. They realize they both need to come to terms with the fact that they're not as young and carefree as they once were, and Ed's final speech, telling Shaun to move on without him, is one of many great goodbyes in the movie. With Ed's blessing, Shaun can finally forge ahead with his romantic relationship with Liz, and though the film ends with Liz and Shaun happily living together, the real end of the movie is Shaun going out to the garden to hang out with his one true love, Ed, who's turned into a zombie but still wants to play video games with his best friend.

Warm Bodies (2013), directed by Jonathan Levine, takes the *Twilight* young adult setting and swaps out the vampires for zombies, which feels both more accessible and slightly less melodramatic; as in *Shaun of the Dead*, the zombies here are slow, meandering, and generally not posing huge threats at first. I think you could make a case for *Warm Bodies* to fit into the so-called cozy horror category (though the subgenre is definitely a source of debate within the publishing sphere). People die, yes, but the story is tightly focused on a small group of people, and the message is that they must learn to find comfort and love in order to save each other. They conveniently ignore some of the consequences that would naturally come from a situation where your new love interest murdered your boyfriend.

Nicholas Hoult plays the lead zombie, a young man who doesn't remember his name but thinks it started with R. We get a voiceover explaining that the world has been zombified for eight years, and R and many of his fellow zombies live at the airport, while the humans have built an enormous wall around what's left of their major city. While voiceovers can sometimes feel a bit overwrought, in this case it goes a long way toward humanizing R, since he can only grunt and speak a few words. It would be much more difficult to see him as a love interest without his inner monologue. Julie (Teresa Palmer), a human whose father is the leader of the pseudo military force in the city, is tasked to go on a supply run with her friends and her boyfriend, Perry (Dave Franco)—they're in a bit of a rough patch, which will soon get much rougher.

The two star-crossed lovers (R and Julie) meet for the first time when R's horde of zombies runs into Julie's recon mission, and for R, it's love at first sight. (In case you hadn't noticed, *Warm Bodies* is very much inspired by Romeo and Juliet, with the two "houses" of zombies and humans standing in for the Capulets and Montagues.) R's attraction to Julie is amplified when he kills Perry and eats his brain, absorbing Perry's happy memories of Julie. He saves her from the rest of the zombies and takes her back to his home, a grounded airplane filled with the detritus of life that he's collected, sentimental trinkets and vinyl records that start to convince Julie that R might still be clinging to his humanity. Hoult is great here, and you can really sense the emotions that are trapped in his corpse-like body, even though he can't express them properly, at least not at first.

As time goes by, Julie begins to think that R isn't like other zombies she's encountered, and she's right. R's heart has started beating. He's starting to feel things, and he's sparked a change not only in himself but in his zombie friends as well. Love is changing the zombies, curing them and transforming them into living beings again. They realize they need to band together with the humans to destroy the Boneys, zombies who have nothing left and have given up, becoming mindless monsters who just want to eat everything, including the corpses who have just begun to change.

The other layer to this film is that Julie's father, played by John Malkovich, is a traumatized, angry man, who's lost everything (his wife was bitten and turned into a zombie) and doesn't think there's any chance of things getting better for the humans or the zombies. He's rigid in his thinking, and he tries to convince Julie that there's no path forward that would include the zombies; there's no hope for them. Julie, on the other hand, is portrayed as an optimist, and she still strongly believes, or at least hopes, that one day they'll be able to find a cure for the zombies and everything can return to some sense of normalcy. *Warm Bodies* uses the setting and trappings of the horror genre, but ultimately is a proper romance, with an HEA not only for R and Julie, but also for the world they live in, as people begin to teach and care for the zombies that are reviving themselves.

Ruben Fleischer's *Zombieland* (2009) is another film that combines horror, comedy, and romance. Meet-cutes combine with a zombie apocalypse, as well as the found-family trope common in many contemporary romance novels, adding depth and emotional resonance to the film. At its heart, this leans more into the comedy than the horror side of things, and the zombies are played more for laughs than for scares. But it certainly follows many rom-com beats to an HEA of some sort for Columbus (Jesse Eisenberg) and Wichita (Emma Stone). The film takes place a few months after a virus causes much of the population to turn into zombies, and people stop using each other's names so they don't get too attached to each other when inevitably one is bitten and turns into a zombie. Columbus meets up with Woody Harrelson's Tallahassee, and together they embark on a road trip back to Ohio to find Columbus's parents. Along the way they meet Wichita and her "sister" Little Rock, played by Abigail Breslin. The two young women con Columbus and Tallahassee out of their vehicle and their weapons, leaving them behind. It's a great enemies (or at least rivals) to lovers setup, where the main characters seem to have a bit of a spark when they first get together, but circumstances and personalities clash too much to be able to act on that spark. Or, in this case, the first inkling of feelings between Wichita and Columbus is a con, and Wichita is absolutely playing Columbus to get what she wants and survive.

The four meet up again, and once more, the rivalry between Columbus and Wichita prevents them from pursuing a relationship, but they're forced to work together and slowly open up to one another. The group begins to form that found-family dynamic mentioned earlier; with a zombie apocalypse taking place around them, they realize they need to come together to survive and might as well try enjoying each other's company. The stakes are raised again, and eventually, Wichita and Little Rock leave Columbus and Tallahassee behind to continue their quest to find Pacific Playland, a supposed zombie-free Eden. Columbus, of course, is heartbroken. He's the puppy dog in this relationship, following Wichita and hoping she'll eventually let her emotional guard down enough to invite him into her life as more than just a travelling companion. As the dark moment plays out, with the two young women trapped in the amusement park as zombies swarm around them, the big declaration of love comes when Tallahassee and Columbus burst in, coming to the rescue. It's not a flowery speech that finally thaws Wichita's heart; it's the fact that Columbus makes the effort to chase after her one last time. The film ends with the two of them embarking on the next stage of their journey with the rest of their family unit, happy for now at least.

There is one last horror romantic comedy I revisited for this book, and it straddles the line between sincere and cynical, veering a little more into the earnest side of things, which is why I enjoyed it quite a lot: 2024's *Lisa Frankenstein*. Directed by Zelda Williams and based on a screenplay by Diablo Cody (of *Jennifer's Body* fame), this is a retro modern retelling of the Frankenstein story set in the 1980s and featuring a gender-swapped Dr. Frankenstein creator in Kathryn Newton's Lisa Swallows.

Lisa is a senior in high school whose life was upended when her mother was brutally killed by an axe murderer who invaded their home. Traumatized by the incident, Lisa is quiet and closed off, despite the attempts by her new stepsister Taffy to draw her out and get her to socialize with other kids at school. Taffy (Liza Soberano) is the quintessential extrovert, cheerleading her way through life with her other popular friends. Lisa, on the other hand, is content to spend time by herself in the abandoned Bachelor's Grove Cemetery, reading and occasionally talking to a headstone with the bust of a young man named Frankenstein. After a freak thunderstorm awakens the Creature (played almost totally silently by Cole Sprouse) from the dead, he seeks out Lisa because he knows she was the one who'd been spending time with him, and he's grown fond of her. Not only does Lisa have to worry about hiding her newfound undead friend from her family, but she also needs to avoid being committed to a mental institution by her stepmother, Janet (who's convinced Lisa is acting out for attention), and she needs to figure out how to get her crush Michael (Henry Eikenberry) to notice her. It's a lot.

Kathryn Newton does a lot of the heavy lifting here: She's wonderfully expressive, often adding somewhat whimsical grand gestures to her physical performance, which goes a long way toward making the audience fall in love with her quirky character. She's clearly struggling not only to live with the grief of losing her mother but also with the subsequent upheaval in her life. Moving to a new school in senior year, dealing with a rather toxic stepmother, and ending up with an instant sibling who's prettier, more popular, and generally very sweet bring up conflicting emotions for Lisa. She throws herself into trying to figure out her love life, and the Creature is there to lend her a sympathetic ear. Only one, because his other ear is missing.

This is an undead creature to friends-to-lovers story, and Lisa seems oblivious to the Creature's growing feelings for her as she opens up to him and talks through her anxieties and attempts to get Michael to like her. The Creature is deep in the friend zone, at first helping Lisa by listening to her problems, but then coming to her rescue when Janet (Carla Gugino) confronts Lisa and tells her she's being shipped to the hospital for her emotional problems. The Creature kills Janet, and all he asks for in return is that Lisa sews on one of Janet's ears so he can hear properly (the mechanism for reanimating the Creature's body parts is an abandoned tanning bed in the backyard that electrocutes the person inside rather conveniently). Once the Creature's hearing is restored, and Lisa realizes how freeing it is to get rid of the problematic people in her life, she and the Creature plot to replace the rest of the body parts he is missing by killing other folks who have wronged Lisa and taking what they need.

Lisa's newfound confidence and subsequent transformation into a slightly goth, much cuter weirdo gets people noticing her at school, but she still isn't able to attract the attention of the artsy Michael. Every time she thinks she's making progress, her flirting is thwarted by Michael's very goth friend or by her stepsister Taffy. Still, she's convinced that Michael is the one for her, ignoring the very available (and getting less dead by the minute) Creature who is hanging on her every word. She casually opens herself to the Creature during their conversations, talking about her grief over her mother and how she isn't afraid of dying, as long as she doesn't die a virgin. As tensions rise when the police start looking for clues about the disappearance of Janet (as well as Doug [Bryce Romero], Lisa's lecherous lab partner whose hand was stolen by the Creature), Lisa realizes she doesn't have much time, and decides she needs to offer herself to Michael so she can lose her virginity in case she's caught by the cops. It seems like a good plan until Lisa walks into Michael's house and finds him in bed with Taffy.

Lisa is shocked and hurt, and once again the Creature channels her rage into violence. He cuts off Michael's penis, killing him, but Lisa restrains him from killing her sister. The Creature leaves the girls behind, and Lisa chases after him once she makes sure Taffy is safe and okay (well, okay as you can be after seeing your lover axe murdered while you were in bed together, I guess). Lisa gives a heartfelt speech to Taffy, telling her she loves her before going to find the Creature. Once she meets him in the cemetery, she understands why he did what he did: He's in love with her. He needed the penis to fulfill her wish of not dying a virgin, and also he was defending her honor. Lisa finally has the quintessential '80s teen movie revelation that your true love was right next to you this whole time, and she and the Creature go back to her bedroom for some suturing and sex. It's incredibly silly and also heartfelt. Newton does a great job acting against Sprouse, making the audience believe that she can interpret his grunts as full dialogue, and really selling their connection. Sprouse, for his part, gets more human and more sympathetic as the story goes on, much like Nicolas Hoult's R in *Warm Bodies*. The love of a woman was what they needed to come back to the world of the living. Well, in *Lisa Frankenstein* he also needed to be electrocuted, but the point still stands.

Lisa knows the law is closing in, and now that she's fulfilled her fondest wish, she's ready to move on from the material world, secure in the knowledge that her love for the Creature will survive beyond death. She enters the cursed tanning bed, tells the Creature to turn it up to Max Bronze, and dies, neatly removing herself from any responsibility for the deaths around her. For his part, the Creature seems sad, but Lisa's final note to him gives him a bit of hope. In an epilogue, Taffy and her stepdad visit Lisa's grave, and after placing flowers there, Taffy notices the gravestone reads "Beloved Wife," and there are scorch marks, as if the headstone has been hit by lightning. The film then jumps to the Creature reading on a park bench by the lake, and as the camera pans around, we see Lisa, bandaged and burned, lying with her head in his lap, having found her true love and coming back transformed into a Creature herself.

As I said, it's a bit of a silly movie, but like the most successful horror rom-coms in this chapter, the earnestness pushes *Lisa Frankenstein* into proper romance territory. There's a real chemistry between Lisa and the Creature, and the underlying pathos of their lives before they met each other suffuses the film with enough emotion that as ludicrous as the premise is, we buy into their relationship. These are two damaged people just looking for love and compassion. Let's ignore the three people they murdered and focus on the HEA, shall we?

GRUMPY/SUNSHINE

The Abominable Dr. Phibes (1971, dir. Robert Fuest)

TOP TROPES: Touch Her and Die: The heartbroken Dr. Phibes avenges his beloved wife's death by concocting increasingly elaborate murders for the doctors who couldn't save her.

DARK MOMENT: Phibes believes he's succeeded in his vendetta and carries out the last part of his plan: committing suicide to remain close to his wife.

HEA? Of a sort; Phibes can't imagine a life without the woman he loves, so he inters himself next to her, replacing his blood with embalming fluid.

Shaun of the Dead (2004, dir. Edgar Wright)

TOP TROPES: Second-Chance Romance: Shaun's girlfriend, Liz, has given up on him because he can't get his life together, but the zombie apocalypse is the perfect chance for him to show her how much he loves her.

DARK MOMENT: Shaun and Liz contemplate suicide when they think there's no hope left and the zombies are going to overwhelm them.

HEA? Yes. Shaun and Liz are seen six months after the zombie infections, living a blissful domestic life (with Shaun's best friend Ed still hanging around even though he's now a zombie).

Lisa Frankenstein (2024, dir. Zelda Williams)

TOP TROPES: Beauty and the Beast: Lisa's love life is a disaster, until a freak lightning strike brings her perfect boyfriend back from the dead. He's a monster, sure, but he's devoted, and he eventually wins her over.

DARK MOMENT: When the police close in while investigating the string of murders perpetrated by the Creature, Lisa asks him to electrocute her in her defective tanning bed, and he reluctantly complies.

HEA? Yes. Lisa is killed by the tanning bed, but the Creature brings her back to life and the two end up together.

CHAPTER ELEVEN

YOU'RE THE WORST

Monsters in Love

In researching this project, I realized just how few films tackle the idea of romance between two monstrous characters, particularly in North American cinema—the vast majority are stories about serial killers, and they're generally more in the drama category than straight-up horror, even if horrific crimes are taking place. Movies like Arthur Penn's *Bonnie and Clyde*, Terrence Malick's *Badlands*, and Oliver Stone's *Natural Born Killers* all feature murderous couples, but the sad fact is that their killing sprees all feel so commonplace and conventional that none of these movies fits the horror genre. While some films feature dual monsters in love (or romance is part of their story), I thought I'd first explore why this trope is so uncommon (especially when in publishing there has been an uptick in novels that explore this very theme).

The romantic horror films in the book so far have most often had a "normal" or at least human character that serves as the audience's way into the story, someone who viewers can relate to. These protagonists allow filmgoers to access the Otherness and/or dread of the rest of the story. For many people, it's more difficult to engage with the horror in a story without the hand-holding provided by a regular person thrust into the frightening aspects of the film. When viewing a movie that's too scary or off-putting without the release valve of a character who can act as a proxy to let off tension by screaming or fighting back, audience members often just disengage rather than being pulled into the story. So, a film with a romance between two monstrous characters, particularly if they're monstrous in action as well as in looks, is a difficult dynamic for many viewers. Another problem with a full-blown romance between two terrible creatures, or even worse, two terrible humans on a rampage, is that for the most part, mainstream moviegoers want a satisfying resolution to the story, and if there is no transformative arc or journey for any character, it's hard to craft a great ending. Where do your characters go if they both start out bad? Seeing an earnest hero brought down by his femme fatale lover (like Fred MacMurray as the hopeless sap powerless to refuse Barbara Stanwyck in *Double Indemnity*) is much more interesting. Likewise, an innocent woman succumbing to the dark side after being seduced by a sexy villain (like Lucy Westenra in *Bram Stoker's Dracula*) is a far more exciting prospect than someone who's been bad from the start.

Though James Whale's version of *Frankenstein* (1931) is more about Dr. Henry Frankenstein and his creation than it is about the romance between the doctor and his fiancée, there is still some romance as Elizabeth tries to bring her love back from the brink of insanity. And in his sequel, *The Bride of Frankenstein* (1935), the romance elements are even stronger, as the Creature (Boris Karloff) yearns for romance and a love of his own. The Creature sees the relationship between Victor and Elizabeth (played by Colin Clive and Valerie Hobson) and realizes that no human will ever fall in love with a monster such as himself. There is such a melancholy feeling that permeates this movie, as the audience veers between horror at the Creature's monstrous, murderous ways and understanding of his obvious desperation to find a companion.

Unfortunately, it takes much of the film's runtime for the Creature to convince the doctor to help him find a mate. While the Creature pines for a friend and partner, Whale spends time further showcasing the relationship between human characters. He does a wonderful job of contrasting the Creature's solitude, which is entirely out of his control, and Victor's deliberate attempts to distance himself from his fiancée. For me, the Creature's fixation on Victor's romance serves to highlight his own loneliness more than the happiness of Victor and Elizabeth. The reality of their partnership is much less perfect than the Creature seems to believe.

Elizabeth decides to stand by her man and nurse him back to health even as he continues to push her away to focus on his work. Though he loves her, Henry is too caught up in his experiments. He doesn't realize that his relentless quest to find a love for his Creature takes him further and further away from his own happiness. The whole thing comes to a truly tragic end, with the Creature realizing that he and his bride are not made for this world and destroying them both after telling Henry and Elizabeth to leave and save themselves. At least Henry and Elizabeth get the chance for an HEA, although it's too bad so many people had to die for them to get there.

Many kinds of monsters fall in love in horror films, from human killers with strange habits, like the cannibals in *Bones and All* to killer dolls in *Bride of Chucky* to werecreatures in incestuous relationships, a theme that turns up not just once in the remake of *Cat People* but twice (!)—see Stephen King's *Sleepwalkers*. Sometimes these films are about outsiders finding community with similarly marginalized folks, and sometimes they're more about bad people in a spiral of violence. Can we find HEA here? In most of these films, the happy ending is more bittersweet, with the couple either joining together in death or one of them having to (lovingly, usually) put the other one out of their misery when they cross a moral line. Sometimes, like in *Sleepwalkers*, it's one member of the original couple finding a better partner in a classic love triangle. Fiction can explore these types of relationships really well, giving characters room to explore the implications of what it means to be monstrous while still being the so-called hero of the story.

In some ways, stories about monsters in love are some of the hardest to portray on film, because the audience is expected to put themselves in the shoes of the invariably monstrous people or creatures who are falling in love. It can be quite difficult to root for them when they're awful. In the case of movies like the *Cat People* remake or *Sleepwalkers* (so I guess movies about werecats?), there is an added layer of transgression and taboo because the romantic couple is also incestuous—brother and sister Paul (Malcolm McDowell) and Irena (Nastassja Kinski) in *Cat People* and mother and son Mary (Alice Krige) and Charles (Bryan Krause) in *Sleepwalkers*. Though I'm sure some viewers can get past the ick factor, by and large filmmakers use this boundary-pushing trope as an added signifier that there's something really wrong with these people. We'll come back to these animalistic creatures, but what about human monsters?

All right, technically the monsters in Ronny Yu's *Bride of Chucky* (1998) aren't exactly human. But both of the reprehensible killers in the film start out as human, and their ultimate goal is to get their souls back into flesh-and-blood bodies instead of the plastic-and-rubber vessels they're housed in. The original *Child's Play* film was, as is often the case for supernatural slasher films, a bit of a darker affair, and Brad Dourif, though he isn't onscreen for long, imbues the serial killer Charles Lee Ray with a menace that remains even when the murderer is transformed into a doll. After the first *Child's Play* trilogy came to a close, writer Don Mancini wanted something a bit different for the fourth installment, and the reinvigoration of the slasher genre with the advent of movies like *Scream* had opened the door for this fresh take on the Chucky mythology. At least, it was considered a fresh take at the time. Of all the movies I rewatched as I sat down to write this book, *Bride of Chucky* feels by far like the movie most stuck in the past. The 1990s were a haven for snark, self-referential navel-gazing, and downright obnoxious pandering to the (mostly young, mostly male) teens who were flocking to see horror, and *Bride of Chucky* fits very well into that space.

The movie opens with Jennifer Tilly as Tiffany Valentine murdering a police officer who has retrieved the broken remains of the Good Guy doll that houses the soul of her old love Charles. She's been hunting for the doll for ten years, hoping she can bring Chucky back to life so he can fulfill his promise to marry her. She's no innocent young woman who has been corrupted by the dark influence of Chucky. At least, that innocence is long gone by the time we meet her in *Bride of Chucky*. Tilly plays Tiffany as a breathy sexpot with a mean streak, casually slitting people's throats and sending infatuated men to their doom while batting her extra-long eyelashes. She repairs the doll as best she can, and when her voodoo spell to bring him back to life works, she reminds him that he was planning to marry her, and that's why she spent all her time saving herself for him. This is no sweet second-chance romance, though; Tiffany soon realizes that Chucky never intended to propose, and she's heartbroken. She retaliates by locking Chucky in a playpen with a bride doll to taunt him while she cries herself to sleep. Tilly is good here and adds a damaged nuance to a character that is written as campy and over the top. Unfortunately, she can't save the film from devolving into a mean-spirited and incredibly cynical portrayal of a meant-to-be relationship that's doomed to fail, just like Frankenstein's Creature and his bride.

Once Tiffany is killed and her soul is transferred into the bride doll, the film really starts to deteriorate. If any of the romance portrayed in the film felt even remotely sincere, I think I might give the movie a little more grace, but every relationship here is toxic, mean, or both. Chucky only comes around to apologizing once he sees that Tiffany is as ruthless a killer as he is, and she quickly caves and agrees to rekindle their love, even though he's treated her so badly up to this point. Whether Tiffany has always been homicidal or changed her personality to appeal to Chucky isn't really relevant; regardless of how she got here, she spends much of her time pretending to be nonchalant but is so obviously trying to impress this rude, insulting, cruel ex-lover of hers. He never fully commits to her, even when he proposes. Tiffany is always seen as a device for Chucky to get himself further ahead, like when she helps him arrange to be delivered to the grave where he can retrieve the amulet to put him back inside a human body. I have no doubt that he'd drop her as soon as he was able, and Tiffany seems to know this as well. But she's stuck in the plastic doll body, so she's out of options, and there is, once again, a real I-can-fix-him attitude that runs through the movie.

As for the other romance in *Bride of Chucky*, it's not much better. Jesse Miller (Nick Stabile) is dating Jade Kincaid (Katherine Heigl), a high school girl, whose uncle and guardian, police chief Warren Kincaid (John Ritter), doesn't want her to see him. Maybe that's because he's older than her, isn't in school, and doesn't have a job. Jesse lives in the trailer park near Tiffany, and he resists her sexual advances but can't say no when she asks him to take her dolls to the cemetery. Jesse's age is never specified, but he's definitely older than Jade, and the idea that they're running away to elope with $500 feels like an incredibly silly way to move the plot forward. Perhaps these plot points would be forgivable if the two had any chemistry, but unfortunately, their romance is somewhat lacking. When they eventually do get married, they both seem so baffled by the entire ordeal that it's a wonder they went through with it. The B-plot comedy of errors where Jade and Jesse each think the other is responsible for the string of murders that follow them on their road trip is less than successful, and I just kept wondering why they didn't leave each other if each thought they were with a serial killer.

Throw in some "jokes" poking fun at other horror franchises, some homophobic slights, and multiple shots of Jennifer Tilly's ample cleavage before she turns into a doll, and that's basically the movie. As unsatisfying as I found the Jesse/Jade romance, their relationship isn't really the point of *Bride of Chucky*. Audiences were there to see Chucky, Tiffany, and the kills they were able to orchestrate. The Beauty and the Beast trope is at play in the film, though Tiffany is no shy and retiring Beauty to Chucky's beast. The seeming lack of interest in telling the love story in anything more than surface detail is wasted potential. There could be a great story here, of how monsters like Tiffany are created, or of how instrumental her love for Chucky is in unleashing her inner demons. But though the movie clearly aspires to *The Bride of Frankenstein*, there's no contest: *Bride of Chucky* is nowhere near as poignant, or as thought-provoking. While the filmmakers hit the requisite slasher beats in decent fashion, the entire thing feels calculated and cynical, setting itself up to build another layer to the franchise and not overly concerned with showing us any emotional depth or connection between anyone. A similar problem affects Yu's other big horror film, *Freddy vs. Jason*, by the way—it's all setup and no substance. I much prefer movies that are sincere in their love for the characters and the genre over sarcastic commentaries on pop culture.

Underworld (2003) is sincere to a fault. This brooding, melodramatic story of vampires, werewolves (called Lycans), and the mysterious human that both groups are hunting is almost the opposite of *Bride of Chucky*—full of shadows, double crosses, and slow-burn romance. On the heels of stylish sci-fi action movies like *The Matrix* and *Equilibrium*, director Len Wiseman used a *Romeo and Juliet*–inspired script by Danny McBride (not the actor) to develop an industrial, gothic-tinged horror action film that is full of over-the-top violence and political machinations. Does it take itself way too seriously? Absolutely. Are the CGI special effects a little janky to rewatch over twenty years later? Sadly, yes. But the vampire action trend of the late '90s and early 2000s (that included movies like John Carpenter's *Vampires*, *Van Helsing*, and my fave of the bunch, *Blade*) needed a little bit of romance, and *Underworld* provides it in the way of a slow-burn, kind of enemies-to-lovers story of forbidden partnerships and a very sexy Kate Beckinsale in latex.

Beckinsale plays Selene, a "Death Dealer." She's part of an elite vampire strike team who is hunting down the remaining Lycans in the unnamed city where she and her vampire coven live. Kraven, a Jim Morrison look-alike played by Shane Brolly, is the unofficial leader of the vampire clan because their elders are either asleep or away. Years ago, he told the vampires that he was responsible for killing the leader of the Lycans, Lucian, after Lucian attacked and murdered the elder vampire Viktor's daughter. The backstory here, by the way, is incredibly detailed, and I think the world-building is one of the reasons *Underworld* has been able to grow itself into a franchise, albeit one with diminishing returns. I won't explain the entire convoluted thing here, but suffice to say there is an ingrained enmity between vampires and Lycans, and each group wants to get rid of the other. The Lycans, led by Michael Sheen's Lucian (who, surprise, is not dead), are searching for a human who holds the key to their survival: a descendant of the Corvinus clan, who were progenitors of both the vampire and Lycan communities. The present-day Lycans believe they've found the remaining family member when they come across Michael Corvin, a medical student played by Scott Speedman. Lucian and his army of werewolves think that they can use Michael to create a vampire/werewolf hybrid, someone who will have all the benefits of both species with none of the drawbacks.

Selene interrupts the Lycans' attempt to capture Michael, and she's instantly drawn to the man and wants to learn more. The reason for her attraction isn't really stated; maybe she likes his hair, maybe they're destined to fall in love. But Selene's a hardcore, take-no-prisoners assassin (as telegraphed by her aforementioned latex outfits and many, many guns); she doesn't have time for love, especially not with a human. Nevertheless, she decides she needs to find out more, and breaks into Michael's apartment. As you do when you're attracted to someone, of course. I am constantly surprised by how often a version of this trope exists in romance novels, by the way. It's not always full-on burglary, but a shocking (to me) number of main characters find themselves engaging in sneaky, borderline stalking behavior in romance, and in the current stalker romance trend, it's one of the biggest turn-ons for the protagonists. Anyway, back to *Underworld*.

Michael finds Selene in his apartment, and before the two of them can have a proper conversation to clear up any confusion, the Lycans arrive. Lucian bites Michael, cursing him to transform into a werewolf at the next full moon. Selene saves him and they escape together, eventually ending up back at the vampires' mansion, where Selene opens up to Michael and helps him deal with the fear and confusion of realizing that (a) vampires and werewolves exist, and (b) they're out to capture and/or kill him. Eventually, the audience learns of the conspiracy between vampires and Lycans to control both clans, and Selene must fulfill the prophecy and bite Michael so he can transform himself into the vampire-Lycan hybrid that the groups were warned about, bringing the destruction of both Lycan and vampire groups in the city. Together they escape, and the story ends on a cliffhanger as the last remaining elder slowly wakes up at the end of the film.

Beckinsale does a great job of selling her growing interest in Michael with intense gazes and softening features as she gives in to her emotions before steeling herself once again in the face of danger. The two are constantly in each other's orbit, and though there's little more than smoldering glances and brief touches in this installment of the franchise, the couple are clearly destined to be together. Though the romance takes a backseat to the action in *Underworld*, it's much stronger here than in many of the other action horror movies of the era, and it does eventually pay off in the sequel, when Michael and Selene finally give in to their feelings and become romantically involved. As I mentioned, this is a slow-burn romance; it's not quite enemies to lovers, since the characters are wary of each other but not outright ready to kill each other when they first meet. And it's less a monster romance or typical vampire movie because it doesn't hit many of the tropes common to those stories, either. Michael may begin the movie as a human, but he's never truly *just* a human, so it feels more appropriate to say that this film is about love between monsters. *Underworld* is one of the early entries into the urban fantasy/paranormal romance trend of the time, and the elaborate backdrop of warring families and forbidden relationships is a time-tested theme that has only become stronger in recent years with the advent of Shifterverses, Omegaverses, and even Mafia romance.

The 1980s and early '90s were also interested in shifters, though in recent years the language used has evolved to become much broader, particularly in the indie publishing and fanfic space. Still, the '80s and '90s gave us a spate of horror films featuring werewolves and various other metamorphosing creatures (*Wolfen*, *The Howling*, and *An American Werewolf in London* are all various forms of the werecreature film, and all much more graphic than Lon Chaney's *The Wolf Man*). And, surprisingly, these included two movies about werecats, both of which focused on more taboo romantic relationships. The 1982 remake of *Cat People*, starring Nastassja Kinski and Malcolm McDowell as estranged siblings with dark secrets, and Stephen King's 1992 film *Sleepwalkers*, featuring Alice Krige and Brian Krause as mother and son, are ten years apart but both focus on incest between the main characters who are werefelines. There aren't enough movies with these same themes to be considered a subgenre of their own, perhaps, but it's interesting to contrast these two films and figure out what they each want to say, not only about monsters, but also about how those monsters deal with each other and the rest of the world around them.

Cat People (1982) was released forty years after the original (discussed in chapter 3). In contrast to the moody, melancholic Irena played by Simone Simon, there are two main werecreatures in the remake: Paul, played by Malcolm McDowell, and his estranged sister, Irena, played by Nastassja Kinski. Directed by Paul Schrader, this version is wildly different from the original. Set in New Orleans, it's a sweaty erotic thriller in the vein of *Body Heat* or *The Big Easy*, with an added horrific element. Kinski's vision of Irena is both more naive and more forward than Simon's; she feels younger and less confident in herself, and she is ripe for exploitation by her brother, whom she travels to reconnect with after growing up in separate countries. She is aware that she and Paul share a heritage of growing up in foster care, but she has no idea of their other secret: The two of them are werecats. They will transform into panthers after mating with humans the first time, and they can only revert to human form once they kill someone. Paul has been navigating his curse by having sex with and then murdering sex workers, and Irena, a virgin, is shocked to find out that she too will change into a panther should she ever have a sexual partner. Paul tells her the only way to avoid transforming is to mate with another werecat, just as their parents did. (Obviously, the other way to stay in human form is to just abstain from having sex altogether, but unlike many of today's sexless blockbusters, it seems that in the 1980s it was unthinkable that anyone would want to give up lovemaking entirely, even if you did end up a murderous predator afterward.)

While Paul is pursuing Irena and trying to convince her he is the only person she should be with, Irena has found someone else who is much more interesting to her. Oliver (John Heard) is a curator at the New Orleans zoo who has been brought in as a consultant on the big cat attacks that have been plaguing the city. When he runs into Irena at the zoo, where she's entranced by the giant cats, he is captivated, blowing off his on-again-off-again girlfriend Alice (Annette O'Toole) to chase after this young woman. For all that Irena is interested in exploring a relationship with Oliver, however, she's hesitant to give in to her desires now that she knows she will turn into a panther and be forced to kill someone to regain human form. Also navigating her brother's increasingly overt advances, Irena is conflicted and runs away from both Paul and Oliver, trying to figure out what she wants and what she's willing to do, but not before terrorizing Alice in a reimagining of the 1942 classic pool scene, with more nudity and less suspense, and then sleeping with Oliver, turning into a panther, and killing the owner of an old cabin in the bayou to turn back into human form.

Here's where I confess that I don't find the romance in *Cat People* terribly compelling. John Heard as Oliver is unconvincing, and he feels almost as slimy and manipulative as Malcolm McDowell's Paul. He treats his ex-girlfriend poorly, and he seems interested in Irena because he finds her attractive but blows off her concerns, more focused on getting her to sleep with him than on helping her deal with her clearly homicidal brother. Paul is even worse, wanting solely to use his sister. I suppose he could make a case that mating with Irena would help him stop killing people, but I don't know that it's a good enough excuse for incest. At least Paul is murdered by Alice after he attacks Oliver, but it's too little too late. Irena feels trapped and out of options, and decides she'd rather transform herself permanently into a cat in order to avoid dealing with the advances of these two terrible suitors. In a scene that feels more exploitative than necessary, Irena convinces Oliver that he needs to have sex with her one last time so she can disappear into her cat form. He ties her up (to protect himself, of course), and they make love, with lots of sweaty close-ups of a young woman in bondage. Irena changes into a panther, giving up on her human life and her chance at love. The film ends with Oliver once again in a relationship with Alice (though he still doesn't seem anywhere near as interested as she does) and caressing a docile black panther in the zoo. This vision of Irena locked up in captivity feels much more bleak than the ending of the original. For a film that is much freer with its depictions of sex, the actual sexual politics of Schrader's movie seem regressive compared to Tourneur's. Irena sacrifices an enormous amount—her agency, her humanity, her sibling—to end up as nothing more than a creature to be possessed and owned. Oliver has learned nothing, content to keep Alice tethered to him even as he refuses to fully let her in. And Paul is dead.

Stephen King's *Sleepwalkers* (1992) might also feature a pair of werecat-like creatures, but there aren't many more similarities between the two films. A rather minor film in the King adaptation canon, it was directed by Mick Garris: the story of the last two survivors of a vampiric race of werecreatures who have holed up in a small town in hopes of remaining undetected and finding a virginal young woman to feed from. Alice Krige is Mary Brady, the mother of Brian Krause's Charles, and the two have a *very* close relationship. We establish early on that in order to sustain themselves, Charles is tasked with finding young female virgins and draining their life force, which he then imparts to his mother by having sex with her. If it were anyone else playing the role of Mary, I'm pretty sure this movie would feel even more silly than it already does, but Krige brings a gravitas to the role that really helps to sell both her relationship with Charles and the certain doom that's awaiting the two of them if they don't feed.

The plot of *Sleepwalkers* is pretty run of the mill: Charles finds a young virgin in Tanya (played by an ethereal Mädchen Amick, who is as bewitching here as she is in *Twin Peaks*), and he must seduce her and steal her energy. I think there's an alternate version of this story that has Tanya helping Charles realize that his mother is evil and turning on her to end up in love with this young woman. That feels like a much more traditional story, one that fits in well with many of the monster romance tropes we've seen in other films discussed in this book. But for all its flaws, *Sleepwalkers* subverts the typical love story themes and fully commits to the relationship between Mary and Charles. It might be wrong to outsiders, but the two characters are portrayed as inhuman, not bound by the rules and morals of the society they're living in. It's a choice that has allowed the film to endure in a way that many smaller films of the '90s horror genre have been unable to.

Where the film really suffers, for me, is in the unfortunately low-budget special effects when we get a full transformation. We've seen some really wonderful morphing makeup, even going back to early horror like the original *Phantom of the Opera*, and makeup effects at the time *Sleepwalkers* was released were generally a selling point for many horror films. A movie like *An American Werewolf in London* is nowhere near as effective without the visceral, wet, excruciating transformation that David Naughton undergoes (created by the fabulous special makeup effects artist Rick Baker). Perhaps part of the problem is that giant werecats don't evoke the same sense of menace as slavering wolves, but the slightly wonky effects in this film rob it of a bit of gravitas and danger. Director Mick Garris instead leans into the absurd and the comedic, and, personally, it softens the blow just a little too much. I think there's potential in the premise of *Sleepwalkers* to really embrace the darkness of the story. The race of vampire cats that Mary and Charles belong to are clearly not long for this world, but we don't really feel a sense of desperation in their actions. I'd love to see a reimagining of this story through a more tragic lens, watching a last gasp of a species trying to claw their way back from extinction.

After *Sleepwalkers* fell flat with audiences, the premise of monsters in love (fantastical monsters, anyway) largely disappeared from mainstream film. Many movies explore relationships between one "normal" person and one monster, but those mostly end with either the monster redeeming themselves in a happy ending, or with the regular protagonist succumbing to the monstrous side. The narrative becomes a much more straightforward and simplistic set of tropes and story beats instead of a messy exploration of two creatures embracing their nature. Of course, many movies still work within the framework of "monsters in love"—it's just that in the '90s and early 2000s, the monsters are often more grounded in reality, à la serial killers Mickey and Mallory in *Natural Born Killers* or *Kalifornia*, or criminals of another sort as in *Bound*.

2022's *Bones and All* marries this more grounded take on monsters with a slightly fantastical premise. It's a coming-of-age story and a first-love story wrapped up in a gory, cannibalistic road trip. Director Luca Guadagnino's film feels of a piece with Terrence Malick's 1973 classic *Badlands*, a movie inspired by real-life killers Charles Starkweather and Caril-Ann Fugate, which stars Martin Sheen and Sissy Spacek as young people who fall in love and then happen to go on a killing spree.

In *Bones and All*, our protagonists are Maren (Taylor Russell) and Lee (Timothée Chalamet). Maren is an Eater, someone who consumes human flesh, and her father has been mostly successful at curbing her impulses after she murdered her babysitter as a young child. But when Maren takes a bite of her friend's finger, her dad knows they need to leave their small town. Soon after she turns eighteen, her father abandons her for good, and Maren sets off to find her missing mother in Minnesota. Along the way she runs into Sully (a very creepy Mark Rylance), and she learns the "rules" of Eaters. He says he smelled her from far away and teaches her how to survive, telling her she can never eat another Eater. Maren becomes uncomfortable with Sully, who seems to want her to be more than just a friend or protégée, and she leaves him.

She meets Lee, and they are drawn to each other, Maren having smelled Lee and realizing they are similar. She decides to go with Lee after they save a woman from being harassed by a man, and Lee eats the man. A road trip ensues, and Guadagnino puts together a lovely film, beautifully shot and quite touching (with a gorgeous score by Trent Reznor and Atticus Ross). Maren and Lee are two characters thrown together, outcasts in the "regular" world and making their own way through dangerous situations, and they fall in and out and back in love along the way.

This story is most certainly romantic, full of longing and tenderness, and Russell and Chalamet are wonderful together, clinging to each other as the only bright lights in each other's worlds as they encounter more and more darkness. Lee's family life was traumatic before he escaped his abusive father and left behind his sister; Maren's mother, it turns out, is also an Eater and tells Maren it would be better to die than be the monster she is. They're monsters, yes, but Guadagnino is gentle with these monsters: They're trying to live by a code as best they can in the face of their affliction. The audience roots for them, even as we see the stomach-churning lengths they must go to in order to survive. This is a beautiful movie, yes, but it's also fairly gory; Guadagnino doesn't hold back much when it comes to portraying the bloody consequences of being an Eater. (As someone with misophonia, which the Cleveland Clinic describes as a disorder where you have a decreased tolerance to specific sounds and things you can sense related to them, the sound design in this film was a real challenge for me, a testament to how good it is.)

While *Bones and All* definitely meets the criteria for a love story, it misses out on the HEA because just as our two main characters come back to each other and commit to a new life together, everything falls apart. Sully returns, having tracked Maren after she rebuffed his advances for a second time, and he's not willing to give her up. When Lee finds Maren and Sully, he helps her kill the older Eater. But the victory is hollow; Lee is fatally stabbed in the process of dispatching Sully. Lee tells Maren she needs to promise to eat his body, bones and all, and she reluctantly agrees. Poor Maren is alone, even more so than she seems at the beginning of the film. She learns about love and experiences brief moments of joy, but they're stolen away from her, and it's a heartbreaking end to this strange and sincere film.

It seems that there is a recent resurgence of interest in this kind of twisted love story in both the horror-film genre and the publishing world. While many bestsellers swing more toward the romance side of things than outright horror, dark romance novels like *Butcher & Blackbird*, featuring two serial killers who must team up and dispatch other killers, prove that there is an appetite for stories with a sinister undercurrent. But what's next for horror in movies? Is there room for more love among the horrors?

MONSTERS IN LOVE

The Bride of Frankenstein (1935; dir. James Whale)

TOP TROPES: Monster Romance: This time, it's monster and monster instead of monster and human, as Dr. Henry Frankenstein must create a companion for his Creature from the original Frankenstein film. The Creature longs for someone to build a life with after seeing Henry's fiancée, Elizabeth, returning to the doctor, nursing him back to health, and deciding to try and rebuild their life together even in the face of turmoil.

DARK MOMENT: When the bride finally encounters the Creature for the first time, instead of feeling love for him, she screams. The Creature's hopes are dashed, realizing that no one will ever feel about him the way Elizabeth feels about Henry.

HEA? No, not really. While Henry and Elizabeth are able to escape to safety, the poor Creature and his bride are doomed to die once again in the ruins of the laboratory.

Stephen King's Sleepwalkers (1992, dir. Mick Garris)

TOP TROPES: Dark Past and Family Secrets: Charles is looking for a new love in Tanya, but little does she know that he has nefarious motives, and his true love is actually his mother, Mary.

DARK MOMENT: Tanya discovers Charles and Mary's true natures: They are werecats who want to drain her life force.

HEA? No. Tanya escapes from Charles and Mary, who both die alone.

Bones and All (2022, dir. Luca Guadagnino)

TOP TROPES: Road Trip: Maren, an Eater, meets Lee, who shares the same affinity for cannibalism, and the two embark on a journey across the country as they fall in love.

DARK MOMENT: Maren runs away from Lee after she discovers the man that he enticed her to eat had a family.

HEA? No. The two end up together, but Lee is killed as they embrace their small-town life together, and Maren must devour him to fulfill his final wish.

CHAPTER TWELVE

THE NEW ROMANTICS

Horror Romance in the 2020s

With the exception of a few big movies in the early part of the twenty-first century, romantic plots in general were few and far between for much of the 2010s. In addition to the aforementioned de-emphasis on sex and love in many movies, the fragmentation of the film industry with the exponential growth of streaming platforms and mega-blockbuster films meant there were fewer studios and distributors interested in making mid-budget so-called "prestige pictures." Whereas a few years earlier, it was a given that we would see the fall festival circuit give us dramas like *The King's Speech*, *Silver Linings Playbook*, or *Eastern Promises*, the 2020s brought significant challenges to the film industry in general and smaller-budget, non-genre productions in particular, in the form of a global pandemic and labor actions from the actors' and writers' guilds.

The COVID-19 pandemic upended lives around the globe, and the film industry was hit with shutdowns in productions as well as lockdowns and social distancing measures that prevented audiences from going to theaters to see finished films. The damage to the global box office was staggering; movies that would have, in previous years, made hundreds of millions of dollars around the world were either shelved or released in very select markets, with much smaller grosses. The lack of opportunities for audiences to screen films on a big screen in a community setting meant that many people gave up their moviegoing habits completely, happy to continue watching films from the comfort of their homes or even on their cell phones rather than going out to a cinema. Streaming services like Netflix capitalized on this shift in audience habits by releasing many of the movies that would otherwise have made a modest profit at the box office. But in order to capture as many viewers as possible, instead of focusing on many smaller films that might appeal to narrow niches, the tentpole blockbuster model shifted to these at-home streaming services as well, leaving less room for mid-size films that may have explored a wider variety of relationships and dynamics.

What did that mean for genre films, which typically would have already been made with smaller budgets? The pandemic hit indies as well, certainly, but we have begun to see a proliferation of "smaller" films once again, and the increase in niche streaming services focusing on indies, foreign films, and genre movies—like Mubi and Shudder—means that fans have more options for seeing horror in all its forms. And smaller independent studios like Blumhouse, A24, and Neon, among others, have championed so-called "elevated horror" and have brought some cachet back to a genre that for much of the 2010s languished in relative obscurity outside of the occasional entry in a well-known franchise, like *Paranormal Activity* or *Insidious*. (I say relative obscurity because anyone who's been interested in the genre knows there have been a ton of great horror films over the decade, but the wider audience has largely ignored the genre other than to pop up every few years with think pieces about how horror is having a "moment.")

In any case, at the beginning of the 2020s there wasn't much in the way of horror romance, at least not in more mainstream films. Overall, we've seen a decrease in sex and romance in films (as I mentioned in a previous chapter, R. S. Benedict's piece in *Blood Knife*, "Everyone Is Beautiful and No One Is Horny," details this phenomenon really well), and genre films are no exception.[1] Online discussions lamenting sex scenes in films as unnecessary because they don't "advance the plot" are rampant; "puriteens" and "tradwives" have chastised and persuaded large movie studios and book publishers alike to veer away from more frank depictions of adults engaging in sex for the joy of it. You can see it in everything from Tom Cruise and Jennifer Connolly's fade-to-black implied lovemaking scene in *Top Gun: Maverick* to the rise of illustrated, cutesy covers on romance novels to the use of euphemisms and code words online to circumvent the algorithms of TikTok and Meta in order to avoid shadow bans on social media accounts. Despite the discourse in mainstream media worrying about the prevalence of sex and nudity (which smarter folks than me have attributed to the growing right-wing Christofascist movement and persecution of queer and trans people in North America and around the world), there really hasn't been that much emphasis on the body in films for the last few years, outside of violence perpetrated on and by people.

That doesn't mean romance in horror is completely dead, though. Films like *Fresh*, *The Invitation*, *Nosferatu*, *Companion*, *Heart Eyes*, *The Gorge*, and *Sinners* all explore various facets of romance and love alongside horror, and they prove that there is still an appetite for films that explore the genres in interesting ways. (As an aside: I have mostly avoided talking about films made outside of North America in this book, with a few notable exceptions, but there are lots of great examples of horror romance from various international filmmakers, and I've added a list at the back of the book for folks to check out.)

The above films, for me, fall into two separate categories: There are the genre mash-ups, where romance elements are combined with horror elements into stories that might not quite fall into either genre neatly; and then there are more straightforward horror romance stories, more traditional in tone, perhaps, and with more recognizable tropes and themes. *Fresh*, *Companion*, *The Gorge*, and *Sinners* are all stories that go beyond a more typical horror story and often subvert common tropes or shift in tone from one scene to the next. *The Invitation*, *Nosferatu*, and *Heart Eyes* are closer to more traditional horror films that feature romantic elements. Now that we've broken these films into two separate groups, we can dive in more deeply.

THE MASH-UPS

Comedy is a uniting element of the mash-up horror romance movies listed here. While I wouldn't call any of these movies full-on rom-coms, each includes moments within that are played for laughs, often speaking directly to the audience, saying yes, we know you've already seen countless movies with this premise, but surprise! We're doing it in a different way.

Though Jordan Peele's first foray into horror is technically not a film from the 2020s, *Get Out* (2017) feels like such a modern film and hasn't lost any of its timeliness even almost a decade later. In any case, it's an essential film, and the themes of the movie place it in conversation with many of the others in this chapter, particularly these genre mash-ups. So it makes sense to me to talk about it first before we dive into the current decade.

Prior to writing, directing, and coproducing *Get Out*, Peele was best known for his sketch comedy show *Key & Peele*, which he wrote and starred in alongside Keegan-Michael Key. While there are certainly moments of levity to be found in the movie (thanks in part to some fantastic casting), *Get Out* is far more horrifying than humorous. Part psychological horror, part satire, Peele's dissection of race relations through the lens of a *Stepford Wives*–style conspiracy electrified horror audiences. The film's tenth-place finish at the box office in 2017 cemented Peele as a new auteur of the modern horror era, and he has gone on to direct two more horror movies, *Us* and *Nope*, as well as producing and championing several Black filmmakers (like Nia DaCosta, who directed the reimagining of *Candyman*).

But where is the romance, you may be asking? Well, though I won't pretend that *Get Out* is particularly full of love, it does take romance tropes and themes and subverts them in fresh ways. Chris Washington (Daniel Kaluuya) is a photographer, and he's about to take a road trip with his girlfriend Rose Armitage (Allison Williams) to meet her family. Audiences familiar with rom-coms will instantly recognize this situation as a source of tension and potential amusement. We quickly relate to Chris feeling nervous about making a good impression with Rose's wealthy parents. But as his friend Rod Williams (Lil Rel Howery) warns him, Chris should be worried about more than just being a good boyfriend to Rose. Chris is Black and Rose is white, and Rose has neglected to tell her parents she's dating a Black man. Though she assures Chris her parents are progressive and will be totally fine with him, Rod is wary and we soon find out he has good reason to be.

Chris's experience at the Armitage estate starts out awkwardly but innocuously enough. Rose's parents, Dean (Bradley Whitford) and Missy (Catherine Keener) welcome Chris into their home, but it doesn't take long for Chris to feel like he might not be as accepted as Rose would like him to believe. Her brother Jeremy (Caleb Landry Jones) is kind of a creep, and a series of unsettling events have Chris worried that the Armitages are out to cause him harm (or at the very least use him as a sex slave, as he tells Rod). The other Black people Chris meets seem almost blank, with dead stares and subservient personalities, and the audience starts to see more parallels with folk horror movies like *The Wicker Man* or *Midsommar* than comedies like *Meet the Parents*.

What Chris (and us as the audience) ultimately discovers is that the Armitage family is part of a cult called the Order of the Coagula. They have been transplanting the brains of old and wealthy white men and women into the bodies of younger, stronger, Black people in order to prolong their lives indefinitely. Chris is hypnotized and immobilized by Missy, a psychologist, so that Dean, a neurosurgeon, can perform surgery. When Chris escapes, he tries to get Rose to give him the car keys so the two of them can escape her horrible family. That's when the real horror sets in: Chris is stunned to find out that not only is Rose aware of her family's nefarious plans; she is a gleeful participant, luring Black men and women to her parents' home so they can be possessed by Coagula members.

There definitely isn't a lot of outright romance in *Get Out*. But one of the reasons the film works so well is that Peele uses the audience's knowledge of romance film tropes to lure us in. We think we know where the plot is going because we want to believe Rose has good intentions. She shrugs off Chris's anxieties at every turn, making us question whether Chris (and the audience) is too suspicious of well-meaning but clueless in-laws. There are many examples of this kind of female protagonist in romance films, from Teri Polo's Pam in *Meet the Parents* (2000) to Lauren London's Amira in *You People* (2023). They deflect criticism and harsh words from their partners about their families, convincing us to fall in love with their quirks. As the story progresses, we realize that these women really do love their heroes despite their suspicious natures. Peele's revelation that Rose is fully committed to the conspiracy is a bigger gut punch because we expect her to be our love interest, and that she'll eventually choose her boyfriend over her family if she has to. (For an excellent critique of Rose's role as a white woman weaponizing her race, read Sophie Hall's "Get Out: The Horror of White Women.")[2]

As you'll see in the rest of this chapter, this new decade of horror romance films is much more likely to dissect and question the romance found within them. Why are filmmakers so wary of love and relationships in the 2020s? Are people in their twenties and thirties warier of falling in love and committing to romance? Is there a bigger cultural shift to be explored here? Probably. That's the case with *Fresh* (2022), which sets out to tell a story about the pitfalls of the modern dating scene before descending into darkness.

The film opens with a woman, Noa (Daisy Edgar-Jones) who has decided to swear off dating apps after a string of terrible matches. She and her friend Mollie (Jonica T. Gibbs) commiserate over Noa's bad dates, and it all feels like a typical 2000s rom-com. When Noa meets Steve (Sebastian Stan) at the supermarket, she finds him refreshingly "nice" and charming, and they exchange numbers. We're hitting all the beats normally found in romance novels and films: woman is tired of being treated poorly, meets a man who's different from her typical boors, and they seem to be hitting it off. Screenwriter Lauryn Kahn and director Mimi Cave do a great job of capturing the disillusionment many women feel about so-called fairytale romances before finding Prince Charmings of their own.

But every romance reader knows there's bound to be a reveal coming, a crisis or so-called Dark Moment. Usually, this is when one member of our couple reveals something about themselves they've been reluctant to bring up (a past breakup that's haunted them, a small misunderstanding that snowballs out of control, a traumatic incident). The reveal causes the other person to question the relationship. In this case, the discovery is quite a lot darker than your quintessential romance: Steve is really Brendan, a married man. Oh, and he also captures women and surgically harvests their bodies to consume and sell human meat, keeping them alive as long as he can so the meat stays fresh.

The tone unsurprisingly shifts from romance to horror after that. Noa is locked up with another woman, Penny (Andrea Bang), who has been harvested multiple times already. Noa tries to escape but is caught, and Brendan punishes her by carving meat from her buttocks. While Noa desperately tries to figure out a way to get out of this nightmarish situation, Mollie, who advised Noa not to go on her weekend away with "Steve," recruits a bartender, Paul (Dayo Okeniyi), to help her figure out what's happened to her friend. She discovers Brendan's wife Ann (Charlotte Le Bon), and family, and in questioning Ann, Mollie realizes Brendan's wife is part of the plot to exploit these women. Before she can act, however, Mollie is also abducted.

Noa comes to realize that Brendan's attraction to her is her greatest advantage, and she devises a plot to seduce him once she discovers that he's also holding Mollie hostage. She pretends to be interested in cannibalism, and later engages in oral sex with him, which he enjoys until she bites his penis, injuring him. The injury allows her to escape with Mollie and Penny, but Brendan chases them into the woods. The women ultimately defeat both Brendan and Ann, with absolutely no help from Paul, who drives up to the house but turns around when he hears gunshots.

The tonal shift to such darkness helps to highlight the dangers of the modern dating scene; sure, accidentally ending up with a cannibal is extreme, but how many women would describe their dating life as being chewed up and spit out by toxic men? The fact that every man in the film is problematic at best is aligned with many women's experiences, and its unapologetic condemnation of both predators and those who willingly or unknowingly abet these terrible men is rather refreshing. Obviously, *Fresh* does not end with an HEA for Noa and "Steve," but the idea of exploring horror through such an explicitly romantic lens is interesting, and is echoed in Drew Hancock's 2025 release, *Companion*.

Sophie Thatcher plays Iris, a woman who's nervous about going to meet her boyfriend Josh's friends for the first time at a secluded cabin. There are flashbacks to Sophie and Josh's meet-cute (at the supermarket, maybe as a cue to the domesticity and unthreatening nature to the men in these stories). Josh seems very keen on reminding Iris that everything will be fine, even if his best girlfriend Kat (Megan Suri) is clearly icy toward Iris. The suspense harkens back to the meeting-the-in-laws pitfalls explored in *Get Out*. It's another common trope in romance, where a secondary female character throws a metaphorical wrench in the couple's relationship, either because she's envious and wants the man for herself or because she suspects there's something threatening about the woman. In this case, both are true, but *Companion* subverts expectations in many other ways.

Things start to go wrong when Kat's boyfriend Sergey (Rupert Friend) attempts to sexually assault Iris, and she kills him. When she gets back to the beach house, everyone is of course freaked out, but that's when the typical storytelling beats are set aside to reveal that Iris is not, in fact, Josh's girlfriend. At least not in the human sense. Iris is an android specifically designed for companionship and sexual partnership, and she is supposed to have a mechanism to prevent her from committing violence against humans. But there is a larger conspiracy in place here, involving Josh, Kat, and their friend Eli (Harvey Guillén), who have come to the house to kill Sergey and take off with his money, and Josh has removed Iris's controls in order to take advantage of her extra strength and intelligence. Of course, Iris is programmed not to know she's a robot; she's fully convinced of her humanity. As she comes to terms with the fact that Josh has been using her both as a sexual companion and in this plot to murder Sergey, she wants not only to end her relationship, but to end Josh altogether.

The tone of the film shifts wildly throughout, especially after the initial reveal of Iris's true nature (I think if I had come in with absolutely no knowledge of the plot, I might have been surprised, but unfortunately the trailer gives the game away). There's dark comedy, heightened by Eli and his boyfriend Patrick (Lukas Gage), who is also revealed to be a Companion. There's adventure and suspense as more bodies pile up and Iris must outsmart Josh, his friends, and the police. There's definitely some horror, not only in the gory ways that people are dispatched, but also in the uncaring nature of Josh's treatment of Iris and her inability to walk away cleanly. Josh abuses Iris's trust, he manipulates and gaslights her into thinking he loves her, and when none of that works, he displays a shockingly cruel streak. If *Fresh* is about the horrors of dating new people, *Companion* takes that one step further, exploring how much scarier it can be to find out the person you thought was your soulmate is anything but.

In stark contrast to *Fresh* and *Companion*, Scott Derrickson's *The Gorge* (2025) features a slightly more optimistic love story housed in a spy thriller slash sci-fi conspiracy slash action-packed journey to Hell. Miles Teller (Levi) and Anya Taylor-Joy (Drasa) star as covert, elite snipers tasked with protecting the world from monsters that were unleashed after a military experiment gone wrong. The two spend the first part of the film living in isolated towers at opposite sides of the titular Gorge, under strict instructions not to talk to anyone for a year, not even each other. They're given brief instructions but are largely left to their own devices as long as they don't socialize. But it's not too long before Levi is intrigued by the woman across the gorge, using his high-tech surveillance equipment to zoom in on her. When Drasa reciprocates, breaking the no-communication rule, the two strike up an incredibly unlikely and still kind of sweet long-distance relationship.

We witness a series of moments where the two get closer and closer, both to each other and to the truth about this strange and sinister posting. Levi and Drasa begin to realize that what they're protecting isn't something in the Gorge: They're protecting the outside world from the monsters within, called Hollow Men. As the two try to uncover the secrets and mysteries surrounding this gorge and the military operations they're tasked with performing, the attraction they feel for each other grows. Six months into their tour, Levi rigs a zipline to traverse the gorge and have dinner with Drasa, and the two share an intimate evening together, consummating the relationship they've been cultivating all this time. This is a hallmark of slow-burn romance—the moment when the couple finally gives in to the feelings that have been simmering for weeks, months, or years, and the release the characters feel is cathartic for the audience too. But since this is a mash-up of a whole host of genres, Derrickson places the culmination of the romance fairly early because many other plotlines need to be resolved.

In contrast to a romantasy (or horrormance, if that's a thing by the time this book comes out), where the various genre tropes and themes are threaded throughout the entire story, *The Gorge* is more akin to a genre shift, going from tense military/spy thriller to cutesy romance to outright science fiction. Each section of the film sticks rather closely to the conventions of its respective genre rather than subverting them to tell other aspects of the story and reveal different layers. This storytelling style is similar to that of both *Companion* and *Fresh*; these stories count on the audience expecting one kind of story and then pulling the rug out from under them. In the case of *The Gorge*, once Drasa and Levi's romantic relationship (as quick and surface level as it may be) is established, the audience is expected to buy into the fact that they are in love with each other and will do whatever they can to save one another from the horrors they'll face. Conveniently, we see just how far they'll go when Levi falls into the gorge on his way back from Drasa's tower and, without thinking, she dives in after him.

The film follows the two as they uncover the secret experiments that took place here, when the military created the Hollow Men and other monsters. The filmmakers alternate between horror action sequences full of jump scares and creatures, and exposition as our heroes find clues. There is little in the way of romantic tension as things move ahead, however. Even more so than in the previous films I mentioned, Derrickson keeps each phase or emotional beat of his story quite separate. It's not really until the very end of the film that the romance comes to the forefront again.

Ryan Coogler's *Sinners* (2025) is not only one of my favorite films in recent memory but also a film that bridges the gap between the aforementioned mash-ups and more traditional horror films with romantic elements. Many, many layers and themes intermingle throughout this tale of juke joints, families, music, and vampires, but in contrast to *Fresh*, *Companion*, and *The Gorge*, the narrative doesn't so much shift in tone as expand, adding more and more elements as the story unfolds while remaining true to the initial premise: two brothers coming back to their hometown with dreams.

Michael B. Jordan plays dual roles as twin brothers Elijah ("Smoke") and Elias ("Stack"), who return home to Clarksdale, Mississippi, after a stint in World War I and then working for (and stealing from) the mob in Chicago. They come home to open a juke joint for Black people in the town and neighboring areas, assembling a group of old friends to help them. Everything goes incredibly well, with one of the most transcendent musical sequences in a film I've ever seen. Until a group of vampires lay siege to the dance hall and everyone is forced to make some very difficult choices.

This is an incredibly top-level synopsis, I know, but as with many of the films in this chapter, I hesitate to recap in lots of detail for two reasons: One, many of you have probably seen some or all of these movies recently, and most are easily accessible at the time of this writing, at least compared to many of the older films I have mentioned. And two, for *Sinners* specifically, *so* many layers and subplots and ideas are at play that it would be impossible to capture everything here. Ryan Coogler has crafted an incredibly rich story, full of details and nuance that reward multiple viewings.

What I really want to focus on is, of course, the romance. Love absolutely permeates *Sinners*, not just familial love or love of culture, but honest-to-goodness romance. Smoke and Stack are each reckoning with women they have loved and are hurt deeply by leaving them behind. Smoke's partner Annie (Wunmi Mosaku) is a woman well versed in Hoodoo, though she wasn't able to save their baby daughter's life. Whether this child's death is the main reason for Smoke's leaving is never revealed, but it's clear that both Annie and Smoke find it painful to be around each other, even though they still care for one another very much, and Smoke tells her so when he returns to her home to recruit her for the juke joint.

Stack's ex-girlfriend is Mary (Hailee Steinfeld), a woman who is biracial and white passing. Stack wants to keep her safe, so he arranges for her to be married to a white man before he leaves for the war. Mary is heartbroken, and when she runs into Stack again, she lets him know how much she hates him. But it's soon clear that neither Stack nor Mary is ready to walk away from the other. Even the brothers' young cousin Sammie (Miles Caton) finds love for a brief time, with a married woman named Pearline (Jayme Lawson) who is a brilliant singer, and who shares a night of passion with Sammie before all hell breaks loose.

Amid all the violence and dread of the vampire siege at the juke joint, we experience moments of pure love and romance; compared to many more recent films, particularly genre films, the three distinct love scenes in this movie are quite notable. This is a movie where we don't see shifts in tone as rigid boundaries but as elements of varying genres that blur and overlap and undulate throughout the course of the story. The climax of the film kicks off when shopkeeper Grace (Li Jun Li) finally cracks. Unwilling to give up both her husband Bo Chow (Yao) and the threat to their daughter Lisa (Helena Hu), she invites the vampires in for their final fight. Even Remmick (Jack O'Connell), the primary vampire antagonist, says he wants to save everyone and have them join in a fellowship of peace and love he's creating with his new vampire clan. Throughout, we hear people say to each other "I love you," whether that's brother to brother or husband to wife.

I really do think this film is one of the best of the decade, and someone smarter and more astute than I is probably on their way to writing a much more detailed and beautiful analysis of Coogler's masterpiece. But at the risk of running well over word count, I'm going to move on to the films of the 2020s that follow more traditional horror narratives.

THE TRIED-AND-TRUE HORROR

The Invitation (2022) could arguably fall under the category of tone or genre shift, but I'm keeping it in the more traditional horror film space because it follows many of the beats common in gothic horror stories and films. Director Jessica M. Thompson's story of a woman uncovering dark family secrets is a modern update of gothics like Hammer's *Vampire Lovers* or Hitchcock's *Rebecca*, loosely (very loosely) based on the story of *Dracula*. Nathalie Emmanuel stars as Evie, a young, struggling artist who discovers a long-lost family member who invites her to an upcoming wedding at the family's large estate in England. Evie longs for connection, and the possibility of gaining a family through her distant cousin Oliver (Hugh Skinner) is too tempting to pass up. So she travels to the town of Whitby and the estate (called New Carfax Abbey, a name that will feel very familiar to many horror readers). In addition to meeting Oliver and the rest of the family ahead of the upcoming nuptials, Evie is attracted to the lord of the estate, Walter De Ville (Thomas Doherty). The smoldering and mysterious Walter also seems to connect with Evie, and the two grow closer, even though she begins to suspect that something mysterious is happening at Carfax.

The romantic elements of the story culminate in Walter and Evie getting intimate after an argument. If we were following a more straightforward romance here, we might see this sexual encounter as the tipping point, where the couple realizes they want to commit to a relationship. In a romantic suspense story, the romance would continue deepening as the mystery is uncovered by the new couple. But since this is a horror romance, the next reveal is much more sinister: Evie learns that the wedding she is going to attend is hers. She's been invited to the abbey because Walter and the wedding party are vampires, and Evie's family has offered up a young woman to him for marriage for centuries in exchange for power and wealth.

Evie, disillusioned and betrayed, spends the rest of the film trying to escape from Walter and the vampires who have captured her. Along the way, audiences are treated to several more references to Stoker's *Dracula*, as Jonathan and Mina Harker make an appearance (though they subvert the audience's expectations here). *The Invitation* isn't a retelling by any means, but having the shorthand that viewers can relate to is both a way to cue certain plot points as well as lull the audience into thinking they know where the story will go before undermining those references. Thompson plays with the lore, giving the monsters in her story some different rules to follow for becoming a vampire, and I would argue that Evie's third act rebellion is a way to take back agency as a horror movie Final Girl. Not only that, the ending also reverses the roles of vampire and prey, allowing Evie to reclaim agency and dominate the monster who has coerced and tricked her earlier in the film.

Once again, we see a movie (also directed by a woman, as *Fresh* was) that serves as a cautionary tale for young women longing for a partner, illustrating the dangers of ignoring potential red flags and letting their loneliness inform their decision making. The romance in both *Fresh* and *The Invitation* feels too good to be true in the initial stages, sweeping the women off their feet even though they are "modern" women who should know better. In contrast to these more contemporary visions of women, relationships, and monsters, Robert Eggers's *Nosferatu* (2024) is a very "old" film in both setting and tone.

I won't rehash the plot of *Nosferatu* here; suffice to say that Eggers tells a very similar tale to those of F. W. Murnau, Browning, Werner Herzog, and Coppola before him (among countless other adaptations of *Dracula*). The names are a little different: Lily-Rose Depp plays Ellen instead of Mina, and Nicolas Hoult is Thomas, not Jonathan. But the overarching story is very much the same: A young man travels to visit a mysterious count in Eastern Europe (Bill Skarsgård) in order to help him buy some property, unaware that the count is actually a vampire. When the monster arrives in the city (here Wisburg instead of London), he fixates on Ellen, and the men around her must rally to defeat the creature. That's where the similarities end.

Unlike *Bram Stoker's Dracula*, or Coppola's stylized and highly romantic version of the Dracula story, Eggers has created a dark, somber, and for me, deeply unromantic take on the classic tale. (Critic Alisha Mughal goes even further, arguing that Eggers has created a story where Ellen's lust must be shamed and sacrificed to bring the patriarchal order to Wisburg.)[3] Instead of a love story between the vampire and Mina, Skarsgård's Count Orlok has groomed Ellen from a young age, appearing to her in nightmares and visions and preventing her from fully accepting a loving relationship with her husband, Thomas, even though she tries to achieve a sense of normalcy and embrace her new husband. The vampire's hold on both Ellen and the town grows (he unleashes a plague that devastates the population, signaled by multiple shots of the count's shadowy hand traveling across the countryside, getting closer and closer to the citizens of Wisburg). Ellen becomes increasingly distraught and Dr. von Franz

(Willem Dafoe) is brought in to help manage her symptoms of seizures and sleepwalking, causing her to be tied and restrained for much of the film.

When she is finally set free (when her husband returns from his horrific encounter with the count), Ellen meets Orlok in a dream. He uses the words of an abuser, trying to isolate Ellen from her husband by claiming Thomas has annulled their marriage, and then threatens her by saying that if she doesn't give herself to him after three days, he will destroy both Thomas and the town of Wisburg. Hardly on par with "I've crossed oceans of time to find you."

Does Ellen possess enough agency and free will to freely make the sacrifice demanded of her? Does she welcome Orlok to her bed because she's drawn to him and in love with him? Eggers seems to signal that Ellen is destined to give up her healthy and loving relationship with Thomas because she's always been captivated by the count. But for me, it hardly seems like a choice. Ellen has been told over and over that her lustful behavior and mental illness are shameful, and she decides she must sacrifice her life to save her love. *Nosferatu* is a beautiful film, but I'm not feeling the romance.

In contrast, *Heart Eyes* (2025) is, on the surface, very much a horror film, rooted in the slashers of the '80s and '90s. But there's a terrifically romantic storyline between the two main characters and even more love throughout. The story centers on the Heart Eyes Killer (HEK), who comes out every year on Valentine's Day to murder couples out on dates. The killer has traveled around the country, and the film opens with a marriage proposal at a winery that ends in gruesome deaths for the couple and their photographer. Director Josh Ruben is quick to establish the rules (a necessity in every slasher film): The HEK is only really interested in killing couples in love (and maybe the people around them if they get in the way), and the police caution everyone to stay home and celebrate their love privately.

This suits Ally (Olivia Holt) just fine, because she has recently broken up with her boyfriend and she's feeling very unromantic. Until she meets Jay (Mason Gooding) at the coffee shop. Their meet is decidedly cute, but Ally runs off to work, where her latest ad campaign is a disaster. Her boss has brought in a freelance consultant to right the shop, and of course it turns out that the consultant is Jay. He tries to charm Ally but she's resistant, until, after a working dinner, she runs into her ex and his new girlfriend, and she kisses Jay to pretend she's also moved on. In the span of half an hour or so, we've hit so many romance tropes: enemies to lovers; mistaken identity; workplace romance; fake relationship. At this point, *Heart Eyes* could very easily remain a cute but silly rom-com. But HEK sees Ally and Jay kiss and is fooled into thinking they're a couple (there is a lot of chemistry in that kiss), and the film veers right back into slasher territory, as Jay and Ally try to escape HEK. Along the way, the two begin to develop feelings for each other, which are amplified by the high stakes of running for their lives.

This raising of stakes is so important in both horror and romance. The danger levels must continue to increase as the killer or danger gets closer and closer to our heroes; similarly, the emotional connection between the romantic partners must deepen as the story progresses in order for the HEA to feel earned. *Heart Eyes* does a solid job in both genres, as Ally and Jay find themselves stuck in and escaping from precarious life-or-death situations, all while slowly revealing their emotional vulnerability and their growing affection for each other. The final reveal adds even more romance to the story when we learn that the killer is no lone wolf but, in fact, is working together with their own true love, and murder is their way of keeping their romance alive. It's an interesting subversion of the typical slasher trope featuring an antagonist, usually male, whose loneliness and jealousy are the impetus for his killing spree.

As we reach the halfway point of the decade, there's one last film I want to touch on before wrapping everything up: *Together*, directed by Michael Shanks and starring real-life couple Alison Brie and Dave Franco. Is this a horror movie? Yes. Is it a romance? Also yes. For me, it encapsulates a run of filmmakers (backed by smaller indie studios like Neon, A24, and Blumhouse) who are once again finally getting some freedom to play with genre in very interesting and invigorating ways. The movie explores the messy and complicated relationship between Millie (Brie) and Tim (Franco). They have been dating and living together for several years but haven't yet committed to marriage; what happens to their relationship when they're forced to decide if they really, truly want to spend the rest of their lives as one?

Shortly after the film opens, Tim and Millie arrive at their new house in a small town outside of New York (just far enough away that Tim can't easily commute to gigs as a fill-in guitarist for an up-and-coming band). Millie, a teacher, is excited to move forward with their new life, but Tim has some misgivings. He feels like he's giving up on his dreams so Millie can pursue hers, and she can sense his trepidation and the undercurrent of resentment that fuels their early days in a strange place. Tim, we learn, hasn't been himself since a traumatic incident involving his parents, which is never fully explained but is hinted at throughout the film. The only thing we know for sure is that his father is dead and his mother has had some sort of mental illness, whether triggered by her husband's demise or something else. Tim doesn't want to talk about it, not even with Millie, and it's one of several breadcrumbs of information that Shanks drops for the audience without fully revealing the backstory. In any case, these two characters definitely love each other, but there are some cracks in their relationship. And as anyone who is well-versed in this kind of story knows, their new surroundings are going to exploit the precarity of the situation.

The trope of new people in a small town isn't just common in romance (where it's often labeled "fish out of water"), but is a staple of the folk horror genre, where the insular community is mistrustful of the newcomers as they uncover sinister secrets. The only person who seems welcoming is Jamie (Damon Herriman), another teacher at the school where Millie works, who conveniently lives just down the street. Jamie tells Millie that she and Tim should explore the great hiking trails near their house, and if you've seen more than a couple of these movies, you can tell that Jamie might not be as kind and helpful as he seems. On a hike, Tim and Millie get lost and end up spending the night in a mysterious cave, filled with church pews and a watering hole (the same cave where a pair of hikers disappeared a month earlier, Tim discovers). Of course, Tim drinks the water and that's where things start to get really weird.

Somehow, the water creates an even deeper connection for Tim and Millie, and he is drawn to her like a magnet. He has a difficult time physically separating himself from her, and the body horror escalates as Tim's metaphorical dependence on Millie manifests itself physically in increasingly horrifying ways. Their situation gets much worse when Millie, who was initially able to resist the pull of Tim's body, begins to reciprocate the magnetism between them. As the two try to figure out what is happening, they uncover an ancient, folk horror–tinged cult who believe that a person's life partner is their literal other half, and the water in the cave allows the two individuals to merge into the single person they're meant to be. This is a prime example of using horror imagery and tropes to explore serious themes, as so many "elevated horror" films of recent years have done. When you embark on a relationship with someone, what are you prepared to give of yourself? How do you change over the course of a marriage, becoming a different person from who you were when you were single? *Together* grapples with the fear that comes with taking the plunge, as Tim and Millie joke, and it does so with a fully fleshed-out (pardon the pun) story with a real, grounded love story at its heart.

AFTER THE HEA: WHERE DOES HORROR ROMANCE GO FROM HERE?

In the publishing world, horror and romance are certainly evolving, and we're seeing more and more stories that feature romantic horror or scary romance each year. Mash-ups between genres are becoming more commonplace, largely building on the success of the romantasy genre, and there's an appetite for blending romance with other genres in a more focused way. There's a push toward darker, more taboo stories in traditionally published romance spaces, imprints acquire new voices from indie and self-publishing spheres; and we're seeing further fragmentation of genres as readers look to cater to increasingly specific tastes, from erotic horror to dark romance to horror romance and everything in between.

What's next in film? Though exploring larger and more complex themes in horror and in romance is hardly new, the 2020s so far have given audiences so many films from a variety of perspectives that critics and media have declared a horror renaissance of sorts.[4] Even in the wake of challenging circumstances both external and internal, the film industry, and particularly indies, have introduced horror audiences to thoughtful, provocative stories, and the fact that some of those stories explore aspects of romance and love in addition to horror is refreshing. As large studios continue developing IP and franchises that appeal to the broadest audience possible, audacious indie projects still sometimes hit it big. For every new *Dracula* remake or *I Know What*

You Did Last Summer sequel, there's someone making *Your Monster* or *Dead Lover*. It seems pointless to try anticipating trends in a book I'm writing in 2024 that won't be on shelves until 2026, so I won't try. But I'm excited to see what develops.

NEW ROMANTICS

Get Out (2017, dir. Jordan Peele)

TOP TROPES: Weekend Getaway: Chris is apprehensive about spending the weekend with girlfriend Rose and her family; he's never met them and worries they won't accept him since he is a Black man and she is white.

DARK MOMENT: Chris discovers that Rose has seduced him in order to trap him so that a wealthy white man can transfer his brain into Chris's body.

HEA? Not for the couple! But luckily, Chris is rescued by his friend Rod, and Rose is left for dead.

The Invitation (2022, dir. Jessica M. Thompson)

TOP TROPES: Rags to Riches: Evie is whisked away to a lavish life when she is invited to join her long-lost family, and she falls in love with the elusive Walter. But the wealthy family holds dark secrets that threaten Evie's life.

DARK MOMENT: Evie finds out Walter is a vampire and he only seduced her because he needs her family bloodline to continue his own.

HEA? No. Evie murders Walter and escapes with her life.

Heart Eyes (2025, dir. Josh Ruben)

TOP TROPES: Forced Proximity and Rivals to Lovers: Ally's job is threatened by rival consultant Jay, but when he takes her out for a conciliatory dinner, the two are targeted by the serial killer in town, and they're forced to stick together to save themselves from the murderous villain who's stalking them.

DARK MOMENT: Once the killer has been caught, Ally rebuffs Jay's advances, wanting to reject him before she is rejected, and he leaves without her.

HEA? Yes. Ally searches for Jay and saves him from the real killers. Jay asks her to move in with him, and Ally decides to propose instead, and the happy couple embrace.

MOVIES DISCUSSED

The Island of Lost Souls (1932; dir. Erle C. Kenton)

King Kong (1933; dir. Merian C. Cooper and Ernest B. Schoedsack)

Dracula (1932; dir. Tod Browning)

The Mummy (1932; dir. Karl Freund)

Freaks (1932; dir. Tod Browning)

The Phantom of the Opera (1943, dir. Arthur Lubin)

The Wolf Man (1941; dir. George Waggner)

Cat People (1942; dir. Jacques Tourneur)

Dr. Jekyll and Mr. Hyde (1941, dir. Victor Fleming)

The Creature from the Black Lagoon (1954; dir. Jack Arnold)

Possession (1981; dir. Andrzej Żuławski)

Candyman (1992; dir. Bernard Rose)

Wolf (1994; Mike Nichols)

The Shape of Water (2017; dir. Guillermo del Toro)

Rebecca (1940; dir. Alfred Hitchcock)

The Uninvited (1944; dir. Lewis Allen)

The Curse of Frankenstein (1957; dir. Terence Fisher)
The Haunting (1963; dir. Robert Wise)
Hellraiser (1987; dir. Clive Barker)
Mulholland Drive (2001; dir. David Lynch)
The Hunger (1983; dir. Tony Scott)
May (2002; dir. Lucy McKee)
Jennifer's Body (2009; dir. Karen Kusama)
Thirteen Women (1933; dir. George Archainbaud)
Peeping Tom (1960; dir. Michael Powell)
Blood and Black Lace (1964; dir. Mario Brava)
Black Christmas (1974; dir. Bob Clark)
Friday the 13th (1980; dir. Sean S. Cunningham)
Sleepaway Camp (1983; dir. Robert Hiltzik)
Psycho (1960; dir. Alfred Hitchcock)
Vertigo (1958; dir. Alfred Hitchcock)
The Birds (1963; dir. Alfred Hitchcock)
The Brides of Dracula (1960; dir. Terence Fisher)
The Vampire Lovers (1979; dir. Roy Ward Baker)
Daughters of Darkness (1971; dir. Harry Kümel)
Ganja & Hess (1973; dir. Bill Gunn)
The Lost Boys (1987; dir. Joel Schumacher)
Lifeforce (1985; dir. Tobe Hooper)
Near Dark (1987; dir. Kathryn Bigelow)
Twilight (2008; dir. Catherine Hardwicke)
The Fly (1987; dir David Cronenberg)

Dead Ringers (1988; dir. David Cronenberg)

Blue Velvet (1986; dir. David Lynch)

Wild at Heart (1990; dir. David Lynch)

Rosemary's Baby (1968; dir. Roman Polanski)

Interview with the Vampire (1994; dir. Neil Jordan)

Mary Shelley's Frankenstein (1994; dir. Kenneth Branagh)

Mary Reilly (1996; dir. Stephen Frears)

Bram Stoker's Dracula (1992; Francis Ford Coppola)

Sleepy Hollow (1999; dir. Tim Burton)

Crimson Peak (2015; dir. Guillermo del Toro)

The Blob (1958; dir. Irvin S. Yeaworth Jr.)

The Tingler (1959; dir. William Castle)

The Abominable Dr. Phibes (1971; dir. Robert Fuest)

The Love Witch (2015; dir. Anna Biller)

Warm Bodies (2013; dir. Jonathan Levine)

Shaun of the Dead (2004; dir. Edgar Wright)

Zombieland (2009; dir. Ruben Fleischer)

Lisa Frankenstein (2024; dir. Zelda Williams)

The Bride of Frankenstein (1935; dir. James Whale)

Bride of Chucky (1998; dir. Ronny Yu)

Underworld (2003; dir. Len Wiseman)

Cat People (1982; dir. Paul Schrader)

Sleepwalkers (1992; dir. Stephen King)

Bones and All (2022; dir. Luca Guadagnino)

Get Out (2017; dir. Jordan Peele)

Fresh (2022; dir. Mimi Cave)

Companion (2025; dir. Drew Hancock)

The Gorge (2025; dir. Scott Derrickson)

Sinners (2025; dir. Ryan Coogler)

The Invitation (2022; dir. Jessica M. Thompson)

Nosferatu (2024; dir. Robert Eggers)

Heart Eyes (2025; dir. Josh Ruben)

Together (2025; dir. Michael Shanks)

INTERNATIONAL HORROR ROMANCE FILMS

Les Diaboliques (1955, dir. Henri-George Clouzot)

Bees Saal Baad (1962, dir. Biren Nag)

The Whip and the Body (1963, dir. Mario Bava)

Kohraa (1964, dir. Biren Nag)

Lake of Dracula (1971, dir. Michio Yamamoto)

Lips of Blood (1975, dir. Jean Rollin)

Delicatessen (1991, dirs. Marc Caro and Jean-Pierre Jeunet)

Braindead (1992, dir. Peter Jackson)

Audition (1999, dir. Takashi Miike)

Raaz (2002, dir. Vikram Bhatt)

Kaidan (2007, dir. Hideo Nakata)

Let the Right One In (2008, dir. Tomas Alfredson)

Thirst (2009, dir. Park Chan-wook)

The Skin I Live In (2011, dir. Pedro Almodóvar)

A Wolf at the Door (2013, dir. Fernando Coimbra)

A Girl Walks Home Alone at Night (2014, Ana Lily Amirpour)

Fatal Frame (2014, dir. Mari Asato)

The Untamed (2016, dir. Amat Escalante)

Extra Ordinary (2019, dirs. Mike Ahern and Enda Loughman)

Little Monsters (2019, dir. Abe Forsythe)

Inhuman Kiss (2019, dir. Sitisiri Mongkolsiri)

Titane (2021, dir. Julia Ducournau)

Huesera: The Bone Woman (2022, dir. Michelle Garza Cervera)

Marry My Dead Body (2022, dir. Cheng Wei-hao)

Humanist Vampire Seeking Consenting Suicidal Person (2024, dir. Ariane Louis-Seize)

FURTHER READING

Bogutskaya, Anna. *Feeding the Monster: Why Horror Has a Hold on Us*. Faber & Faber, 2025.

Boulenger, Gilles. *John Carpenter: The Prince of Darkness*. Silman-James Press, 2003.

Coleman, Robin R. Means. *Horror Noire: A History of Black American Horror from the 1890s to Present*. Routledge, 2022.

Coleman, Robin R. Means, and Mark H. Harris. *The Black Guy Dies First: Black Horror Cinema from Fodder to Oscar*. S&S/Saga Press, 2023.

Duncan, Paul, and Jürgen Müller, eds. *Horror Cinema: The Best Scary Movies of All Time*. Taschen, 2017.

Evry, Max. *A Masterpiece in Disarray: David Lynch's* Dune: *An Oral History*. 1984 Publishing, 2023.

Hughes, Emily C. *Horror for Weenies: Everything You Need to Know About the Films You're Too Scared to Watch*. Quirk Books, 2024.

Nesseth, Nina. *Nightmare Fuel: The Science of Horror Films*. Tor Nightfire, 2022.

Skal, David J. *The Monster Show: A Cultural History of Horror*. Farrar, Straus and Giroux, 2001.

Thorne, John. *Devious Dreams: Reimagining David Lynch's* Mulholland Drive. John Thorne, 2024.

Vallese, Joe, ed. *It Came from the Closet: Queer Reflections of Horror*. The Feminist Press at CUNY, 2022.
White, Edward. *The Twelve Lives of Alfred Hitchcock: An Anatomy of the Master of Suspense*. W. W. Norton, 2021.

ACKNOWLEDGMENTS

To my husband, Steve, for asking me the same question pretty much every single day since we started dating: "What do you want to watch tonight?" You've been unwaveringly supportive, endlessly optimistic, and you track down countless films for me. I wouldn't want to be sitting on the couch or at the cinema watching movies with anyone else.

To Dexter, Henry, and Lucy, for being curious and opinionated and passionate. I am so glad to have kids who are thoughtful and engaged and artistic (even when we don't agree on movies!).

To Elana, Frank, Kerry, Todd: the most creative, enthusiastic, ambitious family, ready to cheer successes and commiserate about failures, and I wouldn't be where I am without you. Thank you.

To my agents, Danai Christopoulou and Lane Heymont. You saw the potential in my work before I did, worked tirelessly to find the best home for this book, and talked me down when I was ready to throw everything in the garbage. Such a pleasure to work with you both.

To my editor, Maya Fernandez. I knew the minute we spoke that you were the best champion for this book, and your thoughtful notes and comments made this whole process so easy. Thank you to everyone at Beacon Press, especially Marcy Barnes, Susan Lumenello, Molly Woodward, Caitlin Meyer, Louis Roe, and Brittany Wallace.

To Andrew, Amy, Annika, Mike, Alex, Matt, Sasha, Theo, Jenny, Joe, Daniel, Hailey, Cina . . . all the writers and editors I know who listened to me complain and then celebrate and then freak out and back again, everyone who encouraged me to call myself a writer, who told me not to self-reject, who encouraged me to get the words on the page. I am a better writer because of you. Thank you.

To Mike at From Beyond Press. Thanks for putting out a call for nonfiction submissions; you spurred me into writing and I'm very grateful. Thank you.

To Clay. Thank you for being my first reader, for every early morning message, every encouraging email written in all caps, every conversation about writing and publishing and horror and romance.

To the filmmakers who created the movies I watched for this book. Watching movies and writing about them is one of my favorite things and I'm grateful for the opportunities to fall in love or hate with your characters and settings and plots.

I would be remiss if I didn't mention the writers who made me fall in love with films and film criticism all over again: Matt Zoller Seitz, Walter Chaw, Katie Rife, Angelica Jade Bastien, BJ Colangelo, Brandon Streussnig, Robert Daniels, Drew Magary, Mo Moshaty. . . . In an era when writers, especially arts and culture writers, are being laid off, it's vital to engage with people who are excited about movies, who want to talk about movies, and who understand that writing about film is an art unto itself. Thank you.

To everyone who's ever talked to me about books, or movies, or writing: Thank you.

NOTES

CHAPTER ONE: MEET CUTE

1. Matthew Bernstein, ed., *Controlling Hollywood: Censorship and Regulation in the Studio Era* (Rutgers University Press, 1999).

2. Robin R. Means Coleman, *Horror Noire: A History of Black American Horror from the 1890s to Present* (Routledge, 2023).

3. Christine Smallwood, "*Island of Lost Souls:* The Beast Flesh Creeping Back," *The Current*, October 25, 2011, https://www.criterion.com/current/posts/2034-island-of-lost-souls-the-beast-flesh-creeping-back.

CHAPTER TWO: FORBIDDEN LOVE

1. Sarah Cook, "Old Movies: The Many Screen Adaptations of Jekyll & Hyde," Film Stories, March 1, 2022, https://filmstories.co.uk/features/old-movies-the-many-screen-adaptations-of-jekyll-hyde/.

2. Robin T. Reid, "The History of the Drive-In Movie Theater," *Smithsonian Magazine*, May 27, 2008, https://www.smithsonianmag.com/arts-culture/the-history-of-the-drive-in-movie-theater-51331221/.

3. Mallory O'Meara, *The Lady from the Black Lagoon: Hollywood Monsters and the Lost Legacy of Milicent Patrick* (Hanover Square Press, 2009).

4. Dominique Brown-Sampayo, "History, Collective Memory, and More in *Candyman* (1922)," *Medium*, April 26, 2024, https://medium.com/black-horrific/history-collective-memory-and-more-in-candyman-1992-15b13cfb5e44.

CHAPTER THREE: DEEP DIVE—ROMANCE AND REPRESSION IN *CAT PEOPLE*

1. See Drew Burnett Gregory, "Monsters & Mommis: *Cat People* and *The Seventh Victim* Come Out of the Closet," *Autostraddle*,

October 8, 2024, https://www.autostraddle.com/monsters-mommis-cat-people-and-the-seventh-victim-come-out-of-the-closet/; and Bee Delores, "*Cat People*: Society's Tethering of Queer Sexuality & Identity," *Bloody Disgusting*, April 20, 2021, https://bloody-disgusting.com/editorials/3661133/cat-people-societys-tethering-queer-sexuality-identity/.

2. Meagan Navarro, "How an Iconic Scene in *Cat People* Created the Cinematic Jump Scare as We Know It Today," *SlashFilm*, November 18, 2020, https://www.slashfilm.com/577856/cat-people-jump-scare/.

CHAPTER FOUR: QUEER REPRESENTATION IN HORROR ROMANCE CINEMA

1. Joe Vallese, ed., *It Came from the Closet: Queer Reflections on Horror* (The Feminist Press at CUNY, 2022); Willow Catelyn Maclay and Caden Mark Gardner, *Corpses, Fools, and Monsters: The History and Future of Transness in Cinema* (Repeater, 2024).

2. Patrick McGilligan, *Alfred Hitchcock: A Life in Darkness and Light* (It Books, 2004).

3. Rhona J. Berenstein, "Adaptation, Censorship, and Audiences of Questionable Type: Lesbian Sightings in 'Rebecca' (1940) and 'The Uninvited' (1944)," *Cinema Journal* 37, no. 3 (Spring 1998): 17–18, https://doi.org/10.2307/1225825.

4. Mark Harris, *Pictures at a Revolution: Five Movies and the Birth of the New Hollywood* (Penguin Books, 2009).

5. Samantha McLaren, "Titillation and Trepidation: Revisiting Hammer's Queer Outings," *Fangoria*, June 21, 2021, https://www.fangoria.com/hammers-queer-outings/.

6. Andrew Pulver, "Martin Scorsese Names His Scariest Films of All Time," *The Guardian*, November 12, 2013, https://www.theguardian.com/film/2013/nov/12/martin-scorsese-scariest-films-the-haunting-shining.

7. Michael Koresky, "Queer Now & Then: 1963," *Film Comment*, October 24, 2018, https://www.filmcomment.com/blog/queer-now-1963/.

8. Carmen Maria Machado, "Both Ways," in Vallese *It Came from the Closet*.

CHAPTER FIVE: SLASHERS—THE ANTI-ROMANCE FILM

1. Carol J. Clover, *Men, Women, and Chainsaws: Gender in Modern Horror Film* (Princeton University Press, 1993); Barbara Creed, *The Monstrous-Feminine: Film, Feminism, Psychoanalysis*, 2nd ed. (Routledge, 2023); Sady Doyle (now Jude Ellison S. Doyle), *Dead*

Blondes and Bad Mothers: Monstrosity, Patriarchy, and the Fear of Female Power (Melville House, 2019).

2. Gita Jackson, "When Joss Whedon Was Our Master," *Vice*, January 13, 2022, https://www.vice.com/en/article/when-joss-whedon-was-our-master/.

3. Stanley Swindling, "Where Is the Final Boy?" FilmUpdates, October 19, 2020, https://filmupdates.net/2020/10/19/where-is-the-final-boy/.

4. Viet Dinh, "Notes on *Sleepaway Camp*," in Joe Vallese, ed., *It Came from the Closet: Queer Reflections on Horror* (The Feminist Press at CUNY, 2022); Alice Collins, "*Sleepaway Camp*: The Elephant in the Room [Trapped by Gender]," *Bloody Disgusting*, August 21, 2020, https://bloody-disgusting.com/editorials/3625816/sleepaway-camp-elephant-room-trapped-gender/.

5. Sean Abley, "Problematic Films: In Defense of *Sleepaway Camp*," *Fangoria*, September 28, 2021, https://www.fangoria.com/problematic-films-in-defense-of-sleepaway-camp/.

CHAPTER SIX: DEEP DIVE—IS HITCHCOCK HORROR, ROMANCE, OR BOTH?

1. Stephen Rebello, *Alfred Hitchcock and the Making of* Psycho (Soft Skull, 2013).

2. Tara Brady, "Vertigo: From Box-Office Flop to 'Greatest Film of All Time," *Irish Times*, July 12, 2018, https://www.irishtimes.com/culture/film/vertigo-from-box-office-flop-to-greatest-film-of-all-time-1.3561982.

3. Clay McLeod Chapman, *Devil Inside: A Novel* (Mira Books, 2026).

CHAPTER SEVEN: VAMPIRES—SEX, DEATH, AND *TWILIGHT*

1. G. G. Graham, "Bloodlust and Blues Beyond Dracula: Ganja & Hess," *Horror Homeroom*, April 28, 2020, https://www.horrorhomeroom.com/bloodlust-and-blues-beyond-blacula-ganja-hess/.

2. Donato Totaro, "The Uniqueness of Bill Gunn's *Ganja & Hess*," *Offscreen* 25, nos. 9–10 (October 2021), https://offscreen.com/view/the-uniqueness-of-bill-gunns-ganja-and-hess.

3. *Lifeforce*, directed by Tobe Hooper (Cannon Films, 1985).

4. Nicholas Chare, Jeanette Hoorn, and Audrey Yue, eds., *Re-reading the Monstrous-Feminine: Art, Film, Feminism, and Psychoanalysis* (Routledge Advances in Film Studies, 2021).

5. Joanne O'Sullivan, "Who Is YA For?" *Publishers Weekly*, October 13, 2023, https://www.publishersweekly.com/pw/by-topic/childrens/childrens-industry-news/article/93417-who-is-ya-for.html.

6. Johnny Compton, *Devils Kill Devils* (Tor Nightfire, 2024); Hailey Piper, *All the Hearts You Eat* (Titan Books, 2024).

CHAPTER EIGHT: DEEP DIVE—THE TWO DAVIDS

1. Walter Chaw, "David Cronenberg Re-examines David Cronenberg: A Retrospective Interview," *Film Freak Central*, March 9, 2003, https://filmfreakcentral.net/2003/03/david-cronenberg-re-examines-david-cronenberg/.

2. Roger Ebert, "*Dead Ringers* Review," September 23, 1988, accessed at https://www.rogerebert.com/reviews/dead-ringers-1988.

CHAPTER NINE: SECOND-CHANCE ROMANCE

1. See R. S. Benedict, "Everyone Is Beautiful and No One Is Horny," *Blood Knife*, February 14, 2021, https://bloodknife.com/everyone-beautiful-no-one-horny/; and Carlee Gomes, "The Puritanical Eye: Hyper-Mediation, Sex on Film, and the Disavowal of Desire," *Specchioscuro*, November 25, 2023, https://specchioscuro.it/the-puritanical-eye-hyper-mediation-sex-on-film-and-the-disavowal-of-desire/.

2. David Moses, "In Defense of Keanu Reeves in *Bram Stoker's Dracula*," *Departures*, September 2, 2024, https://www.departuresblog.com/actors-pov/2023/10/1/hh2sjj9cs753mxoh5pbdpcxohndvab (URL now defunct).

3. Donna Freydkin, "Burton and Depp: Wide Awake in *Sleepy Hollow*," CNN.com, November 16, 1999, https://web.archive.org/web/20230406143151/http://edition.cnn.com:80/SHOWBIZ/Movies/9911/16/sleepy.hollow/.

4. Cat Dippell, "*Crimson Peak*'s Reliance on Visuality as a Means of Storytelling," *Victorian Visual Culture*, December 16, 2023, https://victorianvisualculture.blog/2023/12/16/crimson-peaks-reliance-on-visuality-as-a-means-of-storytelling/.

CHAPTER TEN: GRUMPY/SUNSHINE

1. "The End of the Golden Age and the Rise of Television," Digital Public Library of America, https://dp.la/exhibitions/radio-golden-age/radio-tv, accessed March 4, 2025.

2. John Patterson, "The Love Witch Director Anna Biller: 'I'm in Conversation with the Pornography All Around Us,'" *The Guardian*, March 2, 2017, https://www.theguardian.com/film/2017/mar/02/love-witch-director-anna-biller-conversation-pornography.

CHAPTER TWELVE: THE NEW ROMANTICS

1. R. S. Benedict, "Everyone Is Beautiful and No One Is Horny," *Blood Knife*, February 14, 2021, https://bloodknife.com/everyone-beautiful-no-one-horny/.

2. Sophie Hall, "Get Out: The Horror of White Women," *Video Librarian*, December 8, 2020, https://videolibrarian.com/articles/essays/get-out-the-horror-of-white-women/.

3. Alisha Mughal, "The Triumph of the Patriarchal Order in *Nosferatu*," *Film Daze*, March 1, 2025, https://filmdaze.substack.com/p/the-triumph-of-patriarchal-order.

4. Federico Furzan, "Why the 2020s Will Be the Best Decade for Horror Ever," *Movieweb*, November 13, 2023, https://movieweb.com/2020s-horror-best-decade/.